INTERNATIONAL INCIDENTS

INTERNATIONAL INCIDENTS

The Law That Counts in World Politics

W. MICHAEL REISMAN AND

ANDREW R. WILLARD,

EDITORS

Princeton University Press
Princeton, N.J.

Copyright © 1988 by Princeton University Press
Published by Princeton University Press, 41 William Street,
Princeton, New Jersey 08540
In the United Kingdom: Princeton University Press, Guildford, Surrey

All Rights Reserved
Library of Congress Cataloging in Publication Data will be
found on the last printed page of this book

ISBN 0-691-07772-X
ISBN 0-691-02280-1 (pbk.)

This book has been composed in Linotron Electra

Clothbound editions of Princeton University Press books
are printed on acid-free paper, and binding materials are
chosen for strength and durability. Paperbacks, although satisfactory
for personal collections, are not usually suitable for library rebinding

Printed in the United States of America by Princeton University Press,
Princeton, New Jersey

Contents

CONTENTS

Preface and Acknowledgments

In November 1983, a notice was posted on the Yale Law School bulletin board announcing a new seminar to be offered in the spring semester. The seminar was called "The Incident as a Decision Unit in International Law." Since the words in the title were not exactly terms of art in the trivium and quadrivium, the notice set out, at rather unusual length, what was intended:

> An incident is an international dispute that shapes or reinforces elite expectations about lawfulness, in which the appraisal of lawfulness by relevant international actors occurs in a nonformal setting. The Soviet destruction of KAL 007, the U.S. invasion of Grenada and the Israeli attack on the Iraqi reactor are examples of recent incidents. Because of the structure of the international political system, most international decision is found in incidents rather than cases and judgments. Yet paradoxically, there is no accepted method for recording incidents. The discipline of international law has adopted the notion of the national judgment as its basic if not exclusive epistemic unit; statements of courts are expanded by generative logic into a codex which is taken to be

international law. As a result, much international jurisprudence is not congruent with contemporary elite expectations that are reflected in practice. It serves neither descriptive nor predictive functions, contributing little to the performance of indispensable legal tasks.

This seminar will attempt to develop a concise method for recording and appraising incidents in the hope that it can install a new genre in international law. It will use the research techniques of contemporary historiography and political science in addition to the methods of international law. Each student, alone or in collaboration with another, will be responsible for researching a particular incident. Each will circulate a draft to the other seminar participants and explain and defend it in a session. It is planned that the better papers in the seminar will be collected in a volume and published.

The convenor of the seminar thought it would be useful to have a number of graduate students in international relations and politics. Arrangements were made to give a brief introductory lecture to students in that department and several very able recruits (or conscripts) joined the seminar.

The papers in this volume are part of the product of the seminar. Some were published in successive numbers of the *Yale Journal of International Law*. They have been reedited for the present publication.

The epigraph to Chapter 11 is reprinted with permission from *The Collected Poems of Wallace Stevens* by Wallace Stevens (copyright 1942 by Wallace Stevens and renewed 1970 by Holly Stevens), published by Alfred A. Knopf, Inc.

Many people helped in the preparation of this book. Particular thanks are due to the editors of Volumes 10 and 11 of the *Yale Journal of International Law*, and especially to the Editor-in-Chief of Volume 10, Mark D. Agrast. Though he did not participate in the seminar, he quickly grasped the possibilities of the incident genre and made the journal and his staff available to us for discussion, criticism, and research assistance. Barbara A. Glesner was a powerful force on the journal for this project and worked with us afterward as well. Cheryl A. DeFilippo was indispensable as office manager, secretary, and coordinator. As usual, Myres S. McDougal was always available for discussion and ideas.

Useful insights were also gained from discussions with Richard A. Falk and Burns H. Weston. The editor and staff of Princeton University Press provided substantial and skillful assistance in the final phases of the preparation of the manuscript.

W.M.R.
A.R.W.

New Haven, 1987

Contributors

ALEXANDER F. COHEN is currently a J.D. Candidate at the Yale Law School. He holds B.A. and M.A. degrees from Yale University.

PATRICK J. DESOUZA, J.D. Yale Law School, is currently Law Clerk to the Honorable Thomas Gibbs Gee, United States Court of Appeals for the Fifth Circuit. He is also a Ph.D. Candidate in Political Science at Stanford University.

D. BRIAN HUFFORD is an associate at Davis Polk & Wardwell in New York City. He holds a B.A. and an M.U.A. from Wichita State University and received his J.D. from the Yale Law School.

RONALD J. KUERBITZ is an attorney practicing in Chicago. He received his J.D. from the Yale Law School.

ROBERT MALLEY is currently a D. Phil. candidate in Politics at Oxford University and a J.D. Candidate at Harvard Law School. He holds both B.A. and M.A. degrees from Yale University.

CONTRIBUTORS

CRAIG A. MORGAN is an attorney practicing in Austin, Texas, with the firm of Brown, Maroney, Rose, Barber & Dye. He received his J.D. from the Yale Law School.

STEVEN R. RATNER is Attorney-Adviser, Office of the Legal Adviser, United States Department of State. He received his J.D. from the Yale Law School in 1986. With the exception of minor revisions, his contribution was written while he was a student at the Yale Law School. The views expressed are his own and not necessarily those of the United States government.

W. MICHAEL REISMAN is Wesley Newcomb Hohfeld Professor of Jurisprudence, Yale Law School.

ROMANA SADURSKA is Lecturer, Faculty of Law, University of Sydney. She received her Ph.D. from the Polish Academy of Sciences and her LL.M. from the Yale Law School.

MICHAEL P. SOCARRAS, J.D. Yale Law School, is currently Special Assistant to the Assistant Attorney General for Civil Rights, United States Department of Justice.

ANDREW R. WILLARD is Research Associate in Law, Yale Law School.

INTERNATIONAL INCIDENTS

INTERNATIONAL INCIDENTS:
Introduction to a New Genre in the Study of International Law

W. MICHAEL REISMAN

Theory that can face fact . . . is what we need. *Karl Llewellyn**

The scene is Beijing. You are an international political advisor to the government of the People's Republic of China. The news dominating the cable traffic is that Argentina has invaded the Falkland Islands.[1] Even though the invasion is on the other side of the planet, in a region in which the People's Republic is not directly involved, you will follow the events there with great interest for the next several weeks.

Some of your colleagues will be concerned about the military dimensions of the conflict, for example, problems encountered in launching amphibious attacks on well-defended island positions, establishing supply lines over long distances, and using weapons in hostile

---

* Llewellyn, *The Constitution as an Institution*, 34 Col. L. Rev. 1 (1934).

1. Spanish speakers refer to the islands as Las Malvinas. Because use of the English or Spanish designation generally marks the user as pro-British or pro-Argentine, United Nations documents, in an effort to escape the politics of names, designate the islands as *Falklands/Malvinas*. I have used the English name alone, because it seems awkward to use both; no political implication should be deduced. For historical background of the conflict, see Goebel, The Struggle for the Falkland Islands: A Study in Legal and Diplomatic History (rev. ed. 1982); for a review of recent literature and an analysis of the 1982 war in legal perspective, see Reisman, *Struggle for the Falklands*, 93 Yale L.J. 287 (1983).

3

natural environments. But you will be absorbed in quite a different aspect of the matter: the reactions of the international community to the unilateral assertion by a continental nation of the right to seize an offshore island.

The reason is obvious. The People's Republic has claims (the validity of which is now acknowledged by most other states in the world) to the island of Taiwan,[2] some 100 miles off the Chinese mainland. But even those who concede your claims have admonished you not to use force to regain Taiwan. Although the United Nations Charter prohibits the use of force in general terms, you recognize that force is often used in interstate relations and is sometimes not seriously condemned.[3] The distant war over the Falkland Islands is of great interest to you because it is almost a laboratory test of just how serious the objections are to the use of force in a situation of this sort. A high degree of actual tolerance for Argentina's unilateral action—words and other verbal condemnations notwithstanding—may be a signal that the international community is willing to accept such unilateral military assertions of right. Substantial condemnation of Argentina and effective support for the United Kingdom may indicate exactly the opposite.

POLITICAL INFERENCES AND INTERNATIONAL LAW

In your analysis of a complex event like the Falklands War, you are in fact making inferences about the normative expectations of those who are politically effective in the world community. These expectations constitute significant variables in international political behavior, be-

2. For the American position, see the so-called Shanghai Communiqué, Feb. 27, 1972, in United States Foreign Policy for the 1970's: The Emerging Structure of Peace, A Report by President Richard Nixon to the Congress 28–41 (1972). The United States position was reiterated in the joint communiqué on the establishment of diplomatic relations between the United States and the People's Republic of China, 79 DEP'T ST. BULL. 25–26 (1979). *See also, Statement of the Government of the People's Republic of China*, 18 I.L.M. 274 (1979). But the issue of title is not without controversy: *see* Chen & Reisman, *Who Owns Taiwan: A Search for International Title*, 81 YALE L.J. 599 (1972).

3. *See generally* BLECHMAN & KAPLAN, FORCE WITHOUT WAR: U.S. ARMED FORCES AS A POLITICAL INSTRUMENT (1978). For legal appraisal, see Reisman, *Coercion and Self-Determination: Construing Charter Article 2(4)*, 78 AM. J. INT'L. L. 642 (1984). *See also* Reisman, *Article 2(4): The Use of Force in Contemporary International Law*, 1984 PROC. AM. SOC'Y INT'L L.

cause shared notions of what is right influence perception, reaction, and capacity for mobilization. These inferences about what other actors think is acceptable behavior are not derived from international judgments or from constitutional documents, statutes, or treaties. They are almost entirely derived from the responses of key actors to a critical event. The expectations and demands of those actors themselves may have been shaped, in part, by many of the formal sources of law just mentioned. But whether those formal sources of law have genuine significance or are merely a façade concealing raw and ephemeral political calculations can only be assessed when you have seen how the sources fared in a particular incident.[4]

Political advisors are constantly studying incidents such as the Falkland Islands War and making inferences from them about politically relevant expectations. These inferences are constantly updated by new information gleaned from similar events. In predicting or projecting future behavior, of course, account is taken of a variety of other unique political factors that characterize any event. It is no disservice to law to acknowledge that prescriptions about what one *ought* to do are, alas, only one factor in deciding what one *will* do. Naturally, the weight accorded prescriptive norms will vary with the factual context, the identity of the actors, and the effectiveness of the legal system enforcing the norms.

The normative expectations that political analysts infer from events are the substance of much of contemporary international law. The fact that the people who are inferring norms from incidents do not refer to the product of their inquiry as "international law" in no way affects the validity of their enterprise, any more than the obliviousness of Molière's M. Jourdain to the fact that he was speaking prose meant that he was not. Whatever it is called, law it is. Yet, at least on first consideration, it is startlingly inconsistent with our accepted notions of law to suggest that one ought to orient oneself in the international legal system by reference to these incidents rather than primarily by reference to statutes, treaties, venerable custom, and judicial and arbitral opinions.

4. The problem is not identifying "sources" of law, but being certain that something in a particular source *is* law. "[M]ore traditional approaches, such as the enumeration of sources in the International Court's statute article 38 are not wrong, but are incomplete. Something may fall within one of the formal sources, but simply not be or have ceased to be law." Reisman, *International Lawmaking: A Process of Communication*, 1981 PROC. AM. SOC'Y INT'L L. 101, 119 (1981).

Indeed, as we shall see, the jurisprudential implications of this reorganization of focus are profound, in ways going beyond even Jellinek's disquieting observation about the "normative force of the factual."[5]

INTERNATIONAL LAWYERS AND INCIDENTS

International lawyers frequently lament the fact that they are rarely consulted by foreign policy decision makers. This cannot be attributed to a general, visceral dislike of lawyers, for government officials, when operating in a domestic setting, frequently consult lawyers. They correctly assume that lawyers are reliable specialists in understanding the expectations of those who are politically and legally effective. Why is it that the same decision makers do not resort to international lawyers with comparable frequency?

There are numerous reasons why international lawyers are increasingly irrelevant in many areas of international politics, not all of them attributable to the lawyers themselves. We cannot ignore the advanced decay of the formal legal system that was painstakingly reconstructed after World War II. One is as unlikely to seek and pay for the advice of the votaries of a demonstrably ineffective legal system as one is to seek and pay for the blessings of the high priests of a sect manifestly out of favor with the pertinent divinity. But the problems we call "legal" continue to present themselves for resolution, whatever the state of the system; someone must perform legal functions even in a decaying system.

The reasons for the diminished relevance of international lawyers are attributable less to the system, however, than to the international lawyers themselves and the jurisprudential framework within which they operate. For key areas of public international law, international lawyers make themselves irrelevant by failing to identify what international law in this context is and by failing to report it to those to whom they are responsible. International lawyers pay relatively little attention to the incidents from which political advisors infer their normative universe. Rather, they persist in constructing their normative universe from texts. They thus confine their attention to sources of international law that were either merely ceremonial at their inception, or that, although animated by more normative intentions when they were created, have

5. G. JELLINEK, ALLGEMEINE STAATSLEHRE 308 (1900).

ceased to be congruent with expectations of authority and control held by effective elites.

To be sure, some international lawyers try to examine practice but, as we will see, that exercise is quite a different enterprise from the intuitive legal research of the political advisor. Rather than seeing incidents as norm-indicators or norm-generators, as does the political advisor, the international lawyer generally reacts to them in judgmental fashion, assuming that the norm in question is *a priori* and enduring and examining the incidents in terms of whether they indicate that a particular norm has been violated.

The question the political analyst will ask, in contrast, is not simply whether the acts at issue have violated some preexisting norm but rather, whether expectations entertained by effective elites about what is permissible may be inferred from their behavior. The question is eminently practical, for even those who do not regularly use the word "law" in their discourse, and even those who snicker when others use it, must make estimates about the subjectivities of allies and adversaries alike. These subjectivities necessarily include what those actors think is right. In a world in which allies and adversaries do not submit to intensive interviews and rarely volunteer or are permitted to tell the whole truth (if any part of it), deeds—actions and reactions—become one of the few available windows to what others are thinking, either consciously or unconsciously.

By default, the political advisor becomes a do-it-yourself lawyer.

FINDING THE LAW IN DOMESTIC SYSTEMS

All lawyers, whether domestic or international, face the same core problem in seeking to ascertain the law: to identify the operational norms used by those who are politically and legally relevant in projected situations, so that accurate predictions of how they are likely to characterize and react to different behavioral options can be made, and the most promising plans of action can be fashioned and recommended to the client.

In the United States, identifying the law is simple and relatively routinized. For one thing, the lawyer knows who the decision makers are. Statutes are reliable guides to legal expectations, but it is court decisions that present the real test: experience has taught American lawyers that for almost all of their purposes, lawmaking is what the courts in fact do. That insight has allowed American legal science to adopt, as its basic unit of knowledge, what we might call its "epistemic" unit, the appellate decision. A tremendous and technologically impressive industry has developed to report, catalogue, and analyze these epistemic units, all of which are made available to practitioners and scholars in retrieval systems of increasing speed and sophistication. The systems of inference called "legal reasoning" or "legal logic" are applied to these epistemic units and become an important part of the repertory of the lawyer in predicting future decisions by courts and in trying to influence them.

Why have judicial decisions in the United States been a fairly accurate indicator of the operational norms entertained by politically relevant strata? Some American lawyers, without comparative or historical perspective, have assumed that the answer to that question can be found in the inherent character of courts. This is a misleading oversimplification, for it looks at a result without reference to the causal factors that produced it. In particular, it evades the important prior question of *why* courts are effective in this environment. Not surprisingly, those who accept this apparent insight and have sought to apply it in the international sphere have concluded that the unruliness and violence of international politics is attributable to the absence of courts. For instance, the peace movement in the United States of the late nineteenth century was, in large part, a movement to establish an international judicial system. Indeed, it was a major factor in the creation of the international courts of the twentieth century.[6]

Since 1899, international courts in one form or another have existed, but the unruliness and violence of the arena have persisted. Plainly, it is not the presence or absence of courts that determines whether minimum order will obtain. Other factors are critical.

Courts have been significant political institutions in the United States not because of something inherent in courts or in the law they process but because of the continuing congruence in U.S. politics of expectations of authority and expectations of control. Expectations of authority are subjective images of how power ought to be exercised; expectations of control are subjective images of how power will in fact be exercised. The more congruent those two sets of expectations, the

6. For background, see DAVIS, THE UNITED STATES AND THE FIRST HAGUE PEACE CONFERENCE (1962).

more effective the legal system in question. This is not the only possible constellation of power and authority. In Venezuela, during the nineteenth century, to cite only one contrasting example, a type of *caudillo* system obtained: all of the formal institutions of power—legislature, court, and sometimes even the executive branch—were essentially powerless and were largely ignored by those holding effective power.[7]

In the United States, the relatively stable political system and the preeminent role assigned to courts within it had a striking effect on the sociology of legal knowledge. Coordinately, it was an important factor in stimulating the creation and then in shaping the unique direction of American law schools and the specialized methods developed there for teaching the "science of law." Oliver Wendell Holmes captured the basic spirit of this new legal science when he stated that law was nothing more than the prediction of what courts will do: "The prophecies of what the courts will do in fact, and nothing more pretentious, are what I mean by the law."[8] Obviously, American lawyers were doing and continue to do much more than merely predict what courts will do. But the power of Holmes's insight derived from the regularly validated fact that what courts in the United States were saying was a remarkably reliable indicator of the probable future actions and reactions of effective elites. Given this degree of predictive power, it is hardly surprising that lawyers should have begun to study appellate decisions.

It has been said that a key part of the American genius is the capacity to mass produce and distribute a good idea. Consistent with Holmes's apothegm, Christopher Columbus Langdell established, at the Harvard Law School, a teaching method that assumed that the fundamental epistemic unit of legal science was the appellate opinion. "It seemed to me," Langdell wrote in the introduction to his casebook on contracts, ". . . to be possible to take such a branch of the law as Contracts, for example, and, without exceeding comparatively moderate limits, to select, classify, and arrange all the cases which had contributed in any important degree to the growth, development, or establishment of any of its essential doctrines."[9] Thus, one could organize these opinions

7. *See, e.g.*, R. Perez Perdomo, El Formalismo Juridico y sus Funciones Sociales en el Siglo XIX Venezolano (1978); *see also* Reisman, Book Review, 29 Am. J. Comp. L. 727 (1981) (reviewing R. Perez Perdomo, El Formalismo Juridico y sus Funciones Sociales en el Siglo XIX Venezolano (1978)).

8. Holmes, *The Path of the Law*, in Collected Legal Papers 167, 173 (1921).

9. C. Langdell, A Selection of Cases on the Law of Contracts vii (1871).

9

into a coherent body of law, treating each as a self-contained and self-explanatory unit, consistent in its properties with others. The examination of these epistemic units could provide the basis for a thorough and systematic legal education.

Law schools stimulated the development of a new genre of legal literature, the "casebook," to be used in the institutions of legal education. Casebooks encompassed the legal universe, for Langdell had decreed "[f]irst, that law is a science; secondly [sic], that all of the available materials of that science are contained in printed books."[10] This preoccupation with cases engendered increasingly sophisticated procedures for gathering, processing, analyzing, and retrieving appellate opinions on a national scale. All of these developments combined to enculturate, even more intensely, those trained in American law to think in terms of cases, with all that that implied.

TRANSPOSING DOMESTIC METHODS TO THE INTERNATIONAL SYSTEM

Since the end of the nineteenth century, great efforts have been mounted to create in the international arena a set of institutions comparable to those to be found in Western Europe and North America. Since 1945, the result of this handiwork has been a complex superstructure and administrative apparatus that bears striking resemblance, at least superficially, to national governments in Western Europe and North America. In the General Assembly of the United Nations, some purport to find something comparable to a legislature. The Secretariat of the United Nations is compared to a domestic Executive Branch, and the specialized agencies of the United Nations are likened to the regulatory agencies of modern industrial government. Most reassuring, the International Court of Justice sits in splendor in The Hague, as the "principal judicial organ" of the United Nations.[11]

It is absurd to assume that the mere existence of this network of international institutions means that it is as effective as a domestic government and that its edicts may be relied upon; Holmes could plausibly direct his readers to do no more than study the behavior of courts to predict the development of law because the context within which his

10. Address by Langdell (1886), *cited in* Stevens, *Two Cheers for 1870: The American Law School*, 5 PERSPECTIVES OF AMERICAN HISTORY 405, 436 (1971).
11. UN CHARTER art. 92.

courts operated gave them effective power to prescribe legal rules.[12] Professors who gave the same instructions to their students of international law would be leading their charges into a fantasy world. The sad fact is that the apparent governmental network that has been established internationally has little power. What power it has in certain cases is assigned to it by effective elites who have sometimes found it useful to use the United Nations or a related agency in a particular instance.

Students of international law, like their domestic counterparts, frequently tend to define decisions in terms of the institutions rendering them. In the domestic law systems of Western Europe and North America, courts, for historical reasons, have been deemed to be the authoritative appliers of the law. Hence legal decisions are defined essentially as the handicraft of those courts. Insofar as there is a congruence between actual political power in the community and the authority of courts, that focus can provide a cogent indicator of decisions. In fact, such a congruence is rarely perfect, and the identification of judgments as decisions in a larger sense frequently leads to the distortions characteristic of much academic law.[13]

Indeed, even in effectively organized legal systems, which are characterized by a general convergence of authority and control, key parts of "book law" may fail to approximate the actual normative expectations of elites. This may occur for two major reasons inherent in the very character of law: discrepancies between myth system and operational code and the differential rates of decay of text and context.

In an earlier study, I noted that, in all legal systems, much of what is expressed in legal formulae and is attended by signals of authority is not intended to govern, regulate, or provide effective guidelines for official or private behavior. This part of the "legal system" conveys aspirations and images, not of the way things are, but of the way group members like to believe they are. This is particularly striking in the area of public law:

12. Holmes, *supra* note 8 at 167.
13. Constitutional law in American law schools is identified as the work of the Supreme Court in supervising the discharge of what is decided are the "constitutional functions" performed by all other authorized agencies in the national community. But the Constitution is not a document; it is an institution, as Llewellyn put it. As such, it involves a process in which many other formal and informal, authoritative and functional actors participate. These, alas, are never studied under the rubric of constitutional law. In this respect, there is no comprehensive course on constitutional law in any meaningful sense in American law schools.

The picture produced by control institutions does not correspond, point for point, with the actual flow of behavior of those institutions in the performance of their public function: indeed, there may be very great discrepancies between it and the actual way of doing things. The persistent discrepancies do not necessarily mean that there is no "law," that in those sectors "anything goes," for some of those discrepancies may conform to a different code. They may indicate an additional set of expectations and demands that are effectively, though often informally, sanctioned and that guide actors when they deal with "the real world." Hence we encounter two "relevant" normative systems: one that is supposed to apply, which continues to enjoy lip service among elites, and one that is actually applied. Neither should be confused with actual behavior, which may be discrepant from both.

A disengaged observer might call the norm system of the official picture the myth system of the group. Parts of it provide the appropriate code of conduct for most group members; for some, most of it is their normative guide. But there are enough discrepancies between this myth system and the way things are actually done by key official or effective actors to force the observer to apply another name for the unofficial but nonetheless effective guidelines for behavior in those discrepant sectors: the operational code. Bear in mind that the terms *myth system* and *operational code* are functional creations of the observer for describing the actual flow of official behavior or the official picture.[14]

People who seek legal advice plainly require it with regard to both the myth system and the operational code: myth system because it is applied in part by some institutions, which are, in fact, controlling; operational code because it is applied by others. The myth system is readily retrievable through conventional research in the formal repositories of law. The operational code, in contrast, must be sought in elite behavior.

Even if there is little divergence between myth system and operational code, the differing rate of decay of text and context may limit the usefulness of formal sources of law. The proverbial decrees of the Medes and the Persians still exist; the context in which they were created and in which they had legal relevance is gone. Whether a partic-

14. REISMAN, FOLDED LIES: BRIBERY, CRUSADES AND REFORMS 15–16 (1979).

ular exercise of lawmaking seeks to stabilize or change a situation, if it is concerned not with ornamenting myth but with doing what it says it is doing, there must be a minimum congruence between the sociopolitical context prevailing at the time and the sociopolitical presumptions of the legislation. Once legislation is expressed in relatively enduring textual form, however, its rate of decay is minimal; the rate of decay of the encompassing sociopolitical situation will always be greater and may, indeed, be extremely rapid.

Where fidelity to text acquires in itself a symbolic political value, texts whose literal congruence with the sociopolitical situation is less than when they were created may misguide those who would rely on them. At the very least, those who would rely on them may need a validation technique for determining their degree of accuracy. Courts may serve this purpose, but if they themselves and the ambit of their jurisdiction are creatures of legislation, a functional and noninstitutional test is required.

THE COSTS OF TRANSPOSITION

In the international arena, the law is applied, for the most part, through a variety of informal channels and rarely benefits from formal appraisal by a court or tribunal. The International Court, with its usual load of two or three cases per year, and public international arbitral tribunals, with scarcely more than that, can hardly be deemed to represent international decision.

Despite the relative inactivity of these institutions, many international scholars continue to view them as the virtual apotheosis and most authoritative expression of international law. The deference given ad hoc arbitral tribunals is symptomatic of this general problem and sometimes takes the most extraordinary form. A tribunal established by one party, in the absence of the other, and composed of a single person, let us say a professor of international law, is treated by other scholars as an authoritative oracle of international law. At the same time, commentators who defer to such an award will insist that a contrary General Assembly vote, supported by virtually every member state, is not indicative of international law but is only a "recommendation."[15]

15. See, e.g., the Caltex Award, and the *ipse dixit* of the arbitrator overruling a widely supported vote of the General Assembly. Award on the Merits in Dispute Between Tex-

There are, to be sure, certain methodological advantages in using the international case as an epistemic unit. Part of the attraction lies in its relative simplicity, economy, and availability. Once there is fundamental agreement among scholars that the case is an epistemic unit, there need be no detailed investigation of factual material outside of the case, for the case carries its own authoritative factual statement. Alternative methods of research could require extensive fieldwork or culling through thousands of pages of documents of uneven probative value, in order to determine what the decision actually was. A case presents that decision in a neat "bite-sized" and easily digestible package, creating in the process an illusion of consensus about the underlying events that probably does not exist.

"Stipulating" the facts permits students of this epistemic unit to get on with discussions of the law, freed from complicating political issues. For those who confuse clerical tidiness with scientific method, there is the ecstacy of imagining that the case method is "scientific," an enthusiasm apparently animating many of the consumers of Langdell's work. And of course, there is the latent drive among all who have been given professional legal training to view things in terms of courts. Outside of the United States, admiration for the stability and achievements of the American political-legal system leads many scholars to seek to adopt the American legal style, as if the method of observation can bring about qualitative changes in the things observed.

Yielding to these attractions, contemporary international legal science has adopted a decisional unit that is convenient for scholars but ill-tooled for the subject matter. It is reminiscent of the familiar story of a man, out walking one night on a street in Vienna, who happens on another well-dressed and plainly sober citizen who is crawling about on all fours in the light cast by a street lamp. Naturally, the first fellow stops to find out if there is something wrong. When the man on the ground explains that he has lost his watch, the passerby offers to help him find it and asks exactly where it fell. "Back there," the man on the ground motions, pointing into the darkness on the other side of the street. "Then why aren't you looking there?" the first fellow asks in exasperation. "Because," the man on the ground explains as if it were perfectly obvious, "it's dark over there and I can't see. But here it's light."

aco Overseas Petroleum Company/California Asiatic Oil Company and the Government of the Libyan Arab Republic, 17 I.L.M. 1, 27–31 (1978).

The transposition of the case unit to the international arena has permitted international lawyers to dwell in a comforting pool of light. Yet much of the resulting international legal description is patently out of step with elite expectations. The discrepancy is so painfully obvious that, outside the small circle of international lawyers, it brings discredit upon the very notion of international law.[16] Small wonder that political advisors rarely use their international lawyers.

TOWARD A NEW INTERNATIONAL EPISTEMIC UNIT

Our hypothetical political advisor in Beijing studying the responses of effective elites around the world during the Falkland Islands War is an intuitive Holmesian. Rather than examine what is written in books about law, the advisor located the functional elites whose behavior determined the outcome and made inferences about international law accordingly.

If law is to be found in significant part in the application of norms to particular cases and controversies, it is plain that such applications in international politics must be sought in a much wider range of arenas than the highly formalized and structured judicial fora of domestic systems. If this is done effectively, both scholar and practitioner will have more reliable barometers of prevailing conceptions of law and the realities of the application of norms. Increased realism may aid not only the practitioner advising clients but those attempting to identify pathological features of the international legal system in order to develop alternatives.

One such alternative would take account of the limited cogency in the international arena of the case as an epistemic unit by developing an additional unit that might be referred to generically as the "incident." I define an "incident" as an overt conflict between two or more actors in the international system. It must be perceived as such by other key actors and resolved in some nonjudicial fashion. Finally, and of critical importance, its resolution must provide some indication of what elites in a variety of effective processes consider to be acceptable behavior. Though the incident is "resolved," in a factual if not authoritative sense, without the judicial imprimatur that routinely indicates law in

---

16. Indeed, even from judges in a system in which international law is the "supreme law of the land." *See, e.g.*, separate opinion of Robb, J. in Tel-Oren vs. Libyan Arab Republic, 726 F.2d 774, 823–27 (D.C. Cir. 1984).

domestic settings, the incident may often be a more reliable indicator of international law than are codes or case law.

Note that the inquiry being proposed here is quite different from the routine examination of "practice" in international law. That inquiry seeks to establish the existence of a bilateral or general norm or custom, by examining, ostensibly, a broad pattern of practice of states.[17] There are many intellectual difficulties with the inquiry into practice. Neither the volume nor the degree of uniformity of practice required has ever been stated with precision. Moreover, examinations of practice do not control for the variable of power. They do not seek to identify who, among a large cast of characters, is effective. The incident, in contrast, is not based on a large volume or flow of supposedly "uniform" events, but instead takes a single critical event as a prism through which the reactions of elites to particular behavior may be examined and assessed as an indication of their views of law.

The incident as an epistemic unit does not, of itself, provide a more accurate and reliable indicator of what elites hold the law to be. There must be some systematic and disciplined way of reporting, codifying, and appraising incidents. Without such a systemization, there is little to recommend the incident over the intuitive inferences of political analysts such as our Chinese advisor. Moreover, reliance on a single incident, or a small number of them, can lead to the same skewing effect encountered in making inferences about contemporary international law from a small number of judicial decisions. Indeed, the skewing effect may be even more distorting, because given the political context of the events being examined, only a small segment of the global elite may be involved in a single incident. What is needed is a systematic method for studying and recording incidents so that through their constant preparation, our understanding of elite expectations can be continually refined and corrected. In short, a paradigm must be established and a genre created.

CHOOSING INCIDENTS

Among the formidable challenges posed by this proposal is the development of criteria by which incidents are to be selected. Pending the

17. On the role of practice in the formation of international law, see generally BROWNLIE, PRINCIPLES OF PUBLIC INTERNATIONAL LAW 4-11 (1973); JENKS, THE COMMON LAW OF MANKIND 1-19 (1958); 1 O'CONNELL, INTERNATIONAL LAW 1-22 (1965).

development of a substantial catalogue of incidents, the necessarily subjective choice from among the infinite number of international events may tend to reflect the biases of those making the selection. This problem would not be a novel one for legal epistemology, though at first glance, it might appear to be. At a superficial level, the body of case law, both domestic and international, exhibits a certain random if not haphazard quality. In the domestic sphere, most cases are initiated by private entities seeking to maximize their special interests, and, accordingly, the judicial responses to these private claims may have little to do with central elite concerns. In the international sphere, key actors rarely go to court. If they do, they usually are careful to prescribe in advance the norms to be applied and to circumscribe the potential consequences of the judgment. This randomness would appear to minimize the bias of a formal selection process, though, of course, it also renders case law less reliable as an indicator of elite perspectives.

A closer look at the judicial function reveals a very different picture. Formal decision makers are not passive receivers of the cases they hear or the codes they shape. In the United States, the Supreme Court reserves for itself, in all but a limited category of cases, the power to determine which cases it will certify for appeal before it. In this respect, it is an implicit but nonetheless decisive factor in establishing the contours as well as the content of the normative code it processes. As the agency with the ultimate competence to determine, once parties submit to it, the cases it will hear, the International Court may play a comparable role in its sphere. Hence it is far from unprecedented that those preparing incidents themselves choose, from the sadly abundant harvest of conflict in daily international political life, events that are especially fit for study as incidents.

In fact, the student of incidents may be in a position to make a more neutral choice than that of the formal decision maker and to provide a more accurate picture of the operation of international law. An institution like the International Court of Justice may have to avoid cases which would pit it head on against the power process in order to preserve itself.[18] As a result, the case law it produces may be limited to certain peripheral areas of community organization. In contrast, the student of incidents may chose to study and report as incidents any

18. *See generally* REISMAN, NULLITY AND REVISION: THE REVIEW AND ENFORCEMENT OF INTERNATIONAL JUDGMENTS AND AWARDS 268–418 (1971); *see also* Reisman, *supra* note 4.

congeries of past events. The critical problem is to choose events that accurately reflect key elite expectations. How is this to be done?

In constitutional law, the archetypal "important case" is characterized by an appreciation on the part of all those who are involved in the case that it is "decisive," i.e., that its disposition is likely to reshape the constitutive process or key aspects of public order. Some incidents may be characterized by participants in the same manner; they sense that the issues at stake and the way they are decided will have a decisive effect on expectations of authority with ramifying effects on political processes. But this sense of moment on the part of participants in a situation is not a necessary characteristic of those events that are chosen to be treated as incidents. Their perceptions may be underinclusive, overinclusive, or both. Thus, they may accord little authoritative weight to events that reinforce or make only minor changes in norms, but that are nonetheless of importance in explaining how international decisions are made. On the other hand, they may exaggerate the importance of particular events as a way of mobilizing themselves, their polities, or their allies in a program that serves their own interests. It is, in the final analysis, the perspective of the student of incidents, rather than of the participants in the events themselves, that must be determinative. Important cases are not all constitutional cases; and incidents do not comprise only "constitutive" events.

IDENTIFYING THE RELEVANT FACTS

Napoleon's remark that history is a collection of lies we all agree upon has an especially wicked relevance when we consider as a source of history the recital of the facts contained in judicial opinions. The statement of "relevant" facts determined by a court would rarely satisfy a historian; indeed, what the court leaves out is often of most interest to the student of politics and history. Consider a few examples.

The *Schooner Exchange*[19] judgment of Chief Justice Marshall is usually cited as the cornerstone for the doctrine that the public acts of foreign governments will not be reviewed by the courts of another state even if the effects of the act are felt in that other state. Somehow the judgment never states the extraordinary fact that the case was being decided against the background of the War of 1812, in which the Brit-

19. 11 U.S. (7 Cranch) 116 (1812).

ish had set fire to Washington. France, the real defendant, was the only ally of the United States. It seems most unlikely under these circumstances that any United States court would have risked imperilling that relationship. In the *Corfu Channel Case* (United Kingdom v. Albania),[20] the International Court somehow never mentions the fact that the Greek Civil War was under way, that the United Kingdom was a major supporter of the Royalist cause, and that Albania, as a proxy for another superpower, was supporting the Communist insurgency. The presence of the British ships in the Straits of Corfu unquestionably constituted a manifest military communication to the Albanians and others about the limits of British tolerance, the susceptibility of Albania to coastal attacks, and the capacity of the British fleet to project its force into that arena.

The point need not be belabored. What these cases demonstrate is that there is no authoritative institution to decree or stipulate that the facts that have been assembled in judgments meet the standards of historical accuracy.

Indeed, legal science is often impatient to finish with "the facts" and to get on with "the law." First-instance factual determinations are only rarely reviewed. Subsequent instances simplify the facts even further. In American legal education, the tendency of first-year students to seek to learn more about the facts of the case is often characterized as a frivolous interest; students are urged to get on with the legal analysis.

There are some cogent reasons for this cultivated astigmatism. Every science develops its own specialized lens in order to focus more sharply and intensively on that aspect of life of interest to it. The particular focus of legal science distinguishes it from history and sociology and does, indeed, permit it to concentrate more effectively on the normative or policy dimensions of problems. But sometimes, sticky political problems or issues can be concealed under a bare factual statement and the infinitely obscurantist potentialities of legal language. These selective abbreviations, whatever their intradisciplinary justification, inevitably produce a legal version of the facts that historians and political advisors often see as, at best, thin and brittle, and, at worst, caricatures of what actually transpired. Because a fuller and more accurate understanding of the facts is indispensable to ascertaining what was actually

20. 1949 I.C.J. 4.

decided, the versions of the facts often presented by judges may undermine the effectiveness of the predictive function of case law.

The sporadic fashion in which the facts become available in incidents presents a special problem. Many facts are concealed for years or even generations. The attack on Pearl Harbor, for example, could not be described with any accuracy until the archives in all the relevant capitals were at last made accessible to historians. It took a generation for scholars to provide a comprehensive picture that could demonstrate the incorrectness of many of their initial conclusions about the incident.[21] Similarly, the extent of U.S. involvement in the overthrow of the Mossadegh government in Iran and the reinstallation of the Pahlavi dynasty in 1953 was not established until years later.[22]

If incident studies had been prepared for each of these events, they would, in all likelihood, have been factually inaccurate or incomplete. If a complete statement of the facts were a prerequisite for studying incidents, several of the studies in this volume would be barred. That would be most unfortunate, for whether or not lawyers study incidents, political actors unquestionably do. They use the best information available in making inferences about normative expectations, among other things.

This is not a problem unique to incidents. In some cases, national courts refuse to exercise jurisdiction because information indispensable to judgment cannot be secured. In international law, judgments of the International Court of Justice may be reopened and revised on the basis of new facts or new information.[23] If anything, the problem is considerably less severe in the study of incidents. The student of incidents, it will be recalled, is not involved in judging the lawfulness of the behavior of actors in the incident concerned, but rather evaluates the reactions of other relevant actors and, through those reactions, the subjec-

21. *See, e.g.*, G. PRANGE, AT DAWN WE SLEPT: THE UNTOLD STORY OF PEARL HARBOR (1981).

22. *See* 1 SENATE SELECT COMMITTEE TO STUDY GOVERNMENTAL OPERATIONS WITH RESPECT TO INTELLIGENCE ACTIVITIES, FINAL REPORT ON FOREIGN AND MILITARY INTELLIGENCE, S. REP. No. 755, 94th Cong., 2d Sess. 111 (1976).

23. Statute of the International Court of Justice, art. 61(2). The government of Tunisia recently invoked this provision in seeking a revision of the ICJ's 1982 judgment regarding the delimitation of the continental shelf between Tunisia and Libya. *See* ICJ Application Instituting Proceedings filed in the Registry of the Court on 27 July 1984. Application for Revision and Interpretation of the Judgment of 24 February 1982 in the case concerning the Continental Shelf (Tunisia v. Libyan Arab Jamahiriya).

tive conceptions of right and/or tolerable behavior entertained by those other actors. Hence what is important in this exercise is not so much what happened as what effective elites think happened and how they react.

A related practical difficulty in constructing the genre of incidents is the question of boundaries: where does a particular incident begin and where does it end? A case presupposes a consensus that critical events begin and end at some point. An incident is not bounded with such precision. Because of this, there is some question as to when it ends, if at all. Territorial losses, for example, may be viewed by the party securing acquisition as completed incidents, with title consolidated by adverse possession. But the losing party may continue to view the lost territories as its own and dream and plan for their repatriation. Hence the two parties to an incident may have diametrically opposite conceptions of when or whether the incident has ended. It is the observer of the incident who must, in effect, establish boundaries in time. Those boundaries are determined primarily by the norms the observer chooses to examine.

BIAS IN THE CHOICE AND CONSTRUCTION OF INCIDENTS

Most of the incidents in this volume were prepared by young North American students in a seminar conducted by North American scholars. Every effort was made to be scrupulous in the description of the events and the facts. Yet, without question, factors such as nationality, culture, class, race or ethnicity, interest group, and exposure to crisis influenced the choice of events, their description, and their appraisal. Students of incidents are certainly prone to this pathology, but theirs is not a unique susceptibility. Court personnel are as subject to bias as anyone else, yet, as we have seen, their factual recitations receive remarkably uncritical acceptance by virtue of their presumed neutrality. Precisely because this is a presumption that students of incidents are never likely to enjoy, it is arguably the case that factual bias will prove less of a problem for the incident study than it is for the judicial opinion. The quality of the factual description will be assessed on its merits and, thus, must meet a standard ordinarily not applied to factual statements in judgments. Moreover, the relation of facts to conclusions is qualitatively different in an incident than in a judgment. The incident, after all, is not a judgment of the lawfulness of the behavior of a given actor. It is, rather, an attempt to identify, by an examination of the reaction of all other actors, what norms were actually engaged in a particular incident.

NORMATIVE IMPLICATIONS OF THE APPROACH

The modern notion of law envisions a rational process of organized public deliberation. This is seen as increasing the likelihood of agreement on community goals, with a thorough canvassing of the comparative social costs of alternative methods of securing them. Additionally, such a process ensures equality of treatment and facilitates participation by all interested parties.

Some who endorse this concept of law are apt to find disturbing the fact that the incidents approach draws its normative inferences from no more than the apparent expectations of elites. The approach thus seems to devalue the rational and deliberative elements of lawmaking. It is not the intention of the incidents approach to do so. It strives merely to acknowledge the painful fact that these elements are all too frequently jettisoned by effective elites in their decision-making calculus. It is true that in recognizing the potential desuetude of the formal legal order, the approach may, in the short term, exacerbate the problem. However, insofar as it aids in diagnosis, it may be hoped that the incidents approach will be a positive first step in restoring rational, deliberative lawmaking in the international community.

USING THE RESULTS OF INCIDENT STUDIES

In formal systems based on *stare decisis*, previous judgments of courts are invoked in current disputes in an effort to persuade the court that the facts in the older case are sufficiently similar to those at bar to warrant applying the same legal specification to them. Citation of previous decisions performs a systemic function as well, for it validates the authority and significance of the very institution that has been called upon to render judgment.

It is doubtful that incidents can aspire to a comparable utility in formal decision situations. In the first place, international adjudication and arbitration are creatures of contract. The international tribunal trying a case is frequently bound to apply law, as defined in its constitutive instrument. Thus, the International Court of Justice is admonished in its Statute to apply to the cases before it a wholly anachronistic conception of international law that excludes some of its most dynamic elements. In this context, it would be unavailing and possibly perilous to invite a tribunal to conceive of the law it is to apply in terms of incidents.

In a more profound sense, international tribunals may be expected to resist the very idea of the incident as an epistemic unit of law. After all, its *raison d'être* as a genre, as well as each individual incident study, presupposes the frequent ineffectiveness of formal decision institutions. In this respect, the incident cannot and, indeed, should not be expected to supplant case law. Rather, incidents may serve as a type of "meta-law," providing normative guidelines for decision makers in the international system in those vast deserts in which case law is sparse. The incident study can also aid in evaluating the output of the formal institutions of international law in those rare oases where its growth is luxuriant.

CONCLUSION

This volume contains a set of studies of contemporary incidents. Together they may be taken as a first, experimental effort at establishing a format for a new genre in international legal analysis. It is hoped that the economy of the format and the reliability of the normative descriptions it provides will gain international acceptance for the incidents approach.

A single collection of incidents will be of relatively little value. A genre whose practitioners continue to update and correct the expression of the code of international law is required. If it is established and adopted (and adapted) by a number of other scholars, it can ultimately yield an abundant literature of international appraisal, richer than the limited number of cases decided by courts, more representative of actual decision trends, more indicative of the political context in which decisions are taken and implemented and, most important, more accurate in expressing international normative expectations.

It is to be hoped that this effort will generate interest in the incident as an indicator of law and a form of knowledge, and that volumes will follow on a regular basis, setting out current incidents. Innovative student international law journals in the United States might establish a section of each issue dedicated to incidents, alongside the more conventional case note. By providing a more accurate and comprehensive picture of how international law is made and applied, efforts such as these may aid in the performance of legal tasks and in identifying and bringing about needed constitutive changes in the international legal system.

2 INCIDENTS: An Essay in Method

ANDREW R. WILLARD

In studying incidents for the purpose of monitoring the genesis, modification and termination of international norms, there are advantages to having a broadly homogeneous approach. Although creative efforts in the genre need not conform to rigid specifications, certain general features would seem indispensable to a systematic study. The pieces included in this volume approach the study of incidents in a comparable fashion: each identifies the problem to be covered and its legal importance, presents a detailed account of the facts of the incident and the claims brought by the participants, analyzes how a complex and frequently unorganized decision process resolved the incident, and finally, appraises the international legal significance and implications of the incident.

The preceding can be summarized in tabular fashion:

Suggested Sequence for Research and Writing of Incident Studies

I. *Preliminary Research and Problem Selection.*
   A. Background reading and interviewing.
   B. Problem selection, with a statement of its relevance to international law.

    C. Provisional characterization of the particular problem, facts, and relevant norms.

    D. Clarification of author's standpoint and methodological concerns.

II. *Statement of the facts, including:*

    A. Who participated?

    B. With what perspectives (i.e., expectations, demands, identifications)?

    C. In which situations (e.g., geographic, temporal, institutional, crisis)?

    D. Employing what bases of influence (e.g., control over people, perspectives, situations, values, resources, and strategic instruments)?

    E. Manipulating what strategies (e.g., diplomatic, ideological, economic, military), in what combinations, and in what modalities (e.g., persuasive, coercive)?

    F. With what outcome(s)?

III. *Identification and description of conflicting claims, including fact characterization and legal justifications.*

IV. *"Final" identification of the norm(s) under consideration.*

V. *Description and analysis of the international appraisal of the incident, including:*

    A. Who participated in the international appraisal?

    B. With what perspectives (e.g., notion of lawfulness, criteria for determining lawfulness, method and rationale for applying criteria of lawfulness)?

    C. In what situations?

    D. Employing what bases of influence?

    E. Manipulating what strategies, in what combinations and modalities?

    F. With what outcome(s) (i.e., the impact of the incident on the norm(s) under consideration in terms of intensity, scope, domain, and duration)?

VI. *Author's appraisal.*

    A. Establishment of standpoint and procedures for self-scrutiny.

    B. Delimitation of focus of inquiry (clarifying conceptions of relevant community, with balanced emphasis on perspectives and operations, and conceptions of law, including expectations of authority and control).

    C. *Performance of intellectual tasks.*

        1. Postulation of basic goals and clarification of related community policies.

        2. Evaluation of the contribution of the norm(s) to the achievement of goals and policies.

3. Analysis of factors that determine how the norm(s) translate into practice.
4. Projection of probable courses of development for the norm(s).
5. Design, evaluation, and proposal of alternative means for influencing development of the norm(s) in ways intended to yield results compatible with postulated goals and clarified policies.

METHODOLOGICAL CONCERNS AND THE IMPORTANCE OF CLARIFYING STANDPOINT

A useful incident study draws inferences regarding the expectations of the politically relevant actors.[1] The validity of these inferences depends in part on an understanding of the role the author plays in observing the event (observational standpoint) and of the author's motives in selecting and drawing inferences from the incident (motivational standpoint).

In general, an incident might be viewed from any of four observational standpoints: that of participant, spectator, interviewer, or collector.[2] Because few analysts of international incidents have the opportunity to be involved in the incident immediately as participant or spectator, the most relevant observational standpoints for the purposes of incident study are those of interviewer and collector.

Interviewing the politically relevant actors in an incident usually provides important information about both the facts of the incident and the views of the participants. However, gaining access to the participants can be difficult, and the most accessible persons will usually have been spectators.

Perhaps the most common and certainly the easiest observational standpoint to adopt in studying incidents is that of collector. As a collector, the observer relies on records prepared by participants, interviewers, spectators, and other collectors as well as on news accounts and background studies of the area and the issues of concern. In interpreting those facts, one might also examine the sizable literature that explores the origins, role, and importance of perceptions in international politics, particularly those inquiries focused on the identification and

---

1. Politically relevant actors are those persons or groups whose participation in or reaction to an incident critically affects the outcome.
2. For further discussion, see Lasswell, *Intensive and Extensive Methods of Observing the Personality-Culture Manifold*, 1 YENCHING J. OF SOC. STUD. 72 (1938); *see generally* H. LASSWELL, THE ANALYSIS OF POLITICAL BEHAVIOR: AN EMPIRICAL APPROACH (1948).

function of norms of conduct in transnational and transcultural settings.[3]

The media occupy at various times each of the four observational standpoints. Initially a spectator, the media may become a participant in an incident as reports or the possibility of coverage influences the perspectives and behavior of participants. Under the right circumstances, the power of the media to focus public attention on a situation might be sufficient to transform that situation into an incident. Because the extensive involvement of the media in the events they report aggravates the problems of bias inherent in all reporting, the author should attempt to find independent corroboration whenever possible. For any information source, the author should be alert to the inherent bias in various collection techniques as well as to the relation between each observer and the subject being observed.

Bias may be a function not only of the observational standpoint but also of the motivational standpoint of the observer. It is important to distinguish between the descriptive standpoint of one primarily motivated to observe, and the prescriptive standpoint of one wishing to influence the behavior of the participants. Because most inquiries are motivated to some extent by both descriptive and prescriptive subjectivities, the analyst of international incidents should seek carefully to separate his or her personal appraisal of the lawfulness of the actor's behavior (prescriptive) from the international community's appraisal of lawfulness (descriptive). Moreover, the author should be aware of these motivational biases at each stage of the incident study, from selection of an event for study to the evaluation of the conflicting claims of the

3. *See, e.g.*, G. HOPPLE, POLITICAL PSYCHOLOGY AND BIOPOLITICS: ASSESSING AND PREDICTING ELITE BEHAVIOR IN FOREIGN POLICY CRISES (1980), which includes a good bibliography; STRUCTURE OF DECISION: THE COGNITIVE MAPS OF POLITICAL ELITES (R. Axelrod ed. 1976); *see also* PSYCHOLOGICAL MODELS IN INTERNATIONAL POLITICS (L. Falkowski ed. 1979); R. JERVIS, PERCEPTION AND MISPERCEPTION IN INTERNATIONAL POLITICS (1976); Hart, Cognitive Maps of Three Latin American Policy Makers, 30 WORLD POLITICS 115 (1977); Bobrow, *Transfer of Meaning Across National Boundaries*, in COMMUNICATION AND INTERNATIONAL POLITICS 33 (R. Merritt ed. 1972); Merritt, *Transmission of Values Across National Boundaries, id.* at 3; THOUGHT AND ACTION IN FOREIGN POLICY, PROCEEDINGS OF THE LONDON CONFERENCE ON COGNITIVE PROCESS MODELS OF FOREIGN POLICY (G. Bonham & M. Shapiro eds., 1973); K. GOLDMAN, INTERNATIONAL NORMS AND WAR BETWEEN STATES—THREE STUDIES IN INTERNATIONAL POLITICS (1971); INTERNATIONAL BEHAVIOR: A SOCIAL-PSYCHOLOGICAL ANALYSIS (H. Kelman ed. 1965). *See generally* H. TRIANDIS, THE ANALYSIS OF SUBJECTIVE CULTURE (1972); HANDBOOK OF CROSS-CULTURAL PSYCHOLOGY (H. Triandis ed. 1980).

actors. Certain precautions can be taken to recognize one's biases and to disclose them to the reader. It is generally useful in this connection to discuss one's choice of event or norm, or one's evaluations, with experts from different disciplines or different political or cultural perspectives. Similarly, making explicit the methodology employed in a study and the rationale for the author's choices helps inhibit the tendency to draw broader conclusions than the data support, and discloses to the reader the bases for one's conclusions.[4]

SELECTION OF INCIDENTS FOR STUDY

It is difficult to know whether a particular situation will provide fruitful study as an "incident," that is, as a situation that created, clarified, or changed the expectations of elites regarding international norms. Some events may not have called forth norms in a clear or definitive way so as to affect expectations regarding that norm. Further, a norm perceived by the public at large as having been involved in an event may obscure more subtle effects upon other, less obvious, norms. Hence, in assessing the provisional choice of subject, the author must begin by exploring the facts fully to determine whether the event seriously engaged international norms. Rather than judging the behavior of actors against preconceived norms, the author should focus on how and in what ways the resolution of the event engaged and subsequently shaped the development of those norms.

This provisional process of selection may be demonstrated by taking as an example the Persian Gulf War between Iran and Iraq. Among the innumerable international legal issues raised by the war are those concerning title to islands lying off the Arabian Peninsula, the effect of treaties purporting to delimit an international waterway, the validity of coerced agreements, the use of chemical and bacteriological weapons, and many other problems about the conduct of hostilities. Each of these issues might appear to engage a norm in a way that would provide a fruitful incident for study. Yet certain issues, such as the alleged use of chemical and bacteriological weapons, failed, at first, to generate sufficient international reaction to provide for satisfactory appraisal.

Though silence is not devoid of normative effect,[5] an incident study is better confined to those factual situations that not only attracted in-

---

4. See generally R. DAHRENDORF, ESSAYS IN THE THEORY OF SOCIETY (1969).
5. See, e.g., S. Ratner, "The Gulf of Sidra Incident of 1981: The Lawfulness of Peacetime Aerial Engagements," infra.

ternational attention but also set into motion a complex decision process that considered whether a norm was engaged and then moved toward consideration of a sanction. Having identified a situation meeting these criteria, the author can then begin to examine in detail what normative expectations existed when the incident began and how those norms were affected by the outcome of the incident.

IDENTIFYING RELEVANT NORMS

Some principles of international conduct are codifed in international conventions or expressed in law treatises. But these principles are not norms unless they are reflected in the expectations of political participants and animate their behavior. In other words, the expectations of politically relevant actors are what shape the norm and, therefore, are central to the norm-selection process.

When identifying expectations, one must be careful not to accept unquestioningly participants' assertions as to what they expected and why. First of all, what participants say may be a very poor indicator of what they actually believe or expect. In addition, the actors may not have been conscious of the norms that guided their behavior or were applied in the instance at hand. The researcher is therefore advised to supplement the study of words with a survey of trends in the historical, cultural, and contemporary international context within which the particular events took place.

It may also be necessary to adjust temporarily the time parameters of the study for purposes of selecting the relevant norms. That is, a norm may have been shaped long before the incident took place;[6] or it may have begun to develop only as a result of the incident.[7]

Brainstorming is also a legitimate means of identifying norms or expectations that might have guided the behavior of the participants in particular ways. However, in order to ensure that these norms are relevant, the brainstorming process needs to be disciplined by an understanding of the cultural, historical, and contemporary trends mentioned above. In this way, an adequate balance of creativity and discipline is achieved in the norm-selection process.[8]

6. See, e.g., R. Sadurska, "'Foreign Submarines in Swedish Waters: The Erosion of an International Norm," infra.
7. See, e.g., A. Cohen, "Cosmos 954: The International Law of Satellite Accidents," infra.
8. Each author may have a different method for identifying a norm to be examined.

It should also be emphasized that the initial identification of norms is a provisional exercise. It may be undesirable or indeed impossible to formulate the norms very precisely at the outset. Because the policy content of a norm depends on the factual context, the final specification of the relevant norm(s) follows rather than precedes the statement of the facts. The entire process, from norm selection through international appraisal, should be viewed as an integrated and circular process, with each step informing the previous step and all steps remaining tentative until seen in the light of the entire process.

DESCRIBING THE FACTS

The first step in organizing a description of the facts giving rise to the incident is to identify the relevant participants. This exercise is not always a straightforward one since, in many instances, the individuals most immediately involved in an incident are only minor or subsidiary actors. In the study below of foreign submarines in Swedish waters, for example, it was evident that the submarine commanders—though major figures in creating the events that culminated in the incident—were not critical to the international appraisal of lawfulness; hence, they are mentioned in the statement of facts but appear only marginally in the discussion of the incident's impact on expectations of lawfulness.

Not only might undue emphasis be given to participants of marginal importance to the incident, but, conversely, it is easy to overlook important participants, especially those acting at some remove from the incident itself. A checklist of those parties will minimize the chances of overlooking a relevant participant. Possible actors include nation states, international governmental organizations, transnational political parties and orders, transnational pressure groups and gangs, international nongovernmental associations and enterprises, and individuals. Because individuals, whether as representatives of organizations or as single actors, provide much of the information used to construct an incident study, authors should be sure to determine on whose behalf an individual is operating. To do this, the author should go beyond the

---

Moreover, even authors using the same method to investigate the same basic situation may draw different conclusions because of predispositional influences. Thus it is especially important that authors make explicit the assumptions and criteria underlying selection of a norm.

individual's own self-characterization and independently determine the actor's role and relationship to the events under scrutiny.[9]

Once the participants have been identified, the author must specify the time parameters of the incident. It is not always clear where the boundaries should be drawn. In the study below of the Falklands/Malvinas War, for example, the battle between Britain and Argentina is seen as one episode in a continuum of events, rather than as a discrete occurrence. If, as that essay suggests, it is misleading to isolate a crisis from its historical development, the fact remains that expectations of authority and control usually become stabilized and some kind of temporal demarcation can be drawn. A simple rule may be provisionally to set the parameters in the way that is most likely to provide insight into both the norms at issue and the impact of the incident on the norms. Occasionally, as in the Gulf of Sidra incident, it will be impossible to develop a consistent statement of the facts. The author of the study of this incident below has resolved the problem by providing the few facts that were stipulated and by then presenting the American and Libyan perspectives under the heading of "conflicting claims."

DESCRIBING CLAIMS OF THE PARTIES

As in the domestic context, there are two types of claims made by participants in an incident: factual and legal. Both types are considered appeals to domestic and international audiences, but not all are pertinent to an incident study.[10] Claims made purely for domestic consumption are generally irrelevant, since they do not play a role in shaping the relevant norm. The only claims that must be considered are

9. Other than interviewing individuals and small groups, the primary sources of information in an incident study include newspapers, radio broadcasts, international chronicles, national documents, bilateral and multilateral documents, treaties, conventions, international judgments and awards, diplomatic communications, and the writings of academic commentators. The Foreign Broadcast Information Service (FBIS) is an especially useful source. It monitors and provides ongoing English translations of foreign newspaper and radio reports. *See also* FACTS ON FILE; WORLD NEWS DIGEST WITH CUMULATIVE INDEX (S. Orlofsky ed. Weekly) and KEESINGS CONTEMPORARY ARCHIVES; RECORD OF WORLD EVENTS (R. East ed. Monthly).

10. Determining which claims are pertinent requires a thorough understanding of the historical and contemporary context within which the incident took place, and an ability to discern and make explicit the relationship between the participants' expectations of lawfulness and their expressions.

those that are directed at an international audience and that also bear upon the norm.

Claims are expressed by participants in a variety of ways. Although at times a straightforward pronouncement may be taken at face value, frequently the real claim will be different from the one being stated.[11] This will be the case where the actor's domestic concerns have pressured it to express one claim rather than another; or it may be that the actor's notion of the relevant norm shaped the claim presented. Participants preparing negotiation or litigation strategies will try to fashion their claims to fit what they believe to be the accepted norm rather than argue that other norms apply. In other cases, for tactical reasons, an actor may fashion claims that are overboard. Unsure of the correct interpretation of the norm, the actor will seek to leave available as many courses of action as possible.

When attempting to infer the participants' unarticulated or ill-articulated claims, it is unnecessary to adhere to a strict methodology, as long as the method used is explicitly stated. What is important is that the description of the participants' claims be fashioned by the author; the claims never come prefabricated as in appellate litigation.

DESCRIBING THE OUTCOME: APPRAISAL OF THE INTERNATIONAL COMMUNITY

After provisionally identifying relevant norms that the incident may have engaged and thoroughly canvassing the factual background of the

11. Distortion may result from deliberate efforts, though even these may not generate the expected result. On propaganda, see PROPAGANDA AND PROMOTIONAL ACTIVITIES: AN ANNOTATED BIBLIOGRAPHY (H. Lasswell, R. Casey & B. Smith eds. 1935, 1969); L. DOOB, PROPAGANDA: ITS PSYCHOLOGY AND TECHNIQUES (1935); B. SMITH, H. LASSWELL AND R. CASEY, PROPAGANDA, COMMUNICATION AND PUBLIC OPINION (1946); A. GEORGE, PROPAGANDA ANALYSIS: A STUDY OF INFERENCES MADE FROM NAZI PROPAGANDA IN WORLD WAR II (1959); B. MURTY, PROPAGANDA AND WORLD PUBLIC ORDER: THE LEGAL REGULATION OF THE IDEOLOGICAL INSTRUMENT OF COERCION (1968); and PROPAGANDA AND COMMUNICATION IN WORLD HISTORY 3 volumes (H. Lasswell, D. Lerner & H. Speier eds. 1980). See also H. LASSWELL, N. LEITES AND ASSOCIATES, LANGUAGE OF POLITICS: STUDIES IN QUANTITATIVE SEMANTICS (1949, 1965); I. DE SOLA POOL ET AL., THE PRESTIGE PRESS: A COMPARATIVE STUDY OF POLITICAL SYMBOLS (1955, 1970); Lasswell, The Value Analysis of Legal Discourse, 9 Western Reserve L.R. 188 (1958); W. DAVISON, INTERNATIONAL POLITICAL COMMUNICATION (1965); and S. ARORA & H. LASSWELL, POLITICAL COMMUNICATION: THE PUBLIC LANGUAGE OF POLITICAL ELITES IN INDIA AND THE UNITED STATES (1969).

incident and the claims of the parties, it is appropriate to begin to assess the outcome of the incident. The outcome may be assessed in respect to three sets of variables: the participants' expectations of lawfulness prior to the incident, the reactions of the international community to the incident, and finally, the impact of the incident upon the previously identified norms. The international appraisal of the lawfulness of an incident is the window through which the analyst can gain insight into how the events may have affected the vitality of legal norms and, hence, the development of international law.

In defining a baseline of expectations, the author must draw upon the historical and contemporary context within which the incident occurred. The author should take care to note the factual underpinnings of this analysis. Expectations of authority and control may be quite specific, tailored to such contingencies as: time and place; the immediate participants and their assets, objectives, and identifications; the presence or absence of crisis; and the kinds of strategic instruments employed. Such considerations as these should be used to identify those situations in the past that are factually similar to the incident, and to evaluate the expectations that may have been generated in the earlier contexts.[12] Expectations of lawfulness may be difficult to assess whenever the relevant participants or their actions cannot be specifically identified. When the author confronts this situation, it may be necessary to examine alternative expectations. As in all studies the author should be mindful of the subtle interplay of data accessibility and research objectives.

The statements of participants and international observers may be helpful in identifying their expectations before, during, or after the incident. However, such statements should not be relied upon too heavily because of the difficulties of distinguishing among biases, distortions, and actual expectations. Finally, there may be political reasons that prevent participants from expressing their actual expectations of lawfulness. Because it is such actual expectations that determine the relevance of the incident to international law, the author will want to rely to the greatest possible extent upon consultation with international experts unconnected with the controversy. Given the fluid nature of elite expectations, the author's analysis can be tentative at best. Due

12. See P. DeSouza, "The Soviet Gas Pipeline Incident: Extension of Collective Security Responsibilities to Peacetime Commercial Trade," infra.

caution dictates that the author provide a detailed explanation of the methodology employed, and that an effort be made to separate description from interpretation to the extent possible.

Once a baseline of expectations is established, the author can describe the reaction of the international community to the incident. The author should look not only to the participants in the incident but to other elites within the international community. It may not be immediately obvious whose responses are proper subjects for attention. In some instances, the appraisal of two or three parties is critical in shaping the international expectations of lawfulness. In the Cosmos 954 satellite study below, for example, the crucial actors included the Soviet, Canadian, and American governments. In other situations, the observer will need to canvass the reactions of many different participants. Particular attention should be paid to the appraisals of participants who may be likely to contemplate actions similar to those that precipitated the incident. For example, in the Soviet pipeline study below, Japan's reaction to the conflict between the United States and European governments over trade with the Soviet Union is discussed because Tokyo, a heavy importer of mineral fuels, was a potential purchaser of such fuels from the Soviet Union. A checklist, similar to that recommended for identifying the relevant participants, might profitably be used in locating other relevant elites.

Having identified the politically relevant elites—i.e., those whose appraisal of an incident will affect the norm—the author should then examine the reactions of those actors. First, the verbal reactions to the incident may be examined. Because all participants and observers are communicating with multiple audiences simultaneously, the analyst must focus on those communications that relate most directly to international expectations of lawfulness.

This focus requires an assessment not only of what was said but to whom, through what channels, and with what effects. It is important that the author be attentive to the subjective nature of the words employed. The meaning of "invasion," "international law," "stability," and "erosion" for the various participants will depend on such factors as culture, class, personality, and previous exposure to crisis; the author's own perceptions will be colored by the same factors.

Similarly, the author should keep in mind that silence and apparent inaction may reveal significant attitudes toward lawfulness. Indeed, the adoption of such postures may be a considered response. Where, for example, there was little overt reaction to the Gulf of Sidra incident, discussed below, the author concluded that the international community's "silence" was best understood as reflecting a decision to neither explicitly condemn nor approve the U.S. military action. Through their silence, the study suggests, other parties wished to preserve for themselves the competence to undertake similar exercises. Sometimes, of course, silence will indicate only the absence of international appraisal; in such a case, the events generally will not qualify as an incident since no lawmaking is involved.

Of course actions, as well as words, may reveal elite perspectives. Some actions that are relevant may be far removed in space or time from the incident itself.[13] Because they require a greater mobilization of resources, actions often indicate the resolve of participants better than words; they may also better reveal the intensity of elite expectations. Whether a reaction is expressed in word or deed, the author should evaluate its intensity, duration, and specificity, its intended audience, and the degree to which it has captured the attention of others in the world community.

By generalizing from the baseline expectations and the international reaction, the author may arrive at an overall appraisal of the lawfulness of the incident and of its effect on legal norms. Although the degree of consensus in the international appraisal is significant, the absence of consensus does not necessarily make the appraisal problematic. As in domestic contexts, a pattern of normative expectations may exist without complete agreement on its policy content or complete support for its application in every conceivable context. Unanimity is not required for there to be authoritative and controlling expectations, under which participants are aware of the likelihood of their violating the norms and of the probable costs and benefits of those violations.

Expectations of lawfulness may be affirmed, denied, suspended, attenuated, or elaborated. Affirmation implies that what took place was largely in conformity with existing or emerging expectations of authority and control. Denial implies the opposite. In assessing the effect upon norms, the author should keep in mind that expectations of law-

---

13. One consequence, perhaps ironic, of an interdependent world community is the tremendous increase in the sites for and variety of ways of exerting leverage through the combined use of ideological, diplomatic, economic, and military strategies. The author should consider each strategy because the use or nonuse of each provides insight into the perspectives of participants.

fulness change continuously through the simultaneous processes of normative accretion and erosion. Thus, denial does not imply that a set of expectations has been extinguished, nor does affirmation mean that expectations are crystallized for eternity.

In addition to the extreme effects of affirmation or denial, the analyst should consider less permanent effects upon the norm. Where a set of normative expectations plays no apparent role in an incident that might have been expected to implicate the norm, the norm may be considered suspended, rather than denied. Attenuation of a norm is marked by curtailment of the domain, scope, range, or intensity of existing expectations; elaboration or extension of the norm coincides with an enhancement of these features.

Appraisal of the effect of an incident upon a norm requires the author to make an inference about how participants translate perception into judgment. Determinations of lawfulness by participants are difficult to separate from judgments about the merit of the existing norm or from claims for changes in the norm. This is especially so when the subject matter is as emotionally charged as it frequently is in the study of international incidents. Even when determinations of lawfulness appear straightforward, conclusions regarding the effect on a norm are not absolute predictors of future behavior. Expectations of lawfulness tend to guide rather than predetermine the behavior of participants, and clarifying the state of an international norm does not mean that participants will abide by the norm in all future instances. Even when an incident evokes a strong reaction, its effect on normative expectations will not be indelible. Under such circumstances, conclusions are necessarily contingent, based, as they are, on incomplete data drawn from a specific configuration of events and conditioning factors. They are also general, because the outcome of the appraisal process—a determination of lawfulness—is incorporated by all participants, though with differing degrees of coherence and intensity.

Notwithstanding the contingent nature of the appraisal process, the incident study furnishes both a guide for predicting future behavior and, perhaps more significantly, a coherent picture of the process by which norms are continually redefined through the interaction of competing elites. Comprehension of this process is critical because the activities that comprise it figure prominently in the establishment and maintenance of what reliability there is in a world community characterized by an unceasing flow of reciprocal and oftentimes conflicting claims and a strained but still effective mutual tolerance.

ANALYZING THE SIGNIFICANCE OF THE INCIDENT: THE AUTHOR'S APPRAISAL

The author's personal appraisal of the implications of the incident may take any of various approaches. One approach might examine the significance of the incident in terms of its likely recurrence or its relevance to analogous situations in which similar norms might be engaged. Accomplishing this task requires the author to explore many factors, including the psychological, historical, political, and geographic features of the particular context that comprised the incident, in order to determine the extent to which similar factors and configurations of such factors are likely to appear elsewhere in the future. By performing this exercise, the author will be able to make disciplined statements about the extent to which the present incident can be generalized.

In addition to these projections regarding the outcome of the incident, the author's appraisal might critically examine the outcome in terms of policy goals. The author might ask whether the outcome of the incident serves to promote world order, human dignity, or other values, or how an outcome more conducive to such values might have been achieved. Where the author approves of the policies furthered by the outcome, the appraisal might consider ways in which the world community could build upon this incident to strengthen further desirable norms. The author may propose alternative ways for improving international appraisals and may suggest ways to facilitate incorporation of the proposed method of determining lawfulness into the expectations of participants. Or the author may choose to focus not on alternative methods of appraising lawfulness but rather on alternative actions that participants in the precipitating events could have taken that would have altered the incident's impact on the norm in question. If this is done, the researcher should demonstrate why the proposed actions would have led to a better outcome. In this vein, alternative strategies can also be offered that the author believes would either mitigate or enhance the immediate or subsequent impact of the incident on the norm under consideration. In all formulations, the author must postulate goals against which proposals are to be appraised and explore the personal, cultural, and environmental factors that would affect the out-come of any proposal.

The scientific attraction of incidents should not and need not be maintained at the expense of the contributions that critical intelligence can make to the improvement of world order. It is hoped that those who use the method and those who appraise it in the future will insist upon appraisals that relate the outcome of the incidents studied to net gains or net losses for improved world order and human dignity.

FOREIGN SUBMARINES IN SWEDISH WATERS: The Erosion of an International Norm

3

ROMANA SADURSKA

PROBLEM

It has been a well-settled international norm that the appropriate responses of a coastal state to an intrusion by a foreign submarine into its internal waters or a noninnocent passage through its territorial sea are limited to requiring the intruding ship to leave its waters and to making a protest to the ship's flag state. This norm has been related to the jurisdictional immunity of foreign warships, a norm long deemed vital to the public order of the oceans.

Increasing violations of Swedish internal waters by unauthorized foreign submarines, typified by the incident described below, induced Sweden to change its policy in ways not consonant with the traditional international position. Under this new policy, an intruding submarine found submerged in *internal* waters is to be forced to the surface, by armed force if necessary, and brought to a Swedish port for investigation and further action. A submerged submarine found in Swedish *ter-*

I gratefully acknowledge the comments and criticisms of Professor Ingemar Dörfer of the Swedish National Defense Research Institute. The views expressed herein, however, are my own and are not necessarily representative of the views of Professor Dörfer.

FOREIGN SUBMARINES

ritorial waters is to be turned back to the high seas, regardless of the purposes of its passage, again by armed force if necessary. This policy has received the express approval of several countries and the apparent tolerance of others. No protests, so far, have been voiced. The Swedish actions, coupled with the apparent acquiescence of the international community, mark the beginning of a potentially serious erosion of the international norm proscribing use of force in dealing with intruding submarines, without any explicit appraisal of the consequences.

FACTS

The incident consists of two discrete events, one at Karlskrona and the other at Harsfjärden.[1]

The Karlskrona Event

On October 27, 1981, a Soviet diesel submarine ran aground in Gasefjärden Bay, a restricted military area in the immediate vicinity of the main Swedish naval base at Karlskrona.[2] The vessel was spotted the next day by a fishing boat, and ships from the Karlskrona base hurried to the scene and surrounded the grounded vessel.[3]

The submarine's commander stated that the gyrocompass had failed, causing a navigational error. The Swedish authorities, however, did not believe this statement[4] and immediately delivered a protest to the Soviet

1. The events at Karlskrona and Harsfjärden are only two chapters in a long history of intrusions into Swedish waters by foreign submarines. Between 1962 and 1980 Swedish waters were violated by foreign submarines at least ninety-three times, with the highest number of trespasses in a single year not exceeding nine. In 1981, the number of violations increased only slightly to ten, but in the first eight months of 1982 the number of reported intrusions jumped to forty. SUBMARINE DEFENCE COMM'N, COUNTERING THE SUBMARINE THREAT app. 2 (S.O.U. No. 13, 1983) [hereinafter cited as COMMISSION REPORT].
2. Gasefjärden Bay is located in the Karlskrona Archipelago on the southeast coast of Sweden. For the Swedish account of events and the statement of Swedish policy, see Theutenberg, U 137—*Folkratt och neutralitetspolitik i tillampning*, KUN GL. KRIGSVE-TENSKAPSAKADEMIENS HANDLINGGAR OCH TIDSKRIFT, No. 2, at 85, *et seq.* (1982) (on file with the *Yale Journal of International Law*).
3. Svenska Dagbladet, Oct. 29, 1981; Frankfurter Allgemeine, Oct. 30, 1981.
4. Radio Stockholm Domestic Service [hereinafter cited as RSDS], Oct. 28, 1981; Foreign Broadcast Information Service [hereinafter cited as FBIS] (W. Europe), Oct. 29,

41

ambassador.[5] The Swedish public, fueled by the media, also made angry protests against the event and its implications about Sweden'a ability to protect its national security.[6] The Swedish government announced that Sweden would salvage the submarine, thereby rejecting the USSR's demand that Soviet tugs be allowed to refloat it,[7] and stated that return of the submarine to the Soviet Union would await the results of an investigation to be undertaken by the commander in chief of the Swedish armed forces.[8] As preliminary steps toward return, Sweden requested an apology from the Soviet Union and at least tacit acceptance of the investigation to be conducted by Swedish authorities.[9]

On October 29, the Soviet Union agreed to the Swedish salvage operation,[10] and on October 30 an apology was conveyed by the Soviet ambassador stating that the Soviet Union regretted that the submarine had entered Swedish territorial waters and trespassed in a restricted military area.[11] Although the Soviet government did not explain why the submarine had gone so far into Swedish waters, the Swedish minister of foreign affairs described the apology as significant, particularly in light of the Soviet Union's refusal to apologize for similar intrusions in the past, and expressed the view that the apology demonstrated the Soviet Union's willingness to cooperate.[12]

Despite this official optimism, however, the Soviet Union never acquiesced in a full-scale investigation,[13] although it finally did agree to allow Sweden to conduct a limited inspection of the vessel and to interrogate the submarine commander and crew on board a Swedish vessel in the presence of representatives from the Soviet embassy.[14] After

1981, at 2 (interview with O. Ullsten, Swedish minister of foreign affairs); *accord*, Svenska Dagbladet, Oct. 29, 1981.

5. RSDS, Oct. 28, 1981; FBIS, *supra* note 4.

6. *See, e.g.*, Dagens Nyheter, Oct. 29, 1981 (editorial calling for interrogation of the Soviet submarine's commander).

7. Radio Stockholm International Service [hereinafter cited as RSIS], Oct. 29, 1981 (press conference of the Swedish minister of foreign affairs).

8. RSDS, Oct. 29, 1981; FBIS (W. Europe), Oct. 30, 1981, at 7 (text of the government's communiqué).

9. Radio Stockholm to Europe and the Middle East, Oct. 31, 1981.

10. RSIS, Oct. 30, 1981; FBIS, *supra* note 8, at 8.

11. Radio Stockholm to Europe and the Middle East, Oct. 31, 1981.

12. *Id.*

13. RSIS, Oct. 30, 1981; FBIS, *supra* note 8, at 8.

14. RSDS, Nov. 2, 1981; FBIS (W. Europe), Nov. 2, 1981, at 3.

reaching this agreement on November 2, Swedish tugs pulled the Soviet submarine from the mud to a safer anchorage within Swedish waters.[15]

The testimony of the commander and crew supported the initial Soviet statement that the intrusion was caused by navigational error due to compass failure. The Swedish navy officer who examined the submarine's log book reported, however, that crucial information had been altered by the crew and that the navigational instruments were in good order.[16] The Swedish investigators were not allowed to inspect the forward part of the submarine where torpedoes are usually carried. On November 5, nevertheless, the Swedish authorities announced that experts from the Research Institute of Swedish National Defense, who had examined the submarine externally, were able to establish the presence of uranium 238 on board, from which they concluded that torpedoes with nuclear warheads were present on the Soviet submarine.[17]

The Swedish government sent the Soviet authorities a "sharply worded protest" demanding to know whether the submarine was carrying nuclear arms.[18] The answer was utterly equivocal: the Soviet government stated that "the submarine carries, as do all naval vessels at sea, the necessary weapons and ammunition."[19]

At this point, Swedish authorities decided to close the investigation, and the submarine was returned to the Soviets on November 6.[20]

The Harsfjärden Event

On October 1, 1982, nearly a year after the episode at Karlskrona, Swedish naval units once again were put on a state of alert. A foreign submarine had been spotted in Harsfjärden, near the top-secret Muskö naval base. A depth charge was dropped from a helicopter and the area was searched by patrol boats and helicopters. The following day the search continued and four more depth charges were dropped. The Navy units placed metal barriers across the two main entrances to

15. 1981 FACTS ON FILE [hereinafter cited as 1981 FACTS], 804 A2.
16. RSDS, Nov. 11, 1981.
17. RSDS, Nov. 5, 1981; FBIS (W. Europe), Nov. 6, 1981, at 2.
18. 1981 FACTS, *supra* note 15, at 840 D, E3.
19. *Id.*
20. RSIS, Nov. 6, 1981; FBIS, *supra* note 17, at 5. The bill for the salvage operation totalled 1.6 million kroner and was paid by the Soviet government. Dagens Nyheter, Dec. 23, 1981; RSDS, Mar. 25, 1982.

Harsfjärden through which conventional submarines might leave the area. The rest of the area (50 square kilometers) was not sealed off, and minisubmarines could have escaped easily from the trap.[21]

On October 3, the search units made sonar contact with a submarine and responded with two depth charges. The next day brought further indications of submarine presence: radar and sonar echoes, air bubbles, and a large oil slick that appeared on the surface after twelve depth charges had been dropped.[22] During the following two days similar evidence was noticed and twelve further depth charges had been dropped.[23]

On October 6, minesweepers, a submarine rescue vessel, anticraft units, and military police were brought into action in preparation for a mine detonation. The next day the navy dropped six depth charges outside the northern barrier of Harsfjärden, where there were indications of either a breakout from within or an attempt to force through the barrier from the outside. Thereafter, three mines were detonated in the vicinity of Mälsten. An internment center was prepared for any rescued crew, and hospitals were alerted to prepare for possible injured seamen who, it was assumed, would be suffering from detonation shock. Swedish armed forces were on full alert along the entire coast and prepared for a possible emergency surfacing of the foreign submarine.[24]

The mine detonations, however, produced no results; no evidence of wreckage was found by divers or underwater cameras. In the evening, new sonar contacts were obtained outside the northern barrier and in north Mysingen, which indicated that a submarine might have escaped from the trap in Harsfjärden. Nevertheless, the search continued both inside and outside the barrier, and on October 9 new controlled mines were laid. The same day, indications of possible submarine presence came from Nämdö (north of Harsfjärden), and two days later from Danziger Gatt (south of Harsfjärden). The latter were particularly strong on October 14, when two depth charges were dropped in Danziger Gatt. The search continued until November 1, during which period there was no further sonar contact.[25]

---

21. Agence France Press (Stockholm) [hereinafter cited as AFP], Oct. 3, 1982; FBIS (W. Europe), Oct. 4, 1982, at 4. The first press communiqué was issued by the Defense Staff on the evening of October 2, 1982. *Id.*

22. AFP, Oct. 6, 1982.

23. *Id.*

24. AFP, Oct. 8, 1982.

25. COMMISSION REPORT, *supra* note 1, at 105.

CONFLICTING CLAIMS

The Karlskrona Event

The physical presence of the grounded submarine in Swedish national waters was the only material fact in the Karlskrona event on which the claimants were in agreement. Each gave different answers about the purpose of the submarine's mission, the causes of the accident, and whether nuclear weapons were on board the submarine.

The Soviets claimed that the submarine, "while making a routine training cruise in the Baltic Sea, went off course in conditions of poor visibility and ran aground."[26] The Swedish government, however, maintained from the outset that the submarine was not performing a mere training task but rather was engaged in illegal intelligence-gathering. The Swedish commander in chief, in his report of the Swedish investigation, contended that the Soviet submarine was already in Swedish waters on October 24, 1981, and had carried out exercises for four days inside and outside Sweden's territorial sea before it ran aground.[27] He also concluded that the submarine was on the surface in Swedish waters at least two hours before it was grounded, and that its crew were aware that they were entering a restricted military area.[28]

The Soviet government described the charge of illegal activities as "bewildering" and "a distortion of facts."[29] "What sober-minded person," asked the Soviet government, "to say nothing of military specialists, can suppose that a submarine, in a surface run with its running lights on and operating diesel engines whose noise could be heard for a great distance, at night and in conditions of poor visibility, could engage in such 'activities'?"[30]

It is a puzzling question indeed, and the Swedish commander in chief had to admit that there were no definite indications of the submarine's presence from radar or radio surveillance. His report offered as a possibile explanation the hypothesis that a radar echo was misin-

26. TASS, Nov. 4, 1981, *reprinted in* 33 CURRENT DIG. SOVIET PRESS, No. 44, at 7 (1981).
27. Svenska Dagbladet, Dec. 19, 1981. The report containing the commander in chief's final conclusions was classified as secret and only part of it was published in December 1981.
28. *Id.*
29. 33 CURRENT DIG. SOVIET PRESS, No. 45, at 5 (1981) (statement of the Soviet government issued Nov. 11, 1981).
30. *Id.*

terpreted by the Swedish coast guard. "Therefore, the possibility cannot be excluded that radar surveillance did reveal the submarine, but that this was taken at the time for a merchant ship or a fishing boat. Identification of radar echoes must normally be effected through direct sighting."[31] In other words, the report indicates that it is conceivable that a foreign submarine could perform illegal activities quite openly without being identified by the Swedish coastal surveillance system.

As noted above,[32] the parties also disagreed as to the cause of the intrusion. The Soviet authorities consistently maintained that the intrusion was caused by failure of the vessel's navigational instruments;[33] the Swedish government alleged that the submarine's navigational instruments were in good working order.[34] The Swedes did not believe the submarine could have reached its location in the restricted military zone if its navigational instruments had been inoperative, since this required traversal of twelve nautical miles of Swedish territorial waters through the outer Karlskrona archipelago and around dozens of small islands and bays.[35] The Swedes also pointed to the fact that the submarine did not send any distress signal for seventy-two hours after it had run aground.[36]

Finally, the Swedes asserted that there was a high probability that the Soviet submarine was carrying nuclear warheads.[37] The Soviets never directly denied this statement, although they did challenge the basis for the assertion, dismissing as "absurd" the claims of Swedish nuclear experts that the presence of uranium 238 made it likely that the submarine was carrying nuclear weapons.[38] With regard to the ac-

31. Svenska Dagbladet, Dec. 19, 1982.
32. *See supra* notes 4, 5 & 16 and accompanying text.
33. TASS, Nov. 4, 1981; TASS, Nov. 11, 1981.
34. RSDS, Nov. 11, 1981.
35. Theutenberg, *supra* note 2, at 101–102.
36. *Id.* The Soviet Union's statements also did not offer any explanation for the grounding itself, focusing instead on the reasons for the initial intrusion into Swedish waters. The Soviets may have hoped by this tactic to focus attention on the wandering off course of the submarine, thereby avoiding the embarrassing question of its trespass into the restricted military zone. According to the Swedish Report, the grounding occurred because of an error in maneuvering inside the restricted military area when the submarine attempted a rapid and powerful turn that was executed too late. Svenska Dagbladet, Dec. 19, 1982.
37. RSDS, Nov. 5, 1981; FBIS, *supra* note 17, at 2.
38. TASS, Nov. 11, 1981. TASS quoted Danish and U.S. scientists as saying that

tual presence of nuclear weapons, the Soviet Union merely stated that the vessel carried "necessary weapons and ammunition."[39]

The Harsfjärden Event

The reconstruction of the dialogue between the Soviet and Swedish governments during and after the Harsfjärden event is difficult. The communication between the two resembled a long monologue by Sweden, with only a short, indignant response on the part of the Soviet Union.

During the event itself, the Swedes had been careful to refrain from making claims regarding the nationality of the suspected submarines, and this discretion no doubt helped repair Swedish-Soviet relations, damaged by the occurrences at Karlskrona.[40] The Swedish government, however, embarrassed and under strong internal political pressure to clarify the circumstances of the event, put forward an extensive analysis contained in the Report of the Submarine Defense Commission (Commission Report).

The publication of this document in April 1983 changed the situation abruptly. The Commission concluded that the submarines that had violated Swedish internal waters in September and October 1982 belonged to the Soviet Union.[41] Because no direct evidence of the presence of Soviet submarines was offered, the official Soviet media simply dismissed all accusations as propaganda and falsifications without entering into any factual or legal argument. The Soviet Union charged

---

although uranium 235 and plutonium 238 are used for the production of nuclear weapons, uranium 238 "in principle" is not. *Id.*

39. 1981 Facts, *supra* note 15, at 840 D, E3.

40. For example, on June 16, 1982, TASS reported that the Soviet and Swedish ministers of foreign affairs had met in New York and "declared in favour of developing Soviet-Swedish relations on the foundation of good-neighborliness and in the interest of the people of both countries and the interests of enhancing peace, security and cooperation." TASS, June 16, 1982. Despite official restraint, however, the Swedish media and some representatives of the military establishment speculated about the nationality of the perpetrators and quite openly pointed to the Soviet Union. The Soviet Union ignored these accusations for some time, but eventually Soviet official sources responded by dismissing the "insinuations" as hostile propaganda and "absurd fabrications" orchestrated by Swedish and U.S. militaristic circles in derogation of Sweden's policy of neutrality. Krasnaya Zvezda, Aug. 5, 1982; Radio Moscow (comment in Swedish), Aug. 17, 1982; TASS, Oct. 6, 1982; TASS, Oct. 11, 1982.

41. Commission Report, *supra* note 1, at 41.

that the affair had been manipulated by the media to cause a crisis in Swedish-Soviet relations that might serve to justify military spending.[42] TASS pointed out that the Commission had failed to offer direct proof of the nationality of the submarines, "rashly" concluding that the vessels were Soviet.[43]

Nevertheless, the Commission Report presented a detailed analysis of the maneuvers allegedly conducted by the Soviet submarines at Harsfjärden and of the likely motives for the intrusions, to which the Soviets made no response. From an examination of the seabed, the report concluded that both conventional submarines and minisubmarines of both the "keel" and the "track" type had carried out a series of exercises in the Harsfjärden area for a period of at least three weeks.[44]

The Commission judged the primary reason for Sweden's failure to locate the intruding submarines and force them to the surface to be that the Swedes were unable to determine at the time of the Harsfjärden event that they were dealing with minisubmarines as well as conventional submarines.[45] The Commission Report found that the weapons and equipment used (which were designed for use against conventional submarines in open waters), as well as the Swedish command, communications, and control systems, were inadequate.[46] The traditional hydroacoustic equipment could not cope with the special problems of antisubmarine operations in an archipelago environment with a busy civilian traffic like the Baltic Sea—an environment characterized by shallow water, a rocky and uneven seabed, variations in salinity and temperature, and large amounts of scrap metal on the seabed.[47] The report suggested, moreover, that conducting the search in an area readily accessible to the media had also hindered the operation.[48]

42. TASS, April 27, 1983, *reprinted in* 1983 FACTS ON FILE [hereinafter cited as 1983 FACTS] 336 FG3.
43. *Id.*
44. COMMISSION REPORT, *supra* note 1, at 34–47. The Commission Report concluded that there were six submarines altogether, at least three of which were minisubmarines. *Id.* The submarines operated in pairs, with a conventional submarine serving as mother craft for each minisubmarine. *Id.*
45. *Id.* at 42.
46. *Id.*
47. *Id.* at 45–46.
48. *Id.* at 43–44. The Commission Report stated: "The geographical location of the operations made it possible for the mass media to follow developments in detail on the

As for the intruders' motives, the Commission Report suggested that these were most probably to gather intelligence and to test new technology and military strategy, including the use of sabotage troop units and other special forces and preparations connected with the laying and sweeping of mines.[49]

Of particular note was the Commission's finding that the Swedish forces had shown too much restraint in the Harsfjärden episode, using too few depth charges, for example, to be effective: "It cannot be excluded that some opportunities for effective action . . . could not be fully exploited because of too restrictive firing instructions."[50] The report did not ignore the hazards of more fully "effective" measures, acknowledging that depth charges "are inevitably blunt antisubmarine weapons, with which it is difficult to distinguish between effective fire for the purpose of forcing the submarine to the surface and fire intended to sink the submarine."[51] Moreover, "The step from individual depth charges to multiple drops (on two occasions patterns of four were dropped), like the decision to use mines, was taken in the clear awareness that increased use of fire aimed at forcing submarines to the surface also involved an increasing risk of their being sunk."[52] Nevertheless, these concerns were overridden, in the Commission's judgment, by military necessity. Thus, the report concluded that "multiple drops [of depth charges] . . . must generally be tolerated even knowing the risk of an unintentional sinking—if the depth charge, as a weapon, is to have any real effect."[53]

In addition to the depth charges, five mines were detonated during the Harsfjärden operation. The Commission Report acknowledged that it is highly questionable whether it is possible to detonate mines in such a way as to cause controllable, limited damage that will force a submarine to the surface rather than sink it.[54] According to the report, the decision of the commander in chief to use mines in a situation in

---

spot. This meant that the defense authorities were faced with the time-demanding task of handling a fairly rich flora of rumors and often erroneous material information. In addition, they were required continuously to account for and justify individual measures within the framework of the operation." Id.

49. Id. at 74.
50. Id. at 51.
51. Id. at 52.
52. Id. at 43.
53. Id. at 52.
54. Id.

which the danger of a breakout was judged imminent "was made in the awareness of the risk of doing damage on a scale that could not wholly be foreseen. The Supreme Commander informed the Government to this effect."[55]

Nevertheless, the Commission Report insisted that the purpose of the use of mines was to force the submarines to the surface and that, consequently, the personnel in charge of detonations "deliberately refrained from automatically detonating mines, and attempted instead a flexible, more sophisticated technique of delayed detonation after indication."[56] Despite the unsuccessful Harsfjärden experience, the report recommended the use of mine barrages in the future to combat alien submarines.[57] Moreover, the Commission took the view that the response to future intrusions should be even more forceful, to ensure that the countermeasures would be successful.[58]

CONFLICTING CONCEPTIONS OF LAWFULNESS

The legal arguments of Sweden and the Soviet Union centered around three main issues: (1) the violation of territorial sovereignty; (2) the jurisdictional immunity of alien submarines; and (3) the use of force by a coastal state to protect its interests.

Violation of Swedish Territory

The Swedish government viewed the submarine incidents as infringements of Sweden's exclusive right to control access of aliens to the entirety of its territory, including its territorial waters. In the first Swedish statement regarding Karlskrona, the Swedish minister of foreign affairs described the incursion of the Soviet submarine into the restricted military areas as a "violation of Swedish territory" and termed its entry into Swedish internal waters without permission from the Swedish authorities a "gross violation of entry regulations" that the Swedish government viewed "very seriously."[59] The intrusion was a "deliberate viola-

55. *Id.* at 53.
56. *Id.*
57. *Id.*
58. *Id.* at 81–87.
59. RSDS, Oct. 28, 1981; FBIS, *supra* note 4 at 2 (interview with O. Ullsten). It should be noted that Article 4 of the Swedish Proclamation Concerning the Admission to Swedish Territory of Foreign Naval Vessels and Military Aircraft (1966: 366) provides

tion of Swedish territory for illegal intelligence aims" made "all the more unacceptable as the submarine was in all likelihood equipped with nuclear charges."[60] The Swedes asserted, therefore, that the territorial violation was aggravated by the high security risk resulting from the presence of the vessel within the restricted military area, the performance of intelligence tasks, and the carrying of nuclear weapons.

The response of the Soviet Union focused on the alleged inadvertence of the intrusion and did not mention the contravention of Swedish regulations, the entry into a restricted area, or the presence of nuclear arms.[61] According to the Soviet government, the submarine had no hostile intentions, and thus its presence within Swedish waters "in no way affected Sweden's security interests."[62] Therefore, "the Soviet Government resolutely rejected the protest contained in the Swedish Goverment's statement as devoid of any legal or factual basis."[63]

By limiting its arguments to the absence of hostile intent and the absence of any security risk, the Soviet government avoided engaging in a debate that might undermine principles recognized by its own law, which defend the right of a coastal state to regulate access to its territory. Soviet law does not provide for the general right of innocent passage of alien warships, and requires all foreign vessels passing through its territorial waters to apply thirty days in advance through diplomatic channels for an entry permit and to comply with its strict regulations.[64]

---

that craft in distress can enter Swedish territory without authorization or notification. However, the Soviet submarine was not considered by the Swedish authorities as belonging to this category. *See* Theutenberg, *supra* note 2, at 101.

60. AFP, Nov. 5, 1981.

61. 33 CURRENT DIG. SOVIET PRESS, No. 45, at 5 (1981).

62. *Id.*

63. *Id.*

64. Articles 16 and 17 of the 1960 Statute on the State Boundary and the 1960 Rules for Visits of Foreign Warships to Territorial Waters and Ports of the U.S.S.R., *quoted* in W. BUTLER, THE SOVIET UNION AND THE LAW OF THE SEA 52–54, 64 (1971). The determination of the Soviet Union to use force against an alien warship compelled the United States to cancel in August 1967 the proposed navigation of two U.S. Coast Guard icebreakers (considered as warships under the Soviet rules) through the Vil'kitskii Straits. *Id.* at 66–70. Shortly after the Swedish incidents, a new law on the State Boundary of the U.S.S.R. was enacted and entered into force on March 1, 1983. Article 36 provides for the use of weapons, *inter alia,* "against violators of the U.S.S.R. state boundary on land, water, and in the air in response to the use of force by them or in instances when the cessation of the violation or detention of the offenders can not be effectuated by other means." Text reprinted in 22 INT'L LEGAL MATERIALS 1055 (1983).

Submarines allowed to enter Soviet territorial and internal waters must navigate on the surface.[65] Infringement of either provision by an alien submarine is considered a violation of Soviet sovereignty, and the "Soviet Ministry of Defense has issued instructions that a foreign submarine discovered within the state boundaries of the U.S.S.R. while submerged is to be destroyed."[66]

Jurisdictional Immunity of the Alien Submarine

Immediately following the events at Karlskrona, the Swedish government instituted an investigation and made the return of the submarine contingent upon its results. It is uncertain whether Sweden ever contemplated the possibility of not returning the vessel or of prosecuting its commander or crew, but there were indications that in this particular case the Swedes were inclined to take stronger action than was usual in such situations.[67]

Anxious to provide a legal justification for its actions, the Swedish government adopted an interpretation of the law of sovereign immunity that made the immunity of foreign warships within the waters of a coastal state conditional upon compliance with the coastal state's admission regulations. The legal advisor of the Ministry for Foreign Affairs stated that Sweden recognizes the principle of state immunity granting foreign state-owned ships immunity from Swedish jurisdiction; however, that immunity is conditioned upon permission to enter the territory.[68] A vessel that disregards admission regulations and flagrantly violates the law of a country cannot be granted immunity in accordance with international law, and the violated state has a right to investigate that vessel's activities in its territory.[69]

According to the Swedes, the traditional policy priorities of the law of the sea, which give preference to the inclusive interests of the international community over the exclusive interests of particular participants, is reversed. The justified claim for protection against the possible abuse of the freedom given to alien warships becomes the overriding

---

65. W. BUTLER, *supra* note 64, at 64.

66. BARBOLIA, VOENNO-MORSKOI SPRAVOCHNIK 50, *quoted in* W. BUTLER, *supra* note 64, at 65.

67. *See, e.g.*, RSIS, Oct. 29, 1981 (interview with T. Falldin).

68. Theutenberg, *supra* note 2, at 88.

69. *Id.*

policy consideration, allowing a coastal state to take actions traditionally prohibited out of concern for freedom of passage.

Understandably enough, the Soviet Union, deviating from its own law,[70] declared itself unequivocally in support of the traditional international priorities. After asserting its adherence to the principle of absolute jursidictional immunity for warships, the Soviet Union defined its acquiescence in the Swedish investigation as "a certain exception" to the general rule dictated by a "spirit of good will" and "the nature of Soviet-Swedish relations."[71]

The Use of Force

During the Karlskrona episode, the problem of the use of force against the vessel and its commander and crew was not fully discussed by the representatives of the Swedish political elite. The Swedish government did not make any clear declarations of its intentions. For example, at the press conference during the second day of the affair, Prime Minister T. Falldin said: "We are prepared to use the naval units we have and other units as well to uphold our territory, but there is no reason to start talking about the use of force now."[72] It is reasonable to assume that Sweden did not contemplate any forcible action because there was no real necessity for a resort to force: Sweden could control the situation sufficiently by holding the submarine and its crew hostage. By instilling some uncertainty about its intentions, however, Sweden attempted to exert pressure on the Soviet Union and to strengthen the Swedish bargaining position in the negotiations.[73]

Increasing submarine violations in 1982 and unsuccessful attempts to capture the perpetrators through peaceful methods changed Sweden's attitude toward the use of force. Prime Minister Falldin and the minister of foreign affairs stated that the navy's task was to force the alien vessels to the surface in order to identify their nationality, board them, and take them into port for interrogation of the crew.[74] To

70. *See supra* notes 64–66 and accompanying text.

71. 33 CURRENT DIG. SOVIET PRESS, No. 45, at 5 (1981).

72. RSDS, Oct. 29, 1981.

73. Reportedly, the minister of defense was not cautious enough and stated that force would not be considered. This assurance was thought to explain the hardening of the Soviet attitude toward the end of the negotiations. The Times, Nov. 5, 1981.

74. RSDS, Oct. 5, 1982; FBIS (W. Europe), Oct. 6, 1982, at 3–4; AFP, Oct. 6, 1982 (interview with T. Falldin).

achieve this goal, the Swedish government was ready to resort to armed force. The commander in chief, commenting on the detonations of mines, said, "it was carried out with the clear intention of seriously damaging a submarine. . . . Exploding the mines in the way we did should reasonably have caused a great deal of damage to a submarine."[75] He also confirmed that the armed forces were prepared to repeat the same action in the future, even if the possibility that the crew might die could not be excluded: "There must always be a risk in intruding into Swedish waters," he concluded.[76]

The strongest warning and clearest statement of the new policy came from Swedish Prime Minister Olof Palme, who returned to power after six years in opposition on the day of the Harsfjärden mine detonation. At the press conference during which the appointment of the Submarine Defense Commission was announced, the new prime minister said: "The Swedish Government has the option of ordering the military to sink a foreign submarine in Swedish waters. Whoever is considering a violation of Swedish territory must take into account that the Government will in future use this option. . . . There are greater possibilities to sink a submarine than to expel it or to force it to surface."[77]

The Commission Report supported the prime minister's assertion and began with the premise that "[i]t is of vital importance to Swedish security policy that Swedish territory be protected by all available means against violations. . . . Confidence in our determination and ability to remain neutral must be maintained."[78] To serve these goals, the Commission concluded, the Swedish defenders at Harsfjärden had legitimately resorted to the use of force. The Commission based its appraisal of the lawfulness of the Harsfjärden operation on Chapter 10, Article 9 of the Swedish Instrument of Government, which establishes the government's responsibility for defending the territory against violations by foreign powers: "The Government may authorize the defense forces to use force in accordance with international law and custom for the purpose of preventing any violation of the territory of the Realm in

75. RSIS, Oct. 13, 1982; FBIS (W. Europe), Oct. 14, 1982, at 2.
76. Id.
77. RSDS, Oct. 22, 1982; FBIS (W. Europe), Oct. 25, 1982, at 1–2 (press conference).
78. Minutes of the Swedish government, Oct. 21, 1982, quoted in COMMISSION REPORT, supra note 1, at 7–8.

times of peace, or during a war between foreign states."[79] The Commission Report based this assertion on the right of self-defense embodied in Article 51 of the United Nations Charter, which entitles every state, in the words of the Commission, to defend its sovereignty and its territory, if necessary by recourse to arms.[80] Consequently, the Commission concluded, "measures taken in accordance with the right of self-defense cannot be regarded as aggression."[81]

OUTCOME

On July 17, 1982, the Swedish government published an "Ordinance Containing Instructions for the Armed Forces in Times of Peace and in State of Neutrality,"[82] which replaced General Order 48/1967 and took effect on July 1, 1983.[83]

The evolution of the Swedish doctrine reflects the changes in behavior caused by the frequency and gravity of submarine violations. The 1967 General Order had stated that the purpose of any action taken by the armed forces against an intruding alien submarine was to turn it away from Swedish territory to the high seas. Section 15 of the 1982 Ordinance read as follows:

A foreign submarine which is found submerged within Swedish internal waters shall be forced to surface. It shall then be ordered to stop, be identified, and then taken to an anchorage for further action. If necessary, force of arms may be used. A foreign submarine which is found submerged within the territorial sea shall be turned away from the territory. If necessary, force of arms may be used. Should special circumstances so require, the Supreme Commander may order recourse to force of arms without prior

79. COMMISSION REPORT, *supra* note 1, at 78.

80. *Id.*

81. *Id.* The self-defense argument in favor of a forceful action against a "spying" warship also was advanced by some writers. *See, e.g.*, Delupis, *Foreign Warships and Immunity for Espionage*, 78 AM. J. INT'L L. 72–75 (1984).

82. COMMISSION REPORT, *supra* note 1, at 79.

83. The long period between the adoption and entry into force of the act was due to the need for comprehensive amendment of the detailed regulations promulgated by the commander in chief under the previous General Order. The delay also permitted translation and appropriate publication of the new rules abroad. *Id.* at 79.

warning against a foreign submarine which is found submerged within Swedish waters.[84]

The consistent increase in the number of submarine intrusions coupled with the more openly provocative behavior of the intruding submarines, their more frequent operation within Swedish internal waters and restricted military areas, and their refusal to allow themselves to be turned away, induced the Submarine Defense Commission to recommend further tightening of the 1982 ordinance.[85] Its proposals were adopted by the government on March 3, 1983.[86] Section 15 now reads as follows:

> A foreign submarine which is found submerged within Swedish internal waters shall be forced to surface. It shall then be ordered to stop, be identified and be taken to an anchorage for further action. If necessary, force of arms, shall be used without prior warning. A foreign submarine which is found submerged within the territorial sea shall be turned away from the territory. If necessary, force of arms shall be used. Should special circumstances so require, the force of arms may be used without prior warning pursuant to a decision by the Supreme Commander.[87]

Thus, the new edict authorizes the use of force without warning as a rule rather than as an exception. In explaining the motives for this change, the Commission stated its view that it is impossible for an alien submarine to navigate into Swedish internal waters by mistake. According to the Commission, Sweden's twelve-mile territorial sea ensures that: "if an alien submarine is found in Swedish internal waters, it can be stated with confidence, that both its commander and those who gave the order for its mission are well aware of the submarine's forbidden position and purpose. No warning is required to inform the parties concerned. The same circumstance emphasizes also the extreme improbability of a submarine crew allowing itself to be forced to the surface merely by warning shots."[88] The Commission's opinion was that, in practice, the warnings merely facilitated evasive maneuvers.[89]

84. *Id.* at 79–80.
85. *Id.* at 81–82.
86. *Id.* at 82.
87. *Id.*
88. *Id.* at 84.
89. *Id.*

The lesson gained from the operational experience at Harsfjärden was that these new rules, in order to be effective, had to be matched by improved methods of antisubmarine defense. Since 1958, the navy's share of military spending had decreased from 18 to 13 percent, despite the clear shift in emphasis toward naval units elsewhere.[90] After the Karlskrona event, the Swedish media and the armed forces demanded more effective defense against violations of Swedish territory. The special review of antisubmarine defense resources resulted in a 200 million kroner package, which formed part of the 1982 Defense Act and was meant to improve surveillance, location, and weaponry employed in antisubmarine actions.[91] Although the main emphasis was on new surveillance and location programs, the new weaponry developed and acquired by the Swedish navy is the most important aspect of this defense program from the standpoint of international law.

The two most significant weaponry developments were incident depth charges and antisubmarine torpedoes. Incident depth charges, which are used primarily by patrol boats and missile boat units, are designed to create numerous scattered punctures in a submarine's hull that are not big enough to sink the submarine immediately but make immediate repair impossible, so that the submarine is forced to the surface without harming the crew.[92] The preservation of human life in these circumstances, of course, depends upon the capacity of the vessel to surface as quickly as possible. The new antisubmarine torpedo, which is intended for use by helicopters, missile boats, and submarines, has an explosive head designed to destroy the submarine's screw, thereby impairing its maneuvering capacity.[93]

In addition, the Swedes installed a new permanent underwater surveillance system for certain key areas, which is supplemented by a controlled mine system. The number of mines is being increased and they are being modernized.[94]

The development of a surveillance system and "incident weapons" shows how the events at Karlskrona and Harsfjärden, particularly the latter, influenced Swedish concepts of antisubmarine defense. Before these events, Sweden was not prepared, either in terms of resources or

90. RSIS, Feb. 3, 1982.
91. COMMISSION REPORT, *supra* note 1, at 90.
92. RSIS, Feb. 3, 1982; *see* COMMISSION REPORT, *supra* note 1, at 83.
93. COMMISSION REPORT, *supra* note 1, at 83.
94. *Id.* at 93; Svenska Dagbladet, Nov. 28, 1981.

in policy and strategy terms, to deal with submarine violations. The events of 1981–1982 brought about a new policy of forcing submarines to surface, when possible, without causing loss of life. At that time, however, the resources needed to implement that policy were not available. To put it bluntly, even if a submarine could have been located precisely, the Swedish navy had only two choices: to sink and destroy the vessel with its crew, or to let it go. The high probability of casualties, on the one hand, coupled with the need to demonstrate Sweden's determination to stop the intrusions, on the other, explains in part the confusion and hesitancy of the command and control systems that sought to cope with the submarine intrusions. Sweden's development of "incident weapons" apparently resolved this dilemma. From the Swedish point of view, these weapons represent a rational, balanced response to both the security risk caused by the violations and the difficulty of preventing them, and a way of maintaining the credibility of their policy of neutrality. From the standpoint of users of international oceans, however, they constitute an unprecedented threat to underwater peacetime navigation in foreign waters.

INTERNATIONAL APPRAISAL

The submarine incident provoked the strongest reaction in the Scandinavian countries. During the events at Karlskrona, the ministers of foreign affairs of Denmark and Norway held a joint press conference, on November 6, 1981, in which they condemned the violation of Swedish territory by the Soviet submarine and particularly the presence of nuclear weapons on board.[95] The Norwegian minister warned that if a similar violation occurred in Norwegian waters, the authorities would use depth charges.[96] The governments of Norway, Denmark, and Iceland ordered their ambassadors to the Soviet Union to boycott the annual celebration of the October Revolution as a protest against the presence of nuclear torpedoes on board the submarine.[97] Only the Finnish Ministry of Foreign Affairs failed to express protest, limiting itself to a remark that the submarine affair was regrettable but concerned solely Sweden and the Soviet Union.[98]

The governments of the other Western countries did not speak out.

95. Berlinske Tidende, Nov. 7, 1981.
96. Id.
97. N.Y. Times, Nov. 8, 1981, at 3, col. 4.
98. RSDS, Nov. 6, 1981.

The silence of the major powers can probably be explained by the difficult configuration of interests at stake. On the one hand, a flagrant violation of the territorial sovereignty of Sweden called for condemnation of the Soviet intrusion in Karlskrona. On the other hand, Sweden's determination to stop such incidents, even at the cost of infringing upon established norms, gave rise to apprehension. For some naval powers, the affair was a reminder that they could easily find themselves in the Soviet's predicament.[99]

Sweden's threat to sink foreign submarines in peacetime seemed to have no effect on Soviet-Swedish relations. The Soviet Union did not break the international silence on this subject and appeared to join other nations in implicit tolerance of the new Swedish policy. This tolerance may be construed as acquiescence in the policy's underlying self-defense argument.

The People's Republic of China was not so reticent, and seized upon the occasion of the Karlskrona affair to accuse the Soviet Union of duplicity in supporting Western European nuclear disarmament movements while intruding into Swedish territory with a nuclear-armed submarine.[100]

The Karlskrona event was brought to the attention of the participants in the Madrid Conference on Security and Cooperation in Europe. The chief Swedish delegate stated that the Soviet Union had violated the Helsinki Act of 1975. The Soviet delegation responded to this by repeating the official version of the incident, and the matter was not discussed further.[101]

During the search for submarines in Harsfjarden, the Swedish minister of foreign affairs, speaking in the United Nations General Assembly, said that "Swedish territory will be protected from violations with all available means."[102] Emphasizing the Swedish policy of neutrality, L. Bodstrom added that "such violations will be treated with equal determination no matter where they emanate from."[103] As with Karlskrona, the international community neither questioned nor con-

99. It is presumably out of such considerations that during the *Pueblo* incident the Soviet Union refrained from publicizing the affair and commenting on its legal implications. *See* Butler, *The Pueblo Crisis: Some Legal Reflections*, 63 PROC. AM. SOC. INT'L L. 7–8 (1969).

100. N.Y. Times, Nov. 9, 1981, at A5, col. 1.

101. RSDS, Nov. 10, 1981; FBIS (W. Europe), Nov. 12, 1981, at 4.

102. N.Y. Times, Oct. 16, 1982, at A2, col. 6.

103. *Id.*

demned the Swedish actions. The international media reported both events in a manner generally sympathetic to the Swedish government's actions.

AUTHOR'S APPRAISAL

Swedish policy was approved of by some states (Norway and Denmark) and tolerated by other members of the international community, many of whom face similar problems as coastal states (for example, Argentina, Italy, and Japan). Norway adopted rules permitting the use of force against intruding alien submarines.[104] No member of the international community protested the new Swedish policy.[105] Taking into account the great publicity given to the incident and the careful mutual monitoring by international actors, this silence can be interpreted as acquiescence in the Swedish policy without either express disapproval of Soviet conduct or explicit support for the Swedish action.

The acceptance, however reluctant, of Swedish actions by the world community, notwithstanding their apparent incongruence with well-established international practice, is only partly explained by the special circumstances in which Sweden found itself. It must also be assumed that international elites were aware that, by tacitly approving of the Swedish behavior, they were acquiescing not only in a justified case of self-defense but also in the erosion of a long-standing practice of international law.

The international norm, unequivocal in itself, of jurisdictional immunity for foreign warships, must be considered in the context of norms pertaining to the control of coastal states over access to their territory, an area in which international law *is* equivocal and has undergone a number of recent changes. These changes seem aimed at enhancing protection of the security interests of coastal states at the expense of the rights of other users of the oceans. A brief examination of this context may be useful in explaining the international reaction of the new Swedish policy.

The centuries-old policy of freedom of navigation is animated by a

---

104. Press & Information Department, Royal Ministry of Defense, Foreign Submarines in Norwegian Waters 1, 8 (Fact Sheet No. 0383, May 1983).

105. The USSR did break off ministerial-level relations after publication of the Commission's report; however these relations were soon on the mend. *See, e.g.*, N.Y. Times, Mar. 31, 1984, at A2, col. 3.

conviction that only "a minimum of monopolization of either use or authority" over the oceans "can create the greatest net gains both in the . . . value of general security and the . . . values of wealth, enlightenment, well-being and so on."[106] This implies a right of passage of alien ships through the territorial sea of a coastal state. However, there had been, and to a certain extent still is, doubt whether the policy should imply the right of passage in peacetime of foreign warships. Some states share an opinion, expressed most eloquently by W. Hall, that the passage of warships has different functions than the transit of merchant ships and constitutes an imminent threat to the security of the coastal state. Hence, the coastal state has the right to regulate the passage of warships by requiring that the foreign warship obtain an authorization or at least notify the coastal state of its intention to pass.[107]

Many states, however, contend that the right of passage in peacetime has been recognized from time immemorial as one of the fundamental policies of the law of the sea. L. Oppenheim has written that

> in practice no State actually opposes in time of peace the passage of foreign men-of-war and other public vessels through its maritime belt. It may safely be stated, first, that a usage has grown up by which such passage, if in every way inoffensive and without danger, shall not be denied in time of peace; and, secondly, that it is now a customary rule of International Law that the right of passage through such parts of the maritime belt as form part of the

106. M. McDougal & J. Burke, The Public Order of the Oceans 562 (1962).

107. W. Hall states that "[t]he right of innocent passage does not extend to vessels of war. Its possession by them could not be explained upon the ground by which commercial passage is justified. The interests of the whole world are concerned in the possession of the utmost liberty of navigation for the purpose of trade by the vessels of all states. But no general interests are necessary or commonly involved in the possession by a state of a right to navigate the waters of other states with its ships of war. Such a privilege is to the advantage only of the individual state; it may often be injurious to third states; and it may sometimes be dangerous to the proprietor of the waters used. A state has therefore always the right to refuse access to its territorial waters to the armed vessels of other states, if it wishes to do so." W. Hall, International Law 198 (P. Higgins 8th ed. 1924). The same argument was made by Elihu Root on behalf of the United States in the North Atlantic Coast Fisheries Case: "Warships may not pass and repass . . . because they threaten. Merchant ships may pass and repass because they do not threaten." 11 Proceedings of the North Atlantic Coast Fisheries Arbitration 2007 (1912). See P. Jessup, The Law of Territorial Waters and Maritime Jurisdiction 120 (1927); G. Gidel, Le Droit International Public 284 (1934); Soviet writers quoted by W. Butler, *supra* note 64, at 59 *et seq.*

highways for international traffic cannot be denied to foreign men-of-war.[108]

The 1958 Convention on the Territorial Sea and the Contiguous Zone provides for the right of innocent passage of all ships through the territorial sea,[109] but some states advocated a denial of this right to warships and made reservations accordingly.[110] Although the 1982 United Nations Convention on the Law of the Sea followed the path set by the 1958 Convention in granting the right of innocent passage to all ships,[111] the controversy concerning warships was not extinguished and the uncertainty as to the existence of a general consensus among states concerning the matter was not dispelled.[112] The frequent practice is that a coastal state regularly accords passage to foreign warships, but reserves the right to regulate and even to forbid such passage.[113] In this situation, the question of whether the passage of foreign warships through territorial waters other than straits[114] is a matter of right ac-

108. L. OPPENHEIM, INTERNATIONAL LAW 494 (H. Lauterpacht 8th ed. 1955); cf. C. COLOMBOS, THE INTERNATIONAL LAW OF THE SEA 237 (5th ed. 1962); 1 E. BRUEL, INTERNATIONAL STRAITS 230 (1947) (although the right of innocent passage of warships cannot be assumed to exist, such a right is accorded to them in practice by all states in time of peace); 1 D. O'CONNELL, INTERNATIONAL LAW OF THE SEA 274–76 (I. Shearer ed. 1982); Froman, *Uncharted Waters: Non-innocent Passage of Warships in the Territorial Sea*, 21 SAN DIEGO L. REV. 630–46 (1984).

109. Convention on the Territorial Sea and the Contiguous Zone, April 29, 1958, 15 U.S.T. 1606, T.I.A.S. No. 5639, 516 U.N.T.S. 205 [hereinafter cited as 1958 Convention], § III, art. 14(1).

110. M. McDOUGAL & J. BURKE, *supra* note 106, at 218–20. Sweden is not a party to the 1958 Convention.

111. United Nations Convention on the Law of the Sea, *opened for signature* Dec. 10, 1982, U.N. Doc. A/CONF.62/122 [hereinafter cited as LOS Convention], art. 17. Sweden is a signatory to the LOS Convention.

112. Froman, *supra* note 108, at 639–42 (summary of debates at the Third UN Conference on the Law of the Sea).

113. For the history of state practice, see generally D. O'CONNELL, *supra* note 108, at 277–81. Approximately 50 states support the right of the coastal state to require notification or authorization. Froman, *supra* note 108, at 651–54.

114. The International Court of Justice held in the Corfu Channel Case (United Kingdom v. Albania), 1949 I.C.J. 4, that a coastal state may not prohibit innocent passage of warships through its straits in time of peace. *Id.* at 29. *See* M. McDOUGAL & J. BURKE, *supra* note 106, at 54–69, 202. Judge Azevedo, however, after having quoted the authorities denying a right of passage to warships, stated: "To sum up, it is evident that all the arguments invoked in favour of freedom of passage for warships are clouded in confusion, at any rate sufficiently to bar the recognition of a custom in accordance

corded the flag state, or a matter of tolerance by the coastal state, remains open.

Once a foreign warship is within territorial waters, it enjoys full immunity from the jurisdiction of any state except its flag state.[115] This policy, being a direct offshoot of the doctrine of the sovereign immunity of states, has an exceptionally strong grounding in customary international law. It guarantees that a foreign warship cannot be seized, that no official of the coastal state can board the vessel without the permission of the commander of the ship, and that no judicial proceedings can be brought against the officers and crew.[116] The only protection provided to a coastal state against possible abuses of the immunity privilege is the requirement that the vessel comply with the coastal state's regulations concerning the admission of foreign warships to its waters.[117] If, however, the warship fails to observe these regulations, the coastal state's response is limited to a complaint lodged with the flag state.[118] If the violation persists, the coastal state can only require the vessel to leave its waters.[119] This norm was confirmed by both the 1958 Convention[120] and the LOS Convention.[121] Unlike norms regarding right of passage, which distinguish between territorial and internal waters, leaving to the coastal state the exclusive competence to regulate access to its internal waters, norms concerning jurisdictional immunity apply indiscriminately, notwithstanding the location of the warship.[122]

The policy with respect to the rights of foreign warships first crystalized at a time when a few naval powers were the only effective decision

---

with traditional requirements." 1949 I.C.J. at 101. (Azevedo, J., dissenting). *See also* G. GIDEL, *supra* note 107, at 283–84. The confusion concerning the regime of straits was not totally dispelled by the LOS Convention. *See* Reisman, *The Regime of Straits and National Security: An Appraisal of International Law Making*, 74 AM. J. INT'L L. 48 (1980); Moore, *The Regime of Straits and the Third United Nations Conference on the Law of the Sea*, 74 AM. J. INT'L L. 77 (1980).

115. C. COLOMBOS, *supra* note 108, at 241. Colombos notes, however, that the original entry of the foreign warship must have been expressly or impliedly permitted by the coastal state. *Id.*

116. *Id.* at 241–42.

117. *Id.* at 242.

118. *Id.*

119. *Id.*

120. 1958 Convention, *supra* note 109, § III, art. 23.

121. LOS Convention, *supra* note 111, art. 30.

122. This conclusion seems to be consistent with the lack of such a distinction in customary international law and the scholarly writings.

makers in the international community. It has served an important in-clusive interest, allowing many elites based on coasts to benefit from the "umbrella" provided by naval powers. Nevertheless, this policy pri-marily benefited those major naval powers that had the means to enjoy such freedom through deployment of their warships throughout the world. From the perspective of some coastal states, warships are a weapon of power politics—symbols and instruments of coercive action that pose a threat to their security. The fear of this threat has stimulated several states to react violently in the past.[123]

The development of electronic intelligence gathering and surveil-lance, which in peacetime operate, *inter alia*, from warships, has made the problem more acute. For the coastal states, which often do not have adequate means to counter this sort of activity, intelligence operations within their waters can be seen as violations of their rights and a serious risk to their security.[124] On the other hand, almost all states are in-volved in some form of intelligence gathering, which is deemed indis-pensable to rational decision making and deterrence.[125]

Claims to enhanced protection of the rights of coastal states induced certain restrictions on the right of passage. In the 1958 Convention, coastal states claimed competence to decide whether a passage of a for-eign ship through their territorial waters was innocent—that is, "not

123. Some examples are the 1946 incident in the Corfu Channel (Albania and the United Kingdom), the 1964 incident in the Gulf of Tonkin (the United States and North Korea), and the 1967 U.S.S. *Liberty* incident (the United States and Israel). The impor-tant difference between these events and the Swedish incident consists in the fact that the former took place in conditions of high international tension or even open hostilities in the region.

124. At least one writer considers the gathering of secret information by a warship in the internal waters of a foreign state to be an act contrary to international law. *See* De-lupis, *supra* note 81, at 69. *Cf.* Fitzmaurice, *The Law and Procedure of the International Court of Justice: General Principles and Substantive Law*, 27 BRIT. Y.B. INT'L L. 29 (1950) (commenting on the *Corfu Channel* decision: "It is an inference from certain of the Court's observations . . . that if the motive were espionage, e.g., the observation of the coastal defenses, the passage would not rank as innocent").

125. McDougal, Lasswell & Reisman, *The Intelligence Function and World Public Order*, in INTERNATIONAL LAW ESSAYS: A SUPPLEMENT TO INTERNATIONAL LAW IN CON-TEMPORARY PERSPECTIVE 311 (M. McDougal & W. Reisman eds. 1981) ("the gathering of intelligence within the territorial confines of another state is not, in and of itself, contrary to international law unless it contravenes policies of the world constitutive proc-ess according support to protected features of internal public order"). *But cf. id.* at 310 n.53.

prejudicial to the peace, good order or security of the coastal state"[126]— and to prevent passage which was not innocent.[127]

The general, abstract terms in which these provisions were worded gave the coastal state wide discretion to interpret and apply them in a way that might be detrimental to the inclusive interests of the international community. Hence, there was widespread opinion that a prescription on innocent passage should be formulated "with maximum precision and certainty of reference."[128] The LOS Convention attempted to restrain the discretion of coastal states by providing an exhaustive list of criteria for evaluating whether a passage is prejudicial to the peace, good order, and security of the coastal state.[129]

Although this provision limits the discretion of the coastal states, its scope is wide enough to permit them to regulate navigation in their territorial seas. A tendency to enhance the protection of their interests may be discerned, particularly in the regulation of the passage of submarines. Both the 1958 Convention[130] and the LOS Convention[131] require submarines passing through territorial waters to navigate on the surface and to show their flag. In other words, submerged passage is considered prejudicial to the interests of coastal states, which are understandably apprehensive about "the use of their territory, without their notice or knowledge, by foreign military craft of great strategic and tactical importance."[132] On the other hand, requiring surface passage of submarines may be prejudicial to the security interests of those states employing them, and may aggravate international tensions.[133] For this reason some states have strongly opposed a requirement of surface passage for submarines.

The assumption underlying the requirement of surface passage—that submergence in territorial waters of a foreign state is tantamount to an exercise of noninnocent passage—is overinclusive, since submerged

---

126. 1958 Convention, *supra* note 109, art. 14(4).

127. *Id.* art.16.

128. Burke, *Contemporary Law of the Sea: Transportation, Communication and Flight,* 2 YALE STUD. WORLD PUB. ORDER 210 (1976).

129. LOS Convention, *supra* note 111, art. 19(2).

130. 1958 Convention, *supra* note 109, art. 14(6).

131. LOS Convention, *supra* note 111, art. 20.

132. Burke, *supra* note 128, at 213.

133. Reisman, *supra* note 114, at 48–57; D. O'CONNELL, THE INFLUENCE OF LAW ON SEA POWER 106–107 (1975); Osgood, *U.S. Security Interests in Ocean Law,* 1 OCEAN DEV. & INT'L L.J. 2 (1974).

submarines might be engaged in an innocent passage (that is, one not prejudicial to the peace, good order, and security of the coastal state). Whether a submerged passage is a noninnocent passage must always be a matter of cautious evaluation by the competent authorities of the coastal state: *a fortiori*, the submerged passage does not give the coastal state a license to use arms against the alleged perpetrator.[134]

The development of rules concerning innocent passage has been accompanied by a gradual extension of the width of internal and territorial waters, thus submitting ever larger portions of the oceans to the exclusive authority of coastal states. It seems therefore, that in the past few decades the general trend has been toward enhancing protection of the interests of coastal states and, in particular, their claim to security and wealth, even if there are reasonable doubts as to how widely the consensus on some issues is shared. The Swedish policy with respect to submarine violations and the international tolerance of that policy are a most dramatic chapter in this development.

For many centuries, the unimpeded access of foreign warships to territorial waters in peacetime was considered essential to the maintenance of friendly relations among members of the international community and to the improvement of its security through the limitation of tension and conflicts. It is true that unhindered passage of navies through parts of territorial waters forming straits and other international waterways is of paramount importance to public order, while more extensive restrictions on passage through other parts of the territorial sea, and particularly through internal waters (where coastal states assert an undisputed exclusive competence), are considered justified because international navigation is less likely to be disrupted and important interests of coastal states are involved. If, however, the perceived need for protection leads a coastal state to the general denial of submerged passage in its territorial sea and disregard for the immunity of alien warships found in its internal waters, the likely result may be a destabilizing effect on the security of the international community. This result is particularly probable when the coastal state views itself as justified in using force against such foreign warships. Use of force, even in self-defense, invites use of force.

The Soviet intrusions into Swedish waters clearly demonstrate how the abuse of privileges leads to the erosion of established norms. Al-

134. *Cf.* D. O'Connell, *supra* note 108, at 294–97.

though the Swedish response to these incidents may have been reasonable from the Swedish viewpoint, and though their response received the acquiescence of the international community, a norm permitting the use of force to repel unauthorized passage of foreign warships in peacetime must be viewed with concern. International law, if it is to mean more than merely naked power, must be based on *l'esprit communautaire*—the common awareness that prudence, self-restraint, and reciprocity are in the long run the best means for maximizing and sharing values in the world community.

COSMOS 954: The International Law of Satellite Accidents

4

ALEXANDER F. COHEN

PROBLEM

Falling satellites[1] are an unavoidable hazard of space exploration: at the current level of technology, a certain number of satellites will inevitably fall out of orbit.[2] The traditional sources of international law provide little help in determining what norms would govern a situation in which a falling satellite causes injury.[3] The 1978 crash of the Soviet

1. A satellite is "[a]ny manmade object launched from and revolving around the earth." FUNK & WAGNALL'S STANDARD DESK DICTIONARY 593 (1977). I prefer this term to "space object." Despite its wide currency in legal writing and UN documents, "space object" poses various thorny problems of definition. For a discussion of these difficulties, see Foster, *The Convention on International Liability for Damage Caused by Space Objects*, 1972 CAN. Y.B. INT'L L. 144–47, 158–60; Wilkins, *Substantive Bases for Recovery for Injuries Sustained by Private Individuals as a Result of Fallen Space Objects*, 6 J. SPACE L. 162 (1978).

2. Telephone interviews with U.S. government officials (Mar. 1984).

3. The Cosmos 954 accident was the first instance in the history of space exploration in which the satellite of one nation caused significant injury to a second nation. Legault & Farand, Canada's Claim for Damage Caused by the Soviet Cosmos 954 Satellite 25 (Jan. 1984) (unpublished manuscript available from Canadian Embassy, Washington, D.C.) (on file with the *Yale Journal of International Law*). Hence, no court cases, arbi-

Union's Cosmos 954 satellite, however, has shed some light on the normative expectations of states concerning satellite accidents.

From the events leading up to and following the crash of Cosmos 954, four governing norms emerged: (1) A state that becomes aware that one of its satellites will crash has the duty to forewarn a state that is in danger; (2) the state whose satellite has crashed in the territory of another state has the duty to provide that state with information (regarding the specifications of that satellite) to enable the endangered state to assess the dangers and act to counter them; (3) special procedures govern the duty to clean up the remains of a state's satellite that has crashed in another state's territory; and (4) the state whose satellite has crashed has the duty to compensate a state injured as a result of the crash.

FACTS

The Soviet Union launched the nuclear-powered[4] Cosmos 954 naval surveillance satellite on September 18, 1977.[5] In late November or early December 1977, Cosmos 954's orbit became erratic.[6] The United States soon calculated that the satellite would fall on or about January

---

tral decisions, or any other formal judicial proceedings have dealt with satellite accidents. In addition, it is unclear if the one international treaty that addresses this problem is prescriptive. *See* Convention on International Liability for Damage Caused by Space Objects, Sept. 1, 1972, 24 U.S.T. 2389, T.I.A.S. No. 7762, *reprinted in* 66 AM. J. INT'L. L. 702 (1972). Canada and the Soviet Union seem to have ignored most of the provisions of the Liability Convention during the Cosmos 954 incident. *But cf.* Schwartz & Berlin, *After the Fall: An Analysis of Canadian Legal Claims for Damage Caused by Cosmos 954*, 27 McGILL L.J. 676, 705–712, (1982) (arguing that the 1972 Liability Convention is prescriptive). For a general discussion of the Liability Convention, *see* Foster, *supra* note 1, 137 *passim*; Schwarzchild. *Space Law—Convention on Liability—Procedure Established to Enforce Liability for Damage Caused by Space Objects*, 6 VAND. J. TRANSNAT'L L. 262 (1972); STAFF OF SENATE COMM. ON AERONAUTICAL AND SPACE SCIENCES, 92D CONG., 2D SESS., CONVENTION ON INTERNATIONAL LIABILITY FOR DAMAGE CAUSED BY SPACE OBJECTS: ANALYSIS AND BACKGROUND DATA (Comm. Print 1972).

4. A nuclear reactor containing some 50 kilograms of enriched uranium powered the radar and radio units with which the satellite tracked U.S. navy ships. Krey, Leifer, Benson, Dietz, Hendrikson & Coluzza, *Atmospheric Burnup of the Cosmos-954 Reactor*, 205 SCIENCE 583 (1979); N.Y. Times, Jan. 25, 1978, at A1, col. 6.

5. N.Y. Times, Jan. 25, 1978, at A8, col. 2. *See also* U.N. Doc. A/AC.105/Inf. 365 (1977) (providing information about the launch of Cosmos 954).

6. N.Y. Times, Jan. 29, 1978, at A8, col. 1.

23, 1978,[7] although it was not known where it would land.[8] In response, the United States initiated a series of secret meetings with the Soviet Union in mid-January 1978,[9] during which the Soviets provided the Americans with information about Cosmos 954's reactor.[10] The United States also warned its NATO[11] and Organization for Economic Cooperation and Development (OECD)[12] partners that Cosmos 954 was expected to fall, and offered to help clean up any radioactive contamination that might result.[13]

Cosmos 954 crashed to earth on January 24, 1978:

> [T]he satellite entered the earth's atmosphere intruding into Canadian air space at about 11:53 A.M. Greenwich Mean Time to the north of the Queen Charlotte Islands on the west coast of Canada. On re-entry and disintegration, debris from the satellite was deposited on Canadian territory, including portions of the Northwest Territories, Alberta, and Saskatchewan.[14]

U.S. president Jimmy Carter notified Canadian prime minister Pierre Trudeau within fifteen minutes of the accident, and repeated the U.S. proposal of assistance.[15] Trudeau accepted Carter's offer.[16]

Some hours later, Canada asked the Soviet Union to provide information about the specifications of the Cosmos 954.[17] The USSR re-

7. Aikman, *Operation Morning Light*, 1978 SENTINEL: MAG. CAN. FORCES, No. 2, at 5.

8. N.Y. Times, Jan. 29, 1978, at A1, col. 6. It is apparently quite difficult to predict where a satellite that is falling out of control will land. *See* Doyle, *Reentering Space Objects: Facts and Fiction*, 6 J. SPACE L. 107, 110 (1978). As one U. S. air force officer put it, "we are just not good enough to tell New York City, for instance, that a satellite is coming and will knock King Kong off the Empire State Building at 2 P.M.," *quoted in* N.Y. Times, Jan. 29, 1978, at A8, col. 1.

9. N.Y. Times, Jan. 25, 1978, at A1, col. 6.

10. Wash. Post, Jan. 27, 1978, at A18, col. 2.

11. N.Y. Times, Jan. 25, 1978, at A1, col. 6 and A8, col. 2.

12. Aikman, *supra* note 7, at 5; N.Y. Times, Jan. 26, 1978, at A5, col. 3.

13. Aikman, *supra* note 7, at 5; N.Y. Times, Jan. 26, 1978, at A5, col. 3.

14. Gov't of Canada, Dep't of External Aff., Note from the Secretary of State for External Aff. to the Soviet Ambassador, Jan. 23, 1979, *Annex A: Statement of Claim* [hereinafter cited as *Annex A*], at 1 (on file with the *Yale Journal of International Law*).

15. Aikman, *supra* note 7, at 5; N.Y. Times, Jan. 26, 1978, at A5, col. 3.

16. *Annex A, supra* note 14, at 2.

17. Dep't of External Aff. Note No. FLO–0497 to the Embassy of the USSR (Ottawa), Feb. 28, 1978, *reprinted in* Gov't of Canada, Dep't of External Aff., Note From the Secretary of State for External Aff. to the Soviet Ambassador, Jan. 23, 1979, *Annex B: Texts of Diplomatic Communications Between the Department of External Affairs and*

sponded that day by offering to help clean up Cosmos 954's remains.[18] In contrast to its reaction to the earlier U.S. proposal, Canada declined the Soviet offer.[19]

The joint U.S.–Canadian cleanup operation that resulted from this exchange, dubbed "Operation Morning Light," cost Canada nearly C$14 million;[20] the United States spent some U.S.$2–2.5 million.[21] Canada billed the Soviet Union for C$6 million of its outlay[22] on January 23, 1979,[23] but did not seek reimbursement for the U.S. expenditure.[24] The Soviets paid C$3 million to Canada on April 2, 1981, "in full and final settlement of all matters connected with the disintegration of the Soviet satellite 'Cosmos 954' in January 1978."[25]

CONFLICTING CLAIMS

Canada and the Soviet Union gave different versions of the facts of the accident. First, the USSR blamed the fall of Cosmos 954 on a midspace collision. Academician L. I. Sedov explained:

> On Jan. 6, 1978, for reasons that as yet remain unclear, sudden depressurization of the satellite took place outside the visibility zone of our facilities for tracking space objects. Judging from the fact that the depressurization process was very rapid, it can be assumed that the satellite collided in flight with some other body of natural or artificial origin. As a result the satellite's onboard systems went out of commission, it lost orientation, and began an uncontrollable descent.[26]

---

the Embassy of the Union of Soviet Socialist Republics [hereinafter cited as Annex B] (copy on file with the Yale Journal of International Law).

18. Annex A, supra note 14, at 2.

19. Id.

20. Id. at 3.

21. Telephone interviews with U.S. government officials (Mar. 1984). See also Canada Wants Cash for Cosmos 954 Cleanup, 203 SCIENCE 632 (1979) (citing cost as U.S.$2 million).

22. Annex A, supra note 14, at 3. See infra notes 46–47 and accompanying text for an explanation of why Canada did not seek recovery of the full amount.

23. N.Y. Times, Jan. 24, 1979, at A7, col. 1.

24. Canada Wants Cash for Cosmos 954 Cleanup, supra note 21, at 632.

25. Claims Protocol, April 2, 1981, Canada–USSR, Can. T.S. No. 8, art. 2.

26. Izvestia, Feb. 5, 1978, at 3, reprinted in 30 CURRENT DIG. SOVIET PRESS, No. 5, at 1 (1978).

Canada, in contrast, blamed the fall of the satellite on a faulty motor. "The U.S.S.R. admitted that Cosmos 954 had failed, and that it was not possible to lift the satellite into a much higher orbit, as had been planned in case of an emergency, because of failure of a rocket system."[27]

Second, the Soviet Union claimed that Cosmos 954 had been completely destroyed during reentry. The official Soviet news agency (TASS) stated that "in the afternoon of Jan. 24, 1978, the Kosmos-954 satellite entered the dense layers of the atmosphere over Northern Canada and ceased to exist."[28] Despite this claim, Canada found charred pieces of the satellite that had returned to the ground.[29]

Finally, the Soviet Union declared that the remains of Cosmos 954, if any, posed a minimal radiation hazard. According to Sedov, "[i]t was emphasized [to the Canadian government] that if individual fragments of the satellite did reach the earth's surface, only limited local pollution might occur, and only in the immediate area of the fall, and that this would require the application of ordinary decontamination measures."[30] Canada, in contrast, found that "all but two of the fragments recovered were radioactive. Some fragments located proved to be of lethal radioactivity."[31]

CONFLICTING CONCEPTIONS OF LAWFULNESS

The Cosmos 954 incident suggests that elites in Canada and the Soviet Union held divergent expectations of how states that are involved in satellite accidents should behave. These expectations concerned the interpretation of four governing norms: the duty to forewarn, the duty to provide information, the duty to clean up, and the duty to compensate for injury.

27. Gov't of Canada, Dep't of External Aff., Note from the Secretary of State for External Aff. to the Soviet Ambassador, Jan. 23, 1979, *Annex C: Schedule of Costs Phase I*, at 35 (on file with the *Yale Journal of International Law*).

28. Pravda, Jan. 25, 1978, at 4, *reprinted in* 30 CURRENT DIG. SOVIET PRESS, No. 4, at 7 (1978).

29. *Annex A, supra* note 14, at 1. The Soviet claim was contradicted both by the existence of charred chunks of metal in Canada and by the Soviet Union's later offer to help clean up the remains of the satellite. *See supra* note 18 and accompanying text.

30. *Supra* note 26, at 1.

31. *Annex A, supra* note 14, at 4.

The Duty to Forewarn

It appears from the record that Canadian elites expected the Soviet Union to warn Canada as soon as the USSR had discovered that Cosmos 954 might conceivably land in Canada:

> In the course of the day January 24, 1978, an official of the Department of External Affairs expressed to the Ambassador of the Union of Soviet Socialist Republics the surprise of the Government of Canada that the Government of the Union of Soviet Socialist Republics had failed to give notice of the possible re-entry of the satellite into the earth's atmosphere in the region of Canada, and, subsequently, of the imminent re-entry of the satellite.[32]

Elites in Canada thus seemed to believe that the Soviet Union was obligated to forewarn all potentially endangered states of the hazards posed by its falling satellite, no matter how remote the possibility of injury.

Soviet elites[33] viewed the norm differently. They claimed that the USSR had an obligation to warn only the United States of the impending crash of Cosmos 954:

> Calculations made on the basis of [Cosmos 954's] last orbits within the visibility range of our tracking facilities showed that if, because of the satellite's emergency condition, individual parts of the satellite were not fully consumed in the atmosphere and reached the earth's surface, they might fall into the open sea in the region of the Aleutian Islands. In this connection, the appropriate information was given to the U.S. government.[34]

32. *Id.* at 2. *See also* N.Y. Times, Jan. 25, 1978, at A8, col. 1 (reporting that unnamed Canadian government officials were angry at the USSR's failure to warn Canada of the impending crash of Cosmos 954); telephone interviews with Canadian government officials (Mar. 1984). *But see* Scientific and Technical Sub-Committee of the UN Committee on the Peaceful Uses of Outer Space, 33 U.N. GAOR (190th meeting of the Subcomm.) at 9, U.N. Doc. A/AC.105/C.1/S.R. 190 (1978). Soviet representative Federov claimed that his country had notified Canada as soon as it realized Cosmos 954 would enter the atmosphere over Canadian territory.

33. It was not possible to gauge Soviet elite expectations through direct interviews. I have therefore relied on statements in Pravda, among other sources.

34. *A Tass Correspondent Interviews Academician L.I. Sedov, supra* note 26. Sedov's assertions seem to contradict statements by U.S. officials that it was unclear into what countries Cosmos 954 would fall until shortly before the actual crash occurred. As the

Two possible conceptions of the duty to forewarn may explain this assertion. First, Soviet elites may have interpreted the norm as a requirement that they warn the state in whose territory the satellite was most likely to crash.[35] Alternatively, the USSR may have agreed with Canada that the duty to forewarn required the notification of all *potentially* endangered states. Elites in the Soviet Union may not have believed, however, that they were required to notify these states directly if they were part of a political and military alliance hostile to the USSR.[36] Rather, Soviet elites may have believed that their country could discharge its duty under the norm by notifying the leading state in the hostile alliance—in this case, the United States—which would relay the warning to the other members of that alliance.

The Duty to Provide Information

Consistent with their position regarding the duty to forewarn, Canada's elites believed that the Soviet Union was under an obligation to disclose information. Canada repeatedly questioned the Soviets about Cosmos 954's specifications, and expressed frustration at their refusal to answer the inquiries: "In this regard, Canada has requested the assistance of the Soviet authorities in furnishing information about the nature and characteristics of the nuclear core contained in the satellite. These requests have been conveyed on several occasions. . . . The Canadian authorities regret that they have not to date received answers to these questions."[37]

Elites in Canada also apparently expected that this information be

---

U.S. Department of Energy report on Operation Morning Light stated, "[t]he satellite was being continually tracked by all available U.S. assets until it reentered the earth's atmosphere. Originally it was relatively easy to predict orbital decay, based on prior observation, as long as the satellite remained horizon stable. Later, when the satellite began to tumble, planners were dealing with an uncertain entry window because the geometry, mass, and altitude were unknown. This uncertainty of entry window location precluded the possibility of prior action to protect the health and safety of specific population clusters." U.S. DEPARTMENT OF ENERGY, OPERATION MORNING LIGHT 5 (1978).

35. This interpretation of the duty to forewarn would appear to ignore the difficulty of predicting where a falling satellite will land. *See* Doyle, *supra* note 8, at 110; OPERATION MORNING LIGHT, *supra* note 34, at 5.

36. It would be interesting to know if the Soviet Union warned the members of the Council on Mutual Economic Assistance (CMEA) or the Warsaw Treaty Organization (WTO) about Cosmos 954. I have been unable to discover an answer to this question.

37. Dep't of External Aff. Note No. FLO–0497 to the Embassy of the USSR (Ottawa), Feb. 28, 1978, *reprinted in Annex B, supra* note 17.

publicly disclosed. Indeed, "Canada decided to publish the documents establishing the claim together with texts of its diplomatic exchanges with the Soviet Union on the matter. In so doing, the Canadian government departed from normal practice regarding the confidentiality of diplomatic communications."[38]

Under the Soviet interpretation, however, the duty to provide information imposed a more limited burden. According to this interpretation, they were required to provide only the minimum degree of information that Canada needed to conduct a cleanup. In addition, the Soviet Union reserved the right to determine what that minimum included:

> In connection with the request made by the Canadian side for information regarding the power unit which was on board the Cosmos-954 satellite, the Embassy would remind that the necessary information about the satellite was already made available which, in the opinion of the Soviet side, is sufficient to organize and carry out effective search for possible consequences of its cessation to exist over Canadian territory.[39]

The statements made in *Pravda* seem to show that the Soviet Union also believed that any information it provided should be transmitted secretly. The Soviets chided Canada for the highly public manner in which Canada had handled the Cosmos 954 incident;[40] they appeared particularly displeased at the fact that Canada did not notify them officially of its findings concerning the wreckage for two weeks, a considerable time after such information was released to the press.[41] Indeed, the Soviets charged that Canada was using requests for information as

38. Legault & Farand, *supra* note 3, at 14–15.
39. Embassy of the USSR Note No. 2 to the Dep't of External Aff. (Ottawa), Mar. 21, 1978, *reprinted in Annex B, supra* note 17.
40. *See supra* note 38 and accompanying text.
41. The Russian statement read: "Likewise one cannot but express regret with regard to the fact that the official notification of the Soviet side about the discovery on Canadian territory of objects which are presumed by the Canadian side to be fragments of the Cosmos-954 satellite was made two weeks after the time the satellite ceased to exist and considerably later [than] the information about these objects had been made available to the press and experts from other countries." Embassy of the USSR Note No. 18 to the Dep't of External Aff., Ottawa, Feb. 20, 1978, *reprinted in Annex B, supra* note 17. The fact that the Soviets had complied with the secret U.S. requests for information in January 1978 suggests that they might have been more forthcoming with information had Canada been more discreet in its demands. *See supra* notes 9–10 and accompanying text.

a pretext for intelligence gathering. "The Soviet side finds it also necessary to note that some of the questions put by the Canadian side obviously relate to information which is outside the scope of the amount [sic] necessary to secure the health and safety of persons and the environment."[42]

The Duty to Clean Up

In the Soviet view, the cleanup should have been undertaken jointly by the injured state and the state that had launched the satellite. As the Soviet representative to the Scientific and Technical Sub-Committee of the UN Committee on the Peaceful Uses of Outer Space stated soon after the crash of Cosmos 954, "[i]f a satellite or any spacecraft, when it goes out of control should cause damage to another State, then the launching State is duty-bound to compensate for this damage: it is duty-bound to participate in the search and recovery of the debris of the satellite."[43] The Soviet Union repeatedly expressed frustration at Canada's refusal to allow it to participate in the cleanup.[44]

Under the Canadian version of this norm, the injured state is entitled to choose which country or countries will carry out the cleanup. Accordingly, Canada turned down the Soviet offer of assistance but permitted its American ally to participate in the operation.[45]

The Duty to Compensate for Injury

Canada evidently considered there to be a norm requiring the Soviet Union to make full payment for the cost of repairing the injury caused

42. Embassy of the USSR Note No. 37 to the Dep't of External Aff. (Ottawa), May 31, 1978, *reprinted in* Annex B, *supra* note 17.

43. Statement of Academician Federov, Scientific and Technical Sub-Committee of the UN Committee on the Peaceful Uses of Outer Space (Feb. 14, 1978), *reprinted in* Legault & Farand, *supra* note 3, at 17.

44. *Id.* at 16.

45. *See supra* notes 15–25 and accompanying text. Elites in Canada felt that the country it designated must be a close political ally. One could conclude that Canada never seriously entertained the Soviet offer: "On that occasion [January 24: 1978], the [USSR's] Ambassador expressed his government's readiness to render urgent assistance by sending to Canada a group of specialists to ameliorate the possible consequences and evacuate remnants of the satellite. Canadian officials replied that their urgent need was for immediate and complete answers to the questions posed earlier on January 24, 1978." *Annex A, supra* note 14, at 2.

by its satellite. Although Canada eventually demanded only C$6 million in damages out of an expenditure of C$14 million,[46] it clearly based its claim on the total cost of cleaning up the radioactive debris.[47] Canadian elites also apparently believed that the United States would help pay for the cleanup. If one conceives of the unreimbursed U.S. expenditure on the cleanup of US$2–2.5 million as a form of payment to Canada, the United States "paid" Canada C$2.5–3.125 million as a result of the crash of Cosmos 954.[48] Canada never offered to repay the United States for its outlay on the cleanup, nor did it press the Soviet Union to do so.[49]

Actions by Soviet elites showed partial disagreement with this interpretation. Unlike Canada, the Soviet Union apparently views the duty to compensate for injury as an obligation to reimburse only the incremental costs[50] that the injured state incurred in repairing the injury.[51] Thus the Soviet officials who negotiated their nation's payment to Canada "made it very clear that they wouldn't pay [Canadian] fixed costs."[52] At the same time, Soviet elites seemed to concur in the Canadian view that the United States should not be reimbursed for its role in the

46. Canada reportedly felt that the Soviet Union would reject a claim larger than C$6 million. Telephone interview with Canadian government official (Mar. 1984).

47. For example, it refused to present its claim to the Soviet Union until it had determined exactly how much the entire cleanup operation would cost: "In this regard, the Department of External Affairs wishes to inform the Embassy of the U.S.S.R. that the Government of Canada will submit to the U.S.S.R. a claim for damages, including search and recovery costs incurred by Canada as a result of the presence on Canadian territory of hazardous component parts of the Soviet satellite. . . . Since the necessary search and recovery operations are still underway, the full amount of damages are not yet known. The claim will be submitted in due course." Dep't of External Aff. Note No. FLO–0497 to the Embassy of the USSR (Ottawa), Feb. 28, 1978, *reprinted in Annex B, supra* note 17. Indeed, the Canadian claim included two lengthy memoranda that detailed the entire cost of all aspects of the cleanup, down to such items as car rental and photocopying. *See supra* note 27.

48. *See supra* note 21 and accompanying text. U.S.$2–2.5 million is approximately C$2.5–3.125 million at a rate of exchange of U.S. $1/C$0.80.

49. Indeed, Canadian elites were convinced that the United States did not wish to be repaid. Telephone interviews with Canadian government officials (Mar. 1984).

50. The term "incremental costs" refers to the costs over and above those that Canada would have borne had Cosmos 954 not fallen, such as salaries of Canadian armed forces personnel.

51. This interpretation would appear to exclude nonphysical injury such as mental anguish.

52. Telephone interview with Canadian government official (Mar. 1984).

cleanup. The Soviet Union, therefore, did not offer to reimburse the U.S. expenditure. Indeed, the Soviet refusal to pay Canada's "fixed costs" tends to suggest that the Soviets would have rejected such a U.S. claim.[53]

INTERNATIONAL APPRAISAL

The conflicting expectations of elites in Canada and the Soviet Union were never appraised in a formal judicial setting. Their claims of what constitutes proper action by states that are involved in a satellite accident did, however, receive widespread informal evaluation by a broad range of state and media elites.[54] From the standpoint of the creation of norms, the crucial appraisals were those of elites in the United States.[55]

The legal conceptions expressed by U.S. elites were much closer to those of Soviet than to those of Canadian elites. The United States assumed the burden of notifying its NATO and OECD partners, apparently without the Soviet Union having asked it to do so.[56] Furthermore, the U.S. government never joined in Canada's public criticism of the Soviets[57] for having failed to notify Canada of the impending crash of Cosmos 954.[58] From this it would appear that the United

53. U.S. elites felt that the Soviet Union would reject any such claim. Telephone interviews with U.S. government officials (Mar. 1984).

54. *See, e.g.*, Wash. Post, Jan. 27, 1978, at A18, col. 2; N.Y. Times, Jan. 27, 1978, at A24, col. 1; Can. Embassy Pub. Aff. Div., *Canadian Press Comment*, Feb. 8, 1978. Indeed, Russell Baker commented that "it turns out some fool had put a lot of nuclear reactors in orbit around the Earth while all the environment lovers were distracted down on the ground keeping the electric companies from putting nuclear reactors into power plants. It was a good joke on the environment crowd, I guess." N.Y. Times, Jan. 28, 1978, at A21, col. 1.

55. The United States and the Soviet Union have a near monopoly on space exploration. These two states, for example, launched 98 percent of all satellites that were orbited between 1957 and 1978. Hosenball, *Nuclear Power Sources in Outer Space*, 6 J. SPACE L. 119 (1978). Thus although the views of elites in other states as to what constitutes lawful behavior may be interesting, they are not particularly relevant: these elite expectations are unlikely to exert much influence on the outcome of future satellite accidents unless it is one of their satellites that crashes.

56. *See supra* notes 11–12 and accompanying text.

57. *See supra* note 32 and accompanying text.

58. U.S. elites were also unwilling to criticize the Soviet Union's behavior in private interviews. Telephone interviews with U.S. government officials (Mar. 1984).

States shared the Soviet view that the launching state was under a duty to forewarn only the leading state of a hostile alliance and was not responsible for warning each of its political adversaries individually.

The United States also appeared to agree with the Soviet Union on the issue of how to interpret the second norm, the duty to provide information. U.S. elites interpreted this as an obligation to provide only the information needed to conduct the cleanup. Unlike Canada,[59] the United States chose to question the Soviets about the specifications of Cosmos 954 in secret[60] and, evidently, expected only minimal compliance with U.S. requests for information:

> [M]any American specialists were skeptical that the Soviet Union would provide any information about its out-of-control space satellite, when national security advisor Zbigniew Brzezinski, on Jan. 12, first raised the issue with Soviet Ambassador Anatoly F. Dobrynin. "Frankly, I thought they were likely to tell us to go to hell," said one administration specialist.[61]

The United States again seemed to take the same view as the Soviets of the duty to compensate for injury. The Americans never joined Canada in criticizing the Soviet payment to Canada as too small,[62] apparently conceiving of the norm as imposing an obligation to reimburse the injured state only for the incremental cost of repairing the injury.[63] Since

59. See *supra* note 38 and accompanying text.
60. See *supra* notes 9–10 and accompanying text.
61. Wash. Post, Jan. 27, 1978, at A18, col. 2. The attitude of U.S. elites is comprehensible in light of the extreme secrecy that normally enshrouds reconnaissance satellites. For both the Soviet Union and the United States, any information about surveillance satellites—no matter how seemingly trivial—is closely guarded. The United States did not officially acknowledge the existence of its reconnaissance satellite program until 1978. T. KARRAS, THE NEW HIGH GROUND: SYSTEMS AND WEAPONS OF SPACE AGE WAR 99 (1983). The Soviet Union, for its part, has never admitted that Cosmos 954 was a surveillance satellite.
62. When asked if Canada was satisfied with the settlement, one Canadian official replied; "[w]ell, it's better than a poke in the eye with a stick." Telephone interview with Canadian government official (Mar. 1984). U.S. officials, in contrast, expressed surprise at how large a sum the Soviets paid. Telephone interviews with U.S. government officials (Mar. 1984).
63. Later U.S. behavior seems to suggest that U.S. elites also do not believe that claims for nonphysical injuries are valid under the duty to compensate. The U.S. uniformly rejected the claims for mental anguish that arose from the crash of Skylab in 1979. Telephone interviews with U.S. government officials (Mar. 1984).

the United States did not ask for reimbursement for its share of the cleanup expenses from either Canada or the Soviet Union, it would seem that U.S. elites agreed with both countries that the United States was obliged to pay Canada under the norm.[64]

Although concurring generally in the Soviet formulations of the first three norms, the United States rejected the Soviet interpretation of the fourth, concerning the duty to clean up. There is no indication that the United States ever expected Canada to permit the Soviet Union to play any part in the cleanup operation. Nevertheless, the apparent difference in legal conceptions obscures the possibility that the two superpowers were motivated by similar concerns. It is not unreasonable to suppose, as did some Canadian observers, that each was anxious to participate in the cleanup chiefly to gather intelligence or to prevent the other from doing so.[65] The U.S. eagerness to examine what was left of Cosmos 954[66] was surely matched by Soviet desires to deny the United States just such an opportunity. It would therefore seem misleading to characterize the U.S. appraisal as an affirmation of free choice for the injured state. Rather, it appears to be an assertion of the right of the injured state to invite only its political allies to participate in the cleanup.[67]

OUTCOME

The norms clarified by the Cosmos 954 incident provide that the major satellite-launching nations—the United States and the Soviet Union—notify each other of hazardous events due to satellite failure, relay information to facilitate damage control, assist their political allies in cleanup operations, and share the cost of compensating the state injured by a falling satellite, regardless of whose satellite caused the injury[68] and regardless of fault.

64. *Id.*
65. *See* T. KARRAS, *supra* note 61.
66. Telephone interviews with Canadian government officials (Mar. 1984).
67. It is unlikely that the United States would have quietly acquiesced had Canada decided to allow the Soviets, rather than the Americans, to assist in the operation.
68. Joint compensation may not apply to accidents in all situations. If a Soviet satellite fell on a CMEA or W.T.O. nation, it is unlikely that the United States would contribute to the cost of the cleanup. Similarly, if a U.S. satellite fell on a NATO country, the United States probably would not expect the Soviet Union to pay. It is unclear what

The critical norm is that of joint compensation. This norm would appear to provide compensation only for the incremental costs of cleanup associated with the accident.[69] It may also be limited in application to surveillance satellites.[70]

Although it is possible that the payments made by the United States and the Soviet Union were *ex gratia* and, hence, devoid of normative content, at least the size of the Soviet payment tends to argue otherwise; in the context of negotiations with the Soviet Union, a 50 percent settlement is apparently quite high.[71] Indeed, that the Soviet Union paid anything is striking in light of the fact that it was not obligated to pay under the 1972 Liability Convention.[72] That the United States paid its share without being at fault lends further support to the existence of this norm.

AUTHOR'S APPRAISAL

The Cosmos 954 incident illustrates the paradox of satellite utilization: satellites simultaneously protect and endanger the international community. Reconnaissance satellites play a crucial role in maintaining the

---

would happen if a satellite of either country fell on a nonaligned country: the outcome would probably depend on how "nonaligned" that country truly was.

69. *See supra* notes 50–52 & 63 and accompanying text.

70. This norm may not govern the crashes of all types of satellites. For example, the United States reportedly made extensive preparations to pay for injuries caused by the crash of Skylab in 1979, even to the extent of printing standardized claims forms. U.S. elites did not expect that the USSR would make payments as well. Telephone interviews with U.S. government officials (Mar. 1984). This suggests that compensation for injuries caused by well-publicized scientific satellites may be the responsibility of the state that launched these satellites, whereas joint compensation is the rule for accidents involving secret reconnaissance satellites.

71. Telephone interviews with U.S. and Canadian government officials (Mar. 1984). More generous settlements are generally expected from the U.S. *Id.*

72. It is not clear that the radioactive remains of Cosmos 954 injured Canada under the Liability Convention's definition of injury. *See* Haanappel, *Some Observations on the Crash of Cosmos 954*, 6 J. SPACE L. 147, 147–48 (1978). *But see* Schwartz & Berlin, *surpa* note 3, at 692–93, 695–98. Article I(a) of the Liability Convention provides that, "[f]or the purposes of the Convention: (a) The term 'damage' means loss of life, personal injury or other impairment of health; or loss of or damage to property of states or of persons, natural or juridical, or property of international intergovernmental organizations. . . ." Liability Convention, *supra* note 3, at article I(a). Canadian elites were relieved that the Soviets chose not to avoid payment on these grounds. Telephone interviews with Canadian government officials (Mar. 1984).

stability of the U.S.–USSR nuclear balance.[73] At the same time, nuclear-powered satellites present clear hazards, as the Cosmos 954 incident demonstrated.

One response to this problem would be to prohibit the use of the satellites that are most hazardous. At the time of the Cosmos 954 incident, President Carter suggested a ban on nuclear-powered satellites: "If we cannot evolve those fail-safe methods, then I think there ought to be a total prohibition against [nuclear-powered] earth-orbiting satellites. I would favor at this moment an agreement with the Soviets to prohibit earth-orbiting satellites with atomic radiation material in them."[74]

A ban on nuclear-powered satellites does not seem a realistic solution. In the first place, the United States and the Soviet Union are unlikely to consent to a prohibition, because certain satellites must carry an on-board nuclear power source[75] in order to perform their missions.[76] Indeed, Canada's attempt, in the wake of the Cosmos 954 in-

73. By reducing the potential for a successful surprise attack, these satellites allow both states to keep their nuclear forces at a relatively low level of alert. Any preparations for surprise attack would be difficult to hide, because reconnaissance satellites allow each state to scrutinize the other's territory. For a discussion of the capabilities of current U.S. reconnaissance satellites, see T. KARRAS, *supra* note 61, at 102-16. In addition, early warning satellites would provide quick notice in the event that a nuclear attack were launched. U.S. satellites can detect Soviet ICBMs within three minutes of their launch. Lecture by U.S. government official (Mar. 1984). The Soviet Union similarly employs nuclear-powered satellites for early warning of U.S. nuclear attacks. *See infra* note 78. Satellites also enhance stability by making arms control agreements verifiable and, hence, meaningful. Communications satellites also play an important role in the prevention of accidental war, by offering a reliable means for the leaders of the United States and the Soviet Union to communicate. The U.S.–USSR "hotline," for example, is satellite-based. N.Y. Times, Jan. 17, 1978, at A2, col. 3.

74. N.Y. Times, Jan. 31, 1978, at A10, col. 5.

75. Most satellites are powered by solar panels or chemical fuel cells. These sources are, however, too weak for satellites that carry power-intensive electronic equipment such as radar. N.Y. Times, Jan. 25, 1978, at A1, col. 6; N.Y. Times, Feb. 1, 1978, at A8, col. 3.

76. As a leading aviation weekly noted:

If the Soviet Union were to agree to such a ban [on nuclear-powered satellites] the effect on its ocean surveillance program would be severe. At least 10 Russian fission reactors have been launched into low earth orbits on 16 ocean surveillance missions since 1967.

. . . Any U.S. decision not to pursue development of earth orbiting reactors could limit potential major future programs. . . . A joint Defense Dept./Energy Dept. committee created two years ago to assess future military space power requirements

cident, to impose a new regime on the use of nuclear power sources in space through the United Nations Committee on the Peaceful Uses of Outer Space has made little progress.[77] In addition, the costs of such a ban might well outweigh its benefits, in that restrictions on nuclear-powered satellites could conceivably destabilize the nuclear balance.[78]

The norm of joint compensation that appears to emerge from the Cosmos 954 incident is a better answer to the paradox of satellite utilization. The states with the greatest investment in satellites are exposed to the greatest potential liability, but that liability is limited[79] and is not such as to discourage satellite use. This norm, by requiring payment regardless of fault, takes into account the probability that some satellites will inevitably fall.[80]

The outcome of the Cosmos 954 incident may well have had a pos-

---

identified almost a dozen missions that might need electric power levels of 10-100kw. These power levels could be provided most easily by nuclear reactors in space. *Cosmos Debris Examined in Canada*, 108. AVIATION WEEK AND SPACE TECHNOLOGY, No. 6, at 22–23 (1978).

77. *See* Legault & Farand, *supra* note 3, at 23-25.

78. The United States deploys nuclear weapons–capable aircraft aboard two of its aircraft carriers in the Mediterranean Sea. These aircraft form part of the "forward based systems" (FBS). *See* NEGOTIATING SECURITY: AN ARMS CONTROL READER 127 (W. Kincade & J. Porro eds. 1979). The Soviet Union has apparently long been concerned with the threat of the seaborne component of the FBS, particularly because the aircraft carriers from which the planes are launched are extremely difficult to locate if they maintain radio silence, turn off their radar, and move under cover of clouds. N.Y. Times, Jan. 25, 1978, at A8, col. 2. As a staff report to the now-defunct Senate Committee on Aeronautical and Space Sciences declared in 1976: "We must assume the Russians have a strong motive to develop a technology to locate United States naval vessels at sea even when they maneuver to stay under cloud cover and when they keep their radio transmitters and radar sets turned off. An obvious approach would be to put into space radar equipment capable of making rapid wide area searches in any weather." *Reprinted in* N.Y. Times, Jan. 25, 1978, at A8, col. 2. Cosmos 954 seemed to provide the Soviet Union with precisely this capability. Soviet behavior at the time of the 1980 U.S. hostage rescue mission may indicate that at least some of the later Cosmos satellites function in early warning surveillance of U.S. aircraft carriers: "The military significance and timing of the Soviet launching [of Cosmos 1176], however, may have more immediate significance. The launching came on April 29, four days after the aborted U.S. effort to rescue the American hostages at the Teheran embassy. Just before launching the rescue attempt, the U.S. aircraft carrier Nimitz sped away from a Soviet spy ship that had been trailing it, and apparently was able to launch the rescue helicopters on their secret mission without notice." Wash. Post, May 2, 1980, at A6, col. 1. Cosmos 1176 was reportedly a twin of Cosmos 954. *Id.*

79. *See supra* notes 68–72 and accompanying text.

80. *Id.*

itive effect on world order. The United States and the Soviet Union apparently recognized that it was in their mutual interest to cooperate rather than to turn the incident into a propaganda battle.[81] The two nations thus demonstrated their ability to take joint steps to deal with the dangerous items over which they exercise control. Their continued cooperation should help to increase their mutual security and that of the rest of the world. Although a price is paid for this security by the unlucky victims in such third states as Canada, the norm of joint compensation provides at least for the payment of substantial reparations.

The use of nuclear-powered satellites will continue to threaten the earth with falling debris. The Cosmos 954 incident offers hope that cooperative measures can be taken to offset the damages that result, and to enhance global security in the satellite age.

81. U.S. elites were reluctant to exploit the Cosmos 954 incident for its propaganda value, recognizing that the next falling satellite might well belong to the United States. Telephone interviews with U.S. government officials (Mar. 1984). Elites in the USSR were relieved that the U.S. chose to handle the Cosmos 954 incident in this way:

A realistic approach to the incident has been evident in Washington, Ottawa, and a number of other capitals. Unquestionably, the climate of international detente has had an effect here.

But not everyone likes this. Some press organs and individuals in the West are attempting to present the matter in a different light, from anti-Soviet positions. They would like to take advantage of any occasion, including the Kosmos-954 incident, to fan the flames of mistrust, fear and mutual recrimination. But such a policy is fruitless. Gubarev, *In a Businesslike Fashion*, Pravda, Jan. 28, 1978, at 5, *reprinted in* CURRENT DIG. SOVIET PRESS, No. 4, at 7 (1978).

THE SOVIET GAS PIPELINE INCIDENT:
Extension of Collective Security Responsibilities
to Peacetime Commercial Trade

5

PATRICK J. DESOUZA

PROBLEM

In 1980, the Soviet Union began construction of a 3,000-mile pipeline to supply natural gas to Western Europe.[1] To accomplish this massive undertaking, the Soviet Union sought financial credit, equipment, and technology from the West. On December 29, 1981, while the natural gas pipeline was still under construction, President Ronald Reagan barred U.S. companies from supplying pipeline equipment to the Soviet Union. His decision was motivated by a variety of policy considerations, the most salient of which was the need to respond to the declaration of martial law in Poland. On June 18, 1982, the president broadened the ban to include all pipeline equipment manufactured by Western firms under license from U.S. companies. These restrictions were criticized by both domestic and international elites on political, economic, and legal grounds. The dispute ended when an informal

---

1. The Soviet pipeline, built in part with Western materials and financing, is now complete. On January 1, 1984, France received the first deliveries of natural gas from the Soviet pipeline. *Chronology 1984*, 63 FOREIGN AFF. 678 (1985) (*America and the World 1984*).

understanding was reached among the members of the Atlantic Alliance. On November 13, 1982, President Reagan announced the lifting of the sanctions.

This dispute within the Atlantic Alliance raised questions among international elites about the nature and extent of Alliance members' peacetime responsibilities. The outcome of the incident seemed to affirm an emerging norm that politico-military responsibilities of Alliance members could not be extended automatically to the peacetime trade of commercial goods.[2]

Norm Specification

Identification of an emerging norm is conditioned by many variables and must be studied as part of an ongoing social process in which decisions[3] shaping the norm are made. This constitutive process[4] must be specified more closely in order to understand the impact of the pipeline incident on international legal norms. Central to the task of norm specification in this incident is an examination of the concepts of alliances[5] and "state management of trade."[6]

2. "Commercial goods" are defined here as those goods not having military application. There is, however, an intermediate category of goods, such as aircraft engines, that have both military and commercial applications. A central problem for security alliances is how to distinguish and categorize such goods. This study takes the position that pipeline equipment is inherently a commercial item that indirectly contributes to the development of Soviet military power through the enhancement of Soviet economic power. Since this link is indirect, as well as debatable, it is difficult to gauge the degree to which the commercial trade involved in the pipeline incident contributes to Soviet military power. It seems clear, however, that inclusion of all forms of trade in the military category would mistakenly assume that every transaction with the Soviets contributes to their military position.

3. Law may be conceived of as a function of decisions characterized by expectations of both authority and control that are communicated to target audiences. McDougal, Lasswell & Reisman, *The World Constitutive Process of Authoritative Decision*, in INTERNATIONAL LAW ESSAYS: A SUPPLEMENT TO INTERNATIONAL LAW IN CONTEMPORARY PERSPECTIVE 192 (M. McDougal & W. Reisman eds. 1981) [hereinafter cited as INTERNATIONAL LAW ESSAYS].

4. Law is made within a constitutive process that involves the exercise of authoritative power to provide an institutional framework for decisions and to allocate indispensable functions and values. The particular decisions emerging from this process, which are termed "public order" decisions, may be specialized to the shaping and sharing of particular values, such as wealth. *Id.* at 191–192.

5. An alliance is a group of states, linked either formally through legal codification

The Management of Alliance Behavior

In the post–World War II era, there has been a continuing tension between the degree of independence with which states wish to act and the requirements of alliance participation. The United Nations Charter created a state system intended to facilitate the participation of territorial entities in the international arena. Under Articles 1(2), 2(4), and 55, the purposes of the United Nations were identified as resting on the respect among nations for the principles of equal rights, self-determination, and the territorial integrity of states.[7] Yet, although the UN Charter has promoted state participation in the international system, it also has sanctioned the formation of defensive alliances, ostensibly to protect the integrity of the state system.[8] Although Article 51, which embodies this principle of "collective security," was drafted to cover collective responses to actual attack, the strategic problems of the nuclear age have blurred the distinction between time of war and time of peace and have required the formation of peacetime alliances to deter

---

or informally through common policies, that has as its basis a perceived commonality of interests. Alliances have been distinguished according to their nature and relationship, distribution of benefits and power, coverage in relation to the total interests of the nations concerned, coverage in time, and effectiveness of common policies and actions. H. MORGENTHAU, POLITICS AMONG NATIONS 177 (4th ed. 1967). This incident is concerned with the interaction among the members of the Atlantic Alliance, best known by their military appellation, the North Atlantic Treaty Organization (NATO).

6. "State management of trade" refers to the ability of individual states to control their international transactions with other states. As one of the leading works in the field of international political economy notes: "[T]he nation-state has reaffirmed its power to shape strategies of foreign economic policy." Katzenstein, Introduction: Domestic and International Forces and Strategies of Foreign Economic Policy, in BETWEEN POWER AND PLENTY 4 (P. Katzenstein ed. 1978).

7. Articles 1(2), 2(4), and 55 articulate clearly the goals of a system of public order established in the aftermath of World War II. U.N. CHARTER art. 1, para. 2: "To develop friendly relations among nations based on respect for the principle of equal rights and self-determination of peoples . . . ;" art. 2, para. 4: "All Members shall refrain in their international relations from the threat or use of force against the territorial integrity or political independence of any state, or in any manner inconsistent with the Purposes of the United Nations;" art. 55: "With a view to the creation of conditions of stability and well being which are necessary for peaceful and friendly relations among nations based on respect for the principle of equal rights and self-determination of peoples. . . ."

8. U.N. CHARTER art. 51: "Nothing in the present Charter shall impair the inherent right of individual or collective self-defense if an armed attack occurs against a Member of the United Nations. . . ."

threats both to the security of states and to the state system.[9] The practical effect of the advent of peacetime alliances in the framework of a state system marked by conflict has been to limit independent state participation in the international system.

Alliances have limited the autonomy of national elites in the international process in at least two ways. First, within an alliance there always exist categories of alliance responsibility (e.g., political, military, economic) that are variable in scope and that are subject to extraterritorial management among the members.[10] Second, alliances sometimes have imposed limits upon the political independence of member states or of those states outside the alliance that represent strategic interests important to the alliance. Spheres of influence are set up to communicate to adversaries the intent of the alliance to exclude outside influences and to shape political decisions. Such exclusionary communications have been conceptualized as "critical defense zones" and articulated by alliances in such policies as the Monroe Doctrine, the Brezhnev Doctrine, and the Carter Doctrine with its Reagan Codicil.[11] The limitation of political autonomy through such policies has exacerbated the tension, basic to alliance management, between the need for members to cooperate for collective aims and their desire to pursue independent policies.

Alliance policies have often focused efforts on withholding power—economic, military, and diplomatic—from their adversaries. In order

9. States that possess nuclear weapons and modern delivery systems may be able to exert political influence over other states, especially those without nuclear weapons, within a particularly compressed time horizon. The ability of nuclear powers to use their influence to bring about political results has been popularly referred to as "nuclear blackmail." Blackmail with respect to foreign policy decision making has been conceptualized in terms of "strategic" moves in a dynamic process of communication and enforcement between states. *See* T. SCHELLING, THE STRATEGY OF CONFLICT 119–61 (1963).

10. These categories of responsibility sometimes result from mutual agreement and at other times are the product of the stronger members' imposition of their policy preferences on the weaker members. Note, *Extraterritorial Application of the Export Administration Act of 1979 Under International and American Law*, 81 MICH. L. REV. 1308, 1330 (1983).

11. For an elaboration of the concept of "critical defense zones" and related notions, see Reisman, *Critical Defense Zones and International Law: The Reagan Codicil*, 76 AM. J. INT'L L. 589 (1982). For an examination of the Brezhnev Doctrine, see N. Rostow, *Law and the Use of Force by States: The Brezhnev Doctrine*, 7 YALE J. WORLD PUB. ORDER 209 (1981). *See generally* M. McDOUGAL & W. REISMAN, INTERNATIONAL LAW IN CONTEMPORARY PERSPECTIVE 175–86 (1981).

for an alliance to be effective in carrying out such policies, it mu: t have at its foundation a high degree of shared interests. This cannot always be presumed to exist among the members of peacetime alliances, which tend to confine their concerns to a fraction of the total interests and objectives of their members.[12]

Under a traditional "realist" analysis,[13] an insufficiency of shared interests within an alliance can only be overcome by having strong leadership by a powerful state.[14] An often-quoted remark of Thucydides captures the essence of this view: "The strong do what they have the power to do and the weak accept what they have to accept."[15] In the pipeline incident, under a traditional, realist view of alliance behavior, the United States might have been expected to use its political and military leverage over its allies to enforce trade sanctions. This use of leverage would have prevented the transfer of economic power in the form of credit and pipeline equipment to the Soviet Union and its allies. The inability of the United States to enforce the sanctions suggests that political and military dominance does not give to the leader of an alliance the power to regulate commercial trade between the members of the alliance and their political adversaries.[16]

State Management of Trade

Some analysts have concluded that attempts by the United States to wield economic power through trade restrictions have had limited success in the postwar period.[17] Efforts by the United States to get its allies

12. H. MORGENTHAU, *supra* note 5, at 179. During peacetime, the common interest in unity against a "threat" is weakened, making coordinated policies more difficult to achieve.

13. *Id.* at 13–14.

14. R. KEOHANE & J. NYE, POWER AND INTERDEPENDENCE 44 (1977). For a general treatment of the problem of leadership in a world of fragmented interests, see Rosenau & Holsti, *United States Leadership in a Shrinking World*, 35 WORLD POL. 368, 373 (1983).

15. THUCYDIDES, THE PELOPONNESIAN WAR 402 (R. Warner trans. rev. ed. 1972).

16. Contemporary international relations theory has come to distinguish the effective uses of power by states according to issue-areas such as trade, finance, military, and ideology. Such a mode of analysis is known as "issue structuralism." Its basic premise is that power resources in one issue-area do not predict effective power across issue-areas. R. KEOHANE & J. NYE, *supra* note 14, at 50.

17. For a broad treatment of the uses of economic power in the post–World War II era, see K. KNORR, POWER OF NATIONS 134–65 (1975).

to act in concert for the purpose of denying political adversaries economic power have met with even less success. In fact, attempts to restrict economic activity with such adversaries as the Soviet Union have often resulted in heavy costs, including foregone gains from trade, intra-alliance friction, increased solidarity within the opposing alliance, increased Soviet self-sufficiency, albeit at a higher cost, and the growth of bureaucracy as Atlantic Alliance members have tried to develop procedures and controls for implementing the restrictions.[18]

A historical analysis of attempts by the United States to persuade the Atlantic Alliance to restrict its trade with the Soviet Union reveals heightened levels of strain within the Alliance. European members have shown increasing reluctance to accept limitations on their authority to manage their own trade relations.

The development of the Atlantic Alliance relationship in the economic issue-area may be organized into three phases.[19] During the first phase (1948–1968), U.S. policymakers consistently took the position that the commercial benefits the West might derive from trade with the Soviets would be offset by the consequent strengthening of the Soviet military.[20] Yet the restrictive trade policies unilaterally formulated by the United States received only grudging support from the European countries whose economies were recovering from war and adjusting to peacetime conditions.

The United States sought to achieve compliance, in part, through legislation. The Export Control Act of 1949,[21] Section 117(d) of the Marshall Plan,[22] the Mutual Defense Assistance Control Act of 1951,[23]

18. *Id.* at 145.

19. For a more detailed treatment that divides the period into four phases, see J. Braathu, *Unilateralism and Alliance Cohesion: The United States, Western Europe, and the Regulation of Energy-Related Trade with the Soviet Union*, 18 COOPERATION AND CONFLICT 21, 27–38 (1983).

20. *Id.* at 26.

21. The Export Control Act of 1949 authorized the president to impose sanctions against those countries contravening United States export regulations regarding the communist bloc. Export Control Act of 1949, Pub. L. No. 81–11, 63 Stat. 7 (current version at 50 U.S.C. app. § 2401 (1979)).

22. Section 117(d) of the Marshall Plan provided for the suspension of aid to any country supplying goods embargoed by the United States to communist countries. Economic Cooperation Act of 1948, Pub. L. No. 80–172, 62 Stat. 137 (22 U.S.C. §§ 1501–1523 (repealed 1951 and 1954)).

23. The Mutual Defense Assistance Control Act of 1951, commonly known as the Battle Act, expanded American trade controls and authorized the president to cut off all

and the 1962 congressional amendments to the Export Control Act of 1949,[24] were all efforts to extend U.S. law to the European allies in order to obtain compliance with U.S. trade policies. Intergovernmental efforts to obtain compliance focused on a coordinating committee (CoCom), set up during 1949–1950 to regulate and coordinate Alliance trade with the Eastern bloc countries.[25] The creation of CoCom did not resolve the issue of the degree to which economic decision-making had to be shared in order to achieve mutual security. Because CoCom can act only with the unanimous agreement of its members, the problem for the United States over time has been to get the rest of the Alliance not only to agree on controls but also to implement them accordingly. In this early period, such attempts were difficult; as time went by, agreement became impossible, especially with respect to goods that had purely commercial uses.

A key test in this early period came in 1962, in response to Soviet

---

military, economic, and financial aid to countries that exported embargoed products to any nations "threatening the security of the United States." Pub. L. No. 82–213, 63 Stat. 479 (1961) (current version at 22 U.S.C. §§ 1611–1613d (1970)).

24. The 1962 amendments to the Export Control Act of 1949 granted the president discretionary power to deny trade licenses if the products in question were deemed to make a "significant contribution to the military or economic potential of the adversary." Pub. L. No. 87–515, 76 Stat. 127, § 4 (1962) (codified at 50 U.S.C. app. §§ 2021–2023, 2025 & 2032 (1976)).

25. The Coordinating Committee for Multilateral Security Export Controls (CoCom) includes Japan and all NATO countries except Iceland. CoCom is a forum in which trade decisions are examined. CoCom was created by informal agreement among its members and works on the principle of unanimous agreement. CoCom has three major functions: (1) to establish and update lists of embargoed products and technologies; (2) to act as a clearinghouse for requests submitted by members for shipping goods to proscribed countries; and (3) to coordinate administration and enforcement activity among member nations. See Buckley, *Control of Technology Transfers to the Soviet Union*, DEP'T ST. BULL., Aug. 1982, at 71, 72. There are essentially three categories of controls: (a) munitions; (b) atomic energy; and (c) industrial commercial. There are also three levels of control: (a) total embargo; (b) quantitative limits; and (c) surveillance. See Braathu, *supra* note 19, at 40 n. 13. It is important to remember that CoCom has no formal treaty or charter and is not officially part of any organization. See 3 A. LOWENFELD, TRADE CONTROLS FOR POLITICAL ENDS 11-12 (1977). CoCom functioned, in the past, because of a shared perception of threat from the Soviet Union and its allies. However, as: "1) European countries became less dependent on aid; 2) technological superiority of the United States both vis-à-vis Western Europe and vis-à-vis the East narrowed; and 3) perceptions of the communist threat declined faster in Europe and Japan than in the United States, CoCom and the multilateral denial effort in general became less effective and more subject to disagreements." *Id.* at 13.

attempts to construct the Druzhba oil pipeline to Eastern Europe.[26] The pipeline offered the prospect of increased oil supplies to the West and, more immediately, of increased employment in West Germany and other Western European countries receiving orders for steel pipe. The United States attempted to block the transaction through CoCom and, when this failed, tried to gain leverage over its allies by obtaining an informal NATO resolution opposing the sale. Despite these efforts, the British, Italians, Swedes, and Japanese fulfilled their contracts. Although the West Germans eventually yielded to pressure by the United States, their compliance came at the expense of a parliamentary crisis.[27]

The second period (1969–1974) was marked by a reversal of the U.S. policy of trade denial. As part of its strategy of détente, the United States tried to use trade incentives to influence Soviet foreign policy. The Export Administration Act of 1969[28] narrowed the definition of national security under which the restrictions had been justified.[29] In addition, it removed references to the "economic potential" that American trade would presumably bestow on the Soviet Union.[30]

The interlude provided by détente allowed the Western Europeans to expand their economic ties with the Soviet Union and its allies. Increasing Soviet supply of energy to Western Europe raised the possibility of a link between Europe's energy security and the continuation of nonconfrontational policies toward the Soviet Union. While there remained categories of trade that were subject to restriction, such as nuclear or military technology, independence of action in the commercial area was expanded.

The third phase (1975–present) saw renewed restrictions on United States exports to the Soviet Union. With the Jackson-Vanik amend-

---

26. Braathu, *supra* note 19, at 29. *See also* Mufson, *United States Effort to Block Soviet Gas Pipeline Recalls Failed Embargo of Twenty Years Ago*, Wall St. J., July 14, 1982, at 32, col. 1.

27. Mufson, *supra* note 26.

28. Export Administration Act of 1969, Pub. L. No. 91–184, 83 Stat. 841 (current version at 50 U.S.C. app. § 2401 (1979)).

29. *Id.* at §§ 3–4. The concept and scope of national security has expanded over time. *See* Export Administration Act of 1979, §§ 2, 3 & 5, Pub. L. No. 96–72, 93 Stat. 503 (50 U.S.C. app. §§ 2401–2420 (Supp. III 1979)).

30. Congress limited its findings regarding the adverse impact of unrestricted trade on national security to trade making a contribution to the military potential of other nations. *See supra* note 28, at § 2(2).

ment to the Trade Reform Bill of 1973[31] and the Stevenson amend-ment to the Export-Import Bank Act of December 1974,[32] Congress tied economic exchange to Soviet domestic policies. The United States by this time had come to question the policy of détente and had re-turned to a strategy of trade denial to further the policy goals of the Atlantic Alliance.[33]

This return to a strategy of trade denial was largely the result of the failure of the Carter administration to influence Soviet foreign policy through diplomatic or military channels. In July 1978, the Carter administration retaliated against Soviet treatment of dissidents and American journalists by limiting computer sales and oil drilling equip-ment to the Soviet Union.[34] In December 1979, the adminstration tried broadly to restrict exports to the Soviet Union, including grain and advanced technology, in retaliation for the Soviet invasion of Af-ghanistan.[35] These economic measures only served to bring to the sur-face differences between the United States and its allies over coopera-tion in denying trade to the Soviets. In fact, after both Carter administration decisions, the Soviets were able to fill their needs through trade with other capitalist countries.[36]

FACTS

The construction of the 3,000-mile pipeline to bring natural gas from the Urengoi fields in Siberia to the Western European gas network is

31. After eighteen months of executive–congressional debate starting in 1973, Senator Henry Jackson, in October 1974, announced a compromise, under which Soviet and Eastern European trade benefits would be made conditional upon a relaxation of Soviet and Eastern European emigration policies. J. Spero, The Politics of International Economic Relations 317 (2d ed. 1981); Trade Act of 1974, Pub. L. No. 93–618, 88 Stat. 1978 (19 U.S.C. § 2431 (1982)); see also 119 Cong. Rec. 11,549 (1973).

32. The Stevenson amendment to the Export-Import Bank Act killed both the "North Star" and Yakutsk gas projects, which were crucial to American-Soviet energy coopera-tion, by imposing severe credit limitations. See Braathu, supra note 19, at 33.

33. In response to the Afghanistan invasion, the United States tried without success to obtain the support of its European allies for trade control measures. See Braathu, supra note 19, at 37. For a general analysis of the failures of détente, see Breslauer, Why Dé-tente Failed: An Interpretation, in Managing U.S.–Soviet Rivalry: Problems of Cri-sis Prevention 319 (A. George ed. 1983).

34. Spero, supra note 31, at 319.

35. Id. at 319–20.

36. Id. at 320.

an important part of Soviet political and energy planning. The Soviets plan eventually to export 40 billion cubic meters of natural gas annually to Western Europe, tripling their current export level.[37] Since 1978, when the Soviets first proposed the construction of a natural gas pipeline from Siberia,[38] it was apparent that pipe and equipment from Western Europe and Japan and credit from Western banks would be essential if the pipeline were to be completed on time.[39]

On June 24, 1981, members of Congress, led by Senator Jake Garn (R–Utah), sent a letter to President Reagan expressing concern that the pipeline would endanger Western security and suggesting alternatives to Western European participation in the pipeline.[40] The legislators feared that Western Europe could become susceptible to blackmail if it relied on the Soviet Union for a substantial portion of its supply of natural gas. In July, when a consortium of German banks, led by Deutsche Bank and the AKA Ausfuhrkredit GMbH, agreed to provide some 3.4 billion deutschemarks in credits for the compressor stations, President Reagan tried unsuccessfully at the Ottawa economic summit (July 19–21) to persuade the Western European leaders to abandon their support of the Soviet pipeline.[41] By the end of 1981, Western European countries had become deeply involved in the project, to the frustration of the Reagan administration.

In September 1981, Nuovo Pignone of Italy agreed to supply nineteen compressor stations for the pipeline.[42] Also in September, the Soviet equipment trading agency signed an agreement with Mannesman (FRG) and Creusot-Loire (France) to supply twenty-two compressor stations for the pipeline.[43] In November, the Soviet Union and Ruhrgas

37. J. HARDT & D. GOLD, SOVIET GAS PIPELINE: UNITED STATES OPTIONS 1 (Cong. Research Service Issue Brief 82020, 1982) (copy on file with the *Yale Journal of International Law*).

38. The Urengoi field on the Taz Peninsula in western Siberia is the largest gas field in the world, and will add the equivalent of four million barrels of oil per day to Soviet gas production. Stern, *Specters and Pipe Dreams*, FOREIGN POL'Y, Fall 1982, at 21–22.

39. Soviet motives in seeking Western technology and financing are discussed in Loeber & Friedland, *Soviet Imports of Industrial Installations Under Compensation Agreements: West Europe's Siberia Pipeline Revisited*, COLUM. J. WORLD BUS., Winter 1983, at 51, 57.

40. This fact and others in this section were derived from a chronology set forth in J. HARDT & D. GOLD, *supra* note 37, at 12–20.

41. *See* J. HARDT & D. GOLD, *supra* note 37, at 20.

42. *Id.* at 19.

43. *Id.*

A.G. (FRG) signed an agreement on the price and quantity of natural gas to be delivered by the pipeline until the year 2006.[44] Of greater concern to the United States was French approval, on December 10, of the sale by Thomas-CSF of electronic systems for controlling the flow of gas in the pipeline. Analysts in the United States government felt that this was a particularly dangerous sale because it included computer technology that might be used by the Soviets to further their military development.[45] Europeans, who by this point had become accustomed to making their own decisions about trade with the Eastern bloc, did not share the U.S. attitude. The lack of consensus on this issue foreshadowed the tensions that the 1982 pipeline incident would bring about.

The imposition of martial law in Poland on December 29 served as the catalyst that forced a showdown over the issue of collective trade policy among the members of the Atlantic Alliance. President Reagan declared that the Soviets bore heavy responsibility for the imposition of martial law and announced a series of sanctions against the Soviet Union that included the suspension of exports of oil and gas equipment and other high technology equipment to the Soviets.[46] These sanctions stripped away the image of Alliance "neutrality" and had an immediate impact, not only on the Soviets, but also on Western European countries, many of whose contractors used U.S. licensed technology in completing their contracts with the Soviet Union.

On January 8, 1982, the General Electric Company announced that its application for a license to export $175 million worth of rotors and other components for compressor stations had been denied by the U.S. Commerce Department. The company was a subcontractor for John Brown (England), Nuovo Pignone (Italy), and AEG-Telefunken (FRG), which had agreed to supply compressor stations to the Soviets.[47] European reaction to the implementation of the United States policy was swift. On January 13, 1982, West Germany's economic minister, Otto von Lambsdorff, told the cabinet that their government's pledge not to undermine U.S. sanctions only applied to new contracts and

44. Id.
45. Interviews, U.S. Department of State officials, July 1984 [copies on file with the *Yale Journal of International Law*.].
46. Id. at 18–19. See also Joffe, Europe and America: The Politics of Resentment (cont'd), 61 FOREIGN AFF. 569, 571 (1983) (America and the World 1982).
47. J. HARDT & D. GOLD, supra note 37, at 18.

those contracts for which a U.S. firm was the prime contractor.[48] This distinction appeared to exclude the German compressor contracts, for which General Electric was a subcontractor. On the same day, Gaz de France signed a twenty-five-year agreement with the Soviets to purchase gas from the pipeline beginning in 1986. This agreement was followed by a second one on February 10, by a group of French banks, granting a credit of $140 million to the Soviets to finance purchases of equipment for the pipeline from French companies.[49] On January 29, Italy's state energy agency announced that it had completed a similar agreement on the price and quantity of Soviet gas to be delivered.[50] On February 2, the Japanese Export-Import Bank announced that Komatsu would be allowed to complete its sale of pipe-laying equipment to the Soviet Union.[51] The machines were similar to an embargoed pipelayer made by Caterpillar in the United States. Thus, it seemed as if the response of the United States to the imposition of martial law in Poland would be accompanied by undiminished economic contacts and cooperative ventures between U.S. allies and the Soviets. It was as if a general had charged into battle without the troops.

The Reagan administration tried, without success, to convince its allies that "commercial prudence with the Soviets was needed for maintenance of their security interests."[52] U.S. frustration over the allies' refusal to commit themselves to a policy of trade sanctions peaked on June 6, during the Versailles economic summit, when the most that the Alliance could agree to was a communiqué indicating their good intentions.[53]

Having failed to secure voluntary cooperation, the Reagan administration turned to more coercive measures to achieve a "coordinated" policy. On June 18, President Reagan extended the embargo to encompass not only American pipeline suppliers but also their subsidiaries and licensees in France, Germany, England, and Italy. Unlike the denial of export licenses to U.S. suppliers, this action had a real chance of damaging the gas pipeline by closing off the last conduit for those

48. *Id.*
49. *Id.* at 17–18.
50. *Id.* at 18.
51. *Id.*
52. Joffe, *supra* note 46, at 574.
53. *Id.*

crucial components embodying superior American turbine technology.[54]

The expanded embargo only generated increased European resistance. On June 22, foreign ministers of the European Economic Community (EEC) countries issued a statement asserting that the extended ban on oil and gas equipment violated international law in attempting to impose American jurisdiction over European contracts. On July 22, the French government officially ordered those companies involved in the pipeline deal to honor their contracts despite U.S. actions.[55] On July 24, the Italian Foreign Ministry publicly stated that Italian contracts with the Soviet Union would be honored.[56] On August 3, in accordance with the provisions of the 1980 Protection of Trading Interests Act,[57] Lord Cockfield, the British trade secretary, ordered four companies producing equipment in Britain under U.S. license— American Air Filter, Baker Oil Tools, Smith International, and John Brown Engineering—to honor their contracts with the Soviet Union.[58] Finally, on August 12, the EEC issued a formal protest in response to President Reagan's expansion of the ban on pipeline equipment.[59]

By the end of August, members of the Reagan administration were beginning to realize that the continuing confrontation was counterproductive. On August 31, senior advisors recommended to President Reagan that he look for ways to compromise with those European companies violating the pipeline embargo. On September 9, the Reagan adminstration imposed limited sanctions against the British company John Brown after it shipped six turbines to the USSR.[60] On October 5, the United States imposed limited sanctions against four West German companies.[61] Finally, on November 13, after almost a year of conflict, the Reagan administration lifted the sanctions altogether.[62]

54. *Id.*
55. J. HARDT & D. GOLD, *supra* note 37, at 16.
56. *Id.*
57. Protection of Trading Interests Act, 1980, ch. 11.
58. J. HARDT & D. GOLD, *supra* note 37, at 15.
59. *Id.*
60. U.S. courts deferred to the authority of the political branches during the pipeline dispute. *See* Dresser Industries Inc. & Dresser (France) S.A. v. Baldridge, 549 F. Supp. 108, 110 (D.D.C. 1982) (denying injunctive relief to companies penalized for violation of the Reagan administration pipeline ban).
61. J. HARDT & D. GOLD, *supra* note 37, at 13.
62. *Id.* at 12.

CONFLICTING CLAIMS

The United States and its allies had different perspectives on the strategy of trade denial. The arguments each side offered often reflected narrow conceptions of self-interest rather than any principled basis for alliance policy. In addition, each side engaged in selective distortions of reality and manipulations of "hard" data in order to further its interpretation.

United States Claims

The Reagan administration offered three principal arguments against Western European participation in the pipeline project.[63] These were given varying emphasis at different points in the dispute. Initially, the American case stressed the danger of increasing energy dependence on a powerful opponent.[64] The United States argued that dependence on Soviet natural gas (at least 30 percent of Western European natural gas needs) and equipment orders (between ten and fifteen billion dollars over the next five years) would make Western European participants vulnerable to Soviet threats to cut off supplies or terminate orders in a crisis.[65] Analysts cited Yugoslavia (1948), Israel (1956), Albania (1961), and China (1962) as instances in which the Soviets had interrupted energy exports to achieve political gains.[66] After the imposition of martial law in Poland in December 1981, the Reagan administration couched its arguments for sanctions in terms of political morality. The United States asserted that failure to support sanctions implied consent for the suppression of the Polish trade union Solidarity.[67] Finally, the United States argued that the transfer of Western technology, subsidized credit, and hard currency would aid the Soviet military buildup, making the task of maintaining Atlantic security much harder.[68] Arguing against this "contribution" to Soviet power, the United States tried to distinguish the pipeline situation from its October 15, 1982, decision to sell grain to the Soviet Union. The Reagan administration argued

63. Joffe, *supra* note 46, at 574.
64. *Id.*
65. *Id.* at 570 (U.S. perspective on Western European energy dependence). *See* J. HARDT & D. GOLD, *supra* note 37, at 1 (U.S. estimate of value of equipment orders).
66. Joffe, *supra* note 46, at 570 n. 1.
67. *Id.* at 571.
68. *Id.*

that European gas purchases would contribute vital resources to the Soviet economy, while U.S. grain sales had extracted billions of dollars in cash that would otherwise have been used to support a further Soviet military building.[69]

The administration's arguments not only inspired sharp criticism from abroad but also divided the U.S. foreign policy community. Two schools of thought could be identified.[70] One group, led by Secretary of Defense Casper Weinberger and Senator Garn, stressed that Europe would become hostage to the Soviet Union if the deals were completed, and that the transactions would be beneficial to the Soviet military.[71] The other group, represented by Richard Lesher and Donald Campbell of the United States Chamber of Commerce, argued that American pressure could not stop the pipeline from being built[72] and could only undermine the Atlantic Alliance. The Weinberger group eventually forced this school to yield to its concerns about the possible "Finlandization" of Western Europe.[73]

European Claims

The Western European allies generally supported increased imports of natural gas and oil from the Soviet Union as well as increased sales of energy equipment on competitive credit terms. Three reasons predominated. First, it was argued that any addition of energy to the world market would help hold down prices.[74] Energy security is perceived

69. *Id.* at 572.

70. J. Hardt & D. Gold, *supra* note 37, at 3–4.

71. Members of the "Weinberger" group searched for ways to delay, if not to stop, the pipeline. Some recommendations included: (a) all-out legal and political efforts to use the leverage conferred by the General Electric patents on the pipeline technology; (b) an offer of U.S. coal to replace all or part of the additional deliveries of Soviet gas from the pipeline; and (c) tying human rights requirements to equipment sales for the pipeline with a requirement of proof that "forced labor" was not being used in the construction of the pipeline. *Id.* at 3.

72. Members of the "Lesher" group favored the development of additional coal exports that might serve as a "safety net" against threats of political pressure by the Soviet Union. *Id.* at 5.

73. "Finlandization" refers to that process or state of affairs in which, under the cloak of maintaining friendly relations with the Soviet Union, the sovereignty of a country becomes reduced. Laqueur, *Europe: The Specter of Finlandization*, Commentary, Dec. 1977, at 37.

74. J. Hardt & D. Gold, *supra* note 37, at 3.

differently in the United States than in Western Europe and Japan. In the latter countries, where energy independence is not possible, decision-making elites see energy security as a product of diversification of supply. Analysts questioned how much coal the United States could export to Western Europe in an emergency, and how much coal the Western Europeans could substitute for gas, given their existing energy infrastructure.[75] Second, it was argued that large equipment orders would be beneficial to stagnant European and Japanese metallurgy and machinery sectors, providing certain employment and production prospects for many years to come.[76] Finally, it was asserted that economic interdependence with the East would stabilize political relations and provide room for Western Europe to maneuver in a crisis.[77]

The perceptions of each of the European allies about pipeline policy seemed to vary with the extent of its economic stake in the project.[78] West Germany took the leading role in the pipeline trade, partly because of its experience twenty years earlier in the Druzhba pipeline affair and partly because of its large economic interest in the project. West Germany is expected to buy about 30 percent of the gas and has the largest contracts to provide equipment of any ally. Each year for twenty-five years, beginning in 1986, it will import 370 billion cubic feet of natural gas. Equipment supply contracts for West German companies total about $1 billion and promise at least one thousand new jobs.[79] With so much at stake, it is no wonder that the *Frankfurter Rundschau*, on November 19, 1982, called the American sanctions policy "the biggest flop of the year."[80]

France supported the pipeline project by lending money directly to the Soviet Union. A consortium of three banks, led by Crédit Lyonnais, offered $850 million in credits at 7.8 percent interest to cover 85 percent of the cost of pipeline equipment to be purchased in France. The loan would be repayable over ten years and would be insured by a

75. *Id.* at 5.

76. *Id.* at 3.

77. There is at least one economic model that indicates a negative relationship between the levels of conflict and trade. *See* Polachek, *Conflict and Trade*, 24 J. CONFLICT RESOLUTION 55 (1980).

78. Mufson, *United States Is in a Sharp Fight with European Allies*, Wall St. J., Aug. 31, 1982, at 29, col. 1 (detailing the economic stakes involved for each of the allies).

79. *Id.* at col. 2.

80. *See* Joffe, *supra* note 46, at 575.

quasi-public agency under the supervision of the French government.[81] Gaz de France, a government-owned company, agreed to buy 280 billion cubic feet of natural gas a year from the pipeline over the next twenty-five years. This would double the current level of French gas purchases from the Soviet Union.[82] Not surprisingly, *Le Monde* joined the German press in its condemnation of the American sanctions, asserting that the embargo had done more damage to the cohesion of the Atlantic Alliance, which President Reagan had wanted to strengthen, than to the Soviet Union, which he had wanted to punish.[83]

Great Britain had pipeline contracts valued at about $383 million, spread among a dozen firms. Of that amount, $228 million worth of contracts were affected by the United States regulations.[84]

Italy was also heavily committed to the pipeline project. It agreed to buy about 280 million cubic feet of natural gas a year for twenty years at a price of $4 per thousand cubic feet. This contract gave the Italians the best price of any member of the Alliance. Credit granted by Italy covered as much as 85 percent of the roughly $1 billion in contracts granted by the Soviets to Italian companies.[85] The Italians instructed their companies to fulfill their contracts, but "sincerely" sought "frank and fair discussions"[86] between Washington and the European Community over the dispute.

The dispute over pipeline policy offers an example of the problems of perception and misperception in international relations.[87] The European allies could argue that 5–6 percent dependence on Soviet energy exports (including gas, oil, and uranium) would not possibly lead to European vulnerability in times of political crisis. The United States, on the other hand, could offer the picture of 30 percent dependence on Soviet natural gas (excluding other energy sources) as the more accurate indicator of European vulnerability.[88] The Europeans continually claimed that the U.S. position was inconsistent.[89] They

81. Mufson, *supra* note 78, at col. 3.

82. *Id.*

83. Joffe, *supra* note 46, at 574–75.

84. Mufson, *supra* note 78, at col. 4.

85. *Id.*

86. Painton, *Imbroglio over a Pipeline*, TIME, Aug. 2, 1982, at 30.

87. *See generally* R. JERVIS, PERCEPTION AND MISPERCEPTION IN INTERNATIONAL RELATIONS (1976).

88. Joffe, *supra* note 46, at 570.

89. *Id.* at 571.

questioned whether the link between American sanctions and martial law in Poland, if successful in pressuring the Poles to lift martial law, would also eliminate European dependence and dampen Soviet military capabilities. They also doubted whether assistance to their domestic steel industries in obtaining pipeline equipment sales was any different from President Reagan's appeasement of midwestern grain farmers in the United States with their problems of overproduction and falling prices. These European doubts received additional support from a study by Wharton Econometrics[90] based on the principles of comparative economic advantage, which showed that the Soviet Union, a lackluster grain producer, was better off buying grain abroad and devoting saved resources to energy production. With resources saved from the import of grain, the Soviets could develop more energy supplies. These, in turn, could be sold to Europe, producing profits that might be used either to buy more American grain or to increase military spending.

CONFLICTING CONCEPTIONS OF LAWFULNESS

Both the United States and the European allies developed legal arguments to reinforce and to legitimize their respective policy claims. These arguments illustrated the differing perspectives of the two sides on the nature of the collective security system to which they belonged.

U.S. Claims

The legal claims of the United States were developed along three lines. First, the Reagan administration placed the controls in the context of U.S. foreign policy and the international obligations of the Atlantic Alliance. Second, the adminstration argued that the European allies had accepted the risk of U.S. export controls in contracting for the use of U.S. technology and equipment. Third, the United States claimed that "reasonable" extraterritorial extensions of jurisdiction were permissible under international law and that, given the shared policy of alliance security, U.S. export controls were "reasonable."

With respect to the first claim, the United States crafted a broadly conceived argument based on its reading of an "agreement" by the Alliance. On June 6, 1982, two weeks before the extension of export con-

90. WHARTON ECONOMETRIC FORECASTING ASSOCIATES, COMPARATIVE ADVANTAGE IN SOVIET GRAIN AND ENERGY TRADE (1982). *See also* Joffe, *supra* note 46, at 572.

trols to the European allies, the leaders of the Western Alliance held a summit meeting at Versailles. Despite "some disagreement," the United States expressed satisfaction over the degree to which the allies had managed to agree on a common approach to the management of East–West economic relations. In the American view, the summit countries had agreed to "pursue a prudent and diversified economic approach with respect to the USSR and Eastern Europe, consistent with U.S. political and security interests."[91] One reason for this expansive view of what had been accomplished at Versailles may have been the pledge to improve consultative mechanisms with CoCom in order both to exercise stricter control over exports of strategic goods to Warsaw Pact countries and to coordinate national arrangements for the enforcement of security controls.[92] Given U.S. preoccupation with East–West security considerations[93] and an already inflated view of what was achieved at the summit, the United States may have read into this pledge a solid commitment to the use of sanctions. The United States did acknowledge that East–West trade plays a greater role in the economies of the European allies than in that of the United States, but nevertheless considered the value of a common sanctions policy to outweigh the economic costs to each state.[94]

91. Meissner, *United States Approach to East–West Economic Relations*, DEP'T ST. BULL., Sept. 1982, at 30. *Cf.* Joffe, *supra* note 46, at 574 (describing differing interpretations of the Versailles summit).

92. Meissner, *supra* note 91, at 30.

93. *Id.* at 31. The United States made three principal arguments in support of its broad conception of the "security" threat. First, the United States believed that because of the "heavy responsibility" that the Soviet Union bore for the imposition of martial law in Poland, it could not be rewarded by business as usual in foreign economic relations. *Id.* Second, Soviet "intimidation" served to underline the danger that the European allies would be jeopardizing their security by becoming dependent on Soviet energy supplies. Joffe, *supra* note 46, at 571. Finally, the United States asserted that Soviet ability to affect political outcomes in other states—Soviet power—should not be enhanced through trade with the West in such critical technology. *Id.* Benefits to the Soviets from "exploiting" the West's advanced technology included: (a) saving billions of dollars by acquiring proven Western technology; (b) saving years of research time; (c) narrowing the technological gap with the West; (d) avoiding time-consuming errors; and (e) knowing in advance that new systems would work properly and knowing where to look should a product falter. For an analysis of the advantages of CoCom controls in countering Soviet gains from exploiting Western advanced technology, see Mally, *Technology Transfer Controls*, DEP'T ST. BULL., Nov. 1982, at 52, 54.

94. Buckley, *The Case for Sanctions Against the Soviet Union*, DEP'T ST. BULL., Sept. 1982, at 37, 38. *See also* Dam, *Extraterritoriality and Conflicts of Jurisdiction*, DEP'T ST. BULL., June 1983, at 48, 52.

The second U.S. claim was that the European allies had assumed the risk of sanctions by agreeing to clauses in trade contracts stipulating that the licensee or purchaser would abide by U.S. regulations in selling U.S. technology or products incorporating U.S. technology to third countries.[95] Since these clauses had been in use since the 1950s,[96] the United States could argue that the possibility of sanctions, no matter how unlikely, should have been factored into the assessment of business risk.

The third U.S. claim was that its export control regulations could legitimately be extended to European subsidiaries of American corporations and to licensees of U.S. technology because they involved "reasonable" extensions of jurisdiction.[97] In assessing the "reasonableness" of U.S. jurisdiction, the Legal Adviser to the Department of State attempted to balance U.S. perceptions of the collective interests of the Alliance against allied perceptions of their respective national interests.[98] Although the United States admitted that the balancing approach could not resolve all intra-Alliance controversies, the economic needs of some Alliance members were seen as subsidiary to the overriding concern for collective security.

The United States claimed that its extension of jurisdiction to foreign country activities was part of a pattern of practice long accepted in international relations.[99] This is not to say that the United States was

95. J. HARDT, SOVIET GAS PIPELINE: U.S. SANCTIONS AND THEIR IMPLICATIONS (Cong. Research Service Issue Paper 0219S, 1982) (copy on file with the *Yale Journal of International Law*).

96. *Id.*

97. Robinson, *Economic Regulation and International Jurisdictional Conflict*, DEP'T ST. BULL., Oct. 1982, at 37.

98. *Id.* The Legal Adviser's approach in developing a "rule of reasonableness" required weighing and balancing factors including, *inter alia*: (a) links such as nationality, residence, or economic activity between the regulating state and the persons responsible for the activity taken; (b) the importance of regulation to the regulating state; (c) extent of the "other" states' interests in the activity; and (d) the existence of potential conflict with regulation by other states. *Id.* The State Department acknowledged that its balancing methodology was derived from decisions in U.S. courts such as Timberlane Lumber Co. v. Bank of America N.T. & S.A., 549 F.2d 597 (9th Cir. 1976) and Mannington Mills, Inc. v. Congoleum Corp., 595 F.2d 1287 (3rd Cir. 1979). *Id.* This balancing approach is also reflected in Section 403 of the RESTATEMENT (THIRD) OF FOREIGN RELATIONS LAW OF THE UNITED STATES (Draft No. 7, Jan. 18, 1985).

99. Dam, *Extraterritoriality and Conflicts of Jurisdiction*, DEP'T ST. BULL., June 1983, at 48.

oblivious to the problems created between it and its European allies by extensions of U.S. jurisdiction, particularly in the antitrust area.[100] The adminstration maintained, however, that its assertion of jurisdiction over a foreign subsidiary of a U.S. corporation or the licensee of U.S. technology fit a consistent historical pattern of practice where substantial U.S. interests were involved.[101]

U.S. legal arguments thus focused on the reasonable foreseeability of the extension of sanctions. The U.S. view was that its allies' obligations to the Alliance included a commitment to view their economic cooperation with the Soviets in terms of security goals and politico-military power. Moreover, the contractual stipulations should have put the Europeans on notice that sanctions could be imposed. Finally, the extension of sanctions to European subsidiaries of U.S. firms should have been expected, given the historical pattern of U.S. extensions of jurisdiction.

European Claims

Although the dispute among the allies began with the announcement of sanctions on December 29, 1981, from the European point of view, the real conflict did not begin until the extension of sanctions to American subsidiaries and license-holders in Europe on June 18, 1982. These restrictions were crucial because they directly affected European companies and threatened to cut off a vital conduit for equipment needed for the pipeline.

European legal arguments focused on two claims.[102] First, the allies asserted that the U.S. regulations, as amended June 22, 1982,[103] con-

100. *Id.* at 48, 49.

101. *Id.* at 50.

102. For a full elaboration of the European legal arguments, see *European Communities: Comments on the U.S. Regulations Concerning Trade with U.S.S.R.*, 21 I.L.M. 589, 891–904 (1982).

103. On June 22, 1982, the Department of Commerce, at the direction of President Reagan and pursuant to para. 6 of the 1979 Export Administration Act, *supra* note 29, amended §§ 376.12, 379.8, and 385.2 of the Export Administration Regulations. 15 C.F.R. §§ 376.12, 379.8, 385.2. These amendments expanded coverage of existing United States controls on the export and reexport of goods and technical data relating to oil and gas exploration. The Europeans understood the regulations, as amended, to provide that: (a) persons (individuals, corporations, and partnerships) within a third country could not reexport machinery of U.S. origin without the permission of the U.S. government if it was for the exploration and production of oil and natural gas; (b) persons subject

tained sweeping extensions of U.S. jurisdiction violative of international law. Second, they claimed that the new regulations, and the way in which they affected contracts in the course of performance, ran counter to the guidelines of the 1979 Export Administration Act[104] and to "principles of U.S. public law."[105]

The first claim, concerning extension of U.S. jurisdiction, was analyzed by the Europeans under four different jurisdictional principles of international law—the territoriality principle, the protective principle, the nationality principle, and the effects principle. Analysis of each principle led the Europeans to conclude that U.S. measures were unacceptable under international law. The territoriality principle[106] supports the right of each state, as part of the state system created by the UN Charter, to organize and to develop freely its social and economic system. The Europeans argued that U.S. measures infringed upon this principle by attempting to regulate the activities of European companies that were not within the territorial jurisdiction of the United States. Anticipating American arguments about their security obligations under the Atlantic Alliance, the Europeans noted that the United States might have grounded its claims on the "protective principle" of jurisdiction. This principle allows a state jurisdiction over acts committed outside its territory that threaten its security.[107] Whether or not this principle might have been available to the United States, the Europeans pointed out that it "was not invoked by the U.S. government,

---

to United States jurisdiction were required to get prior written authorization by the Office of Export Administration for the export or reexport to the Soviet Union of non–United States goods and technical data related to oil and gas exploration; and (c) no person in the United States or in a foreign country could export or reexport to the Soviet Union foreign products directly derived from United States technical data relating to machinery utilized for the exploration and production of oil or natural gas. I.L.M., *supra* note 102, at 891–92 (1982) (summary of regulations).

104. *See supra* note 29.

105. I.L.M., *supra* note 102, at 891.

106. RESTATEMENT (SECOND) OF FOREIGN RELATIONS LAW § 17 (1965) [hereinafter cited as RESTATEMENT (SECOND)]. *See also* M. McDOUGAL & W. REISMAN, INTERNATIONAL LAW IN CONTEMPORARY PERSPECTIVE 1295 (1981). The territoriality principle has been interpreted to mean that a state should restrict its rulemaking to persons and goods within its territory. It also means that an organization such as the European Community should restrict applicability of its rules to the territory to which the treaty creating it applies. I.L.M., *supra* note 102, at 893.

107. RESTATEMENT (SECOND), *supra* note 106, § 30.33. *See also* M. McDOUGAL & W. REISMAN, *supra* note 106, at 1319.

since the regulations were based on § 6 (foreign policy controls) and not on § 5 (national security controls) of the 1979 Export Administration Act."[108]

The nationality principle, authorizing prescriptions of rules for nationals wherever they are,[109] was also rejected by the Europeans as a basis for the extension of U.S. jurisdiction. The Europeans objected to the notion that the United States could impose its corporate nationality controls on European companies given that "the great majority were incorporated in European states."[110] They added that there were no rules for determining the nationality of goods and technology under international law[111] and that judicial decisions indicated that U.S. jurisdiction did not follow goods of U.S. origin once they had been discharged in the territory of another country.[112] Finally, the Europeans argued that the "effects principle"[113] was not applicable because exports from European members were deemed to have no "direct, foreseeable, and substantial" effect on U.S. trade.

The second European claim was that the U.S. controls did not satisfy the criteria laid down in the 1979 Export Administration Act.[114] The Europeans argued that there was little probability that controls would achieve foreign policy purposes.[115] They urged that there was no reason to assume that the Soviets would be unable to develop their own technology, albeit at a greater cost, in order to complete the project and make the U.S. pipeline policy ineffective. The Europeans also argued that the probable reaction of other countries to the imposition or expansion of export controls had received insufficient consideration as

108. *See supra* note 29.

109. RESTATEMENT (SECOND), *supra* note 106, § 30. *See also* M. McDOUGAL & W. REISMAN, *supra* note 106, at 1370–72.

110. I.L.M., *supra* note 102, at 894.

111. *Id.*

112. *Id.*

113. RESTATEMENT (SECOND), *supra* note 106, § 18. The Europeans referred to the "effects doctrine," which grants jurisdiction over conduct outside the territory that causes direct, foreseeable, and substantial effects within the territory. I.L.M., *supra* note 102, at 896 (citing RESTATEMENT (SECOND), *supra* note 106).

114. Congress attempted to circumscribe presidential power by requiring the application of specified criteria when imposing, expanding, or extending export controls for foreign policy reasons. For an elaboration of these criteria, see 50 U.S.C. § 2405(b) (1982).

115. I.L.M., *supra* note 102, at 901–902.

required by the act.[116] Finally, the Europeans claimed that the export controls would cast doubt on the United States as a reliable supplier, both in sales of equipment and in technology licensing arrangements.[117]

OUTCOME

The ban on the sale of pipeline equipment to the Soviet Union by U.S. firms, foreign subsidiaries of U.S. firms and foreign companies manufacturing under U.S. licenses was lifted on November 13, 1982. President Reagan, in a radio address to the nation, announced that the United States and its allies had come to an informal agreement on trade policy with the Soviet Union.[118] The president claimed that this "understanding" with the European allies would be more effective than the sanctions,[119] and that the latter were now obsolete. He highlighted three aspects of this agreement that established a "policy in the economic area to complement our policies in the security area."[120] First, no new contracts for the purchase of Soviet natural gas would be signed during the course of an Alliance study of alternative Western sources of energy. Second, the United States and its allies would strengthen controls on the transfer of strategic items to the Soviet Union. Third, procedures would be established for monitoring financial relations with the Soviet Union which would be consistent with Alliance export credit policies.[121]

In order to put this outcome in the proper focus so that it might be appraised for its impact on community expectations,[122] two points must be made. First, as mentioned above, the natural gas contracts that the European allies signed with the Soviet Union were all long-term agreements: for West Germany, twenty-five years; France, twenty-five years; Italy, twenty years. As a result, the first aspect of this "informal agreement" had no operative significance, because the allies' present needs

116. *Id.* at 902.
117. *Id.*
118. *East–West Trade Relations and the Soviet Pipeline Sanctions*, DEP'T ST. BULL., Jan. 1983, at 28. (Text of President Reagan's address to the nation, Nov. 13, 1982) [hereinafter cited as Presidential Address].
119. *Id.*
120. *Id.*
121. *Id.*
122. McDougal, Lasswell & Reisman, *supra* note 3, at 285.

would be satisfied by existing contracts. Second, this "informal agreement" contained no mention of future limitations on sales contracts of pipeline equipment. Thus, while U.S. policy changed with the lifting of the sanctions, it is important to note that European behavior remained basically unaltered.

INTERNATIONAL APPRAISAL

Although the political rhetoric on each side of the Atlantic still reflected the differing perspectives of the parties, the arguments used by each in appraisal of the outcome indicated a recognition that politico-military responsibilities of Alliance members could not automatically be extended to the peacetime trade of commercial goods.

U.S. Appraisal

U.S. appraisal of the pipeline incident was marked both by reluctance to admit the rejection of its policies by its allies and by uncertainty over how to address European assertions of independence in the choice of trading partners. The Reagan administration originally couched its decision to lift the pipeline sanctions in language that gave the impression of a united Alliance in agreement over a future course of action that would be even more effective against the Soviet Union.[123] Yet it is apparent that this settlement was less a shift from one agreed-upon policy to another than a realization by the United States that it could not effectively translate Alliance responsibilities in the politico-military issue-area into the economic issue-area. As President Reagan admitted in lifting the sanctions: "It's no secret that our allies don't agree with [the sanctions policy]."[124] What the "agreement" demonstrated was that in the future such matters would be determined, not through unilateral action on the part of the Alliance leader, but through allied consensus.[125]

The reappraisal by U.S. elites that was stimulated by the incident

123. President Reagan, in his radio address announcing the end of the pipeline sanctions, asserted: "I believe this new agreement is a victory for all the allies. It puts in place a much needed policy in the economic area to complement our policies in the security area . . . an agreement with our allies which provides for stronger and more effective measures." Presidential Address, *supra* note 118.

124. *Id.*

125. Dam, *supra* note 99, at 51.

may be illustrated by the difficulties encountered in attempting to revise the 1979 Export Administration Act and to formulate a coherent export control policy. The administration, the Senate, and the House of Representatives brought divergent approaches to the task.[126]

In April 1983, the Reagan administration submitted a bill to Congress that indicated a greater respect for its allies' economic independence than had been the case at the outset of the incident.[127] The bill stated that it would be U.S. policy to minimize the impact of export controls on preexisting contracts and business activities in allied countries when these controls are imposed for foreign policy reasons. The administration bill also explicitly recognized the sanctity of contracts as a limitation that would insulate many contracts from foreign policy export controls. Specifically, an "overriding national interest" exception protected existing sales contracts requiring delivery within 270 days of the imposition of restrictions. Although the bill strengthened the enforcement of national security controls, the concessions on foreign policy controls indicated that elite opinion in the executive branch had shifted. Although the congressional position is still in a state of flux, the administration's position indicated an awareness that consultation with the allies and increased information flow regarding Alliance objectives, rather than the use of political power by the United States, has become the norm of behavior on trade issues within the Atlantic Alliance.[128]

European Appraisal

European reaction to the lifting of the pipeline sanctions was uniform. The incident consolidated European expectations of what their alliance obligations were in peacetime concerning trade issues. Such consolidation capped a process of norm formation that had accelerated during the period of détente.

126. As of June 1985, Congress has yet to reenact an updated version of the Export Administration Act. *Compare* S. 2342, 98th Cong., 2d. Sess. § 2 and H.R. Rep. No. 257, Part I, 98th Cong., 1st Sess. (1983). On June 27, 1985, the Congress passed and sent to President Reagan a bill extending the current version of the Export Administration Act until Sept. 30, 1989. N.Y. Times, June 28, 1985, at D4, col. 4. Extension of the status quo reflects both congressional uncertainty over how to proceed and a temporary acceptance of the proposed norm.

127. Dam, *supra* note 99, at 51.

128. Robinson, *supra* note 97, at 37–38.

In the Federal Republic of Germany, the lifting of the sanctions was interpreted by the *Frankfurter Allgemeine Zeitung* as the end of "intervention into the sovereignty of foreign countries."[129] The value of East–West trade was reaffirmed by West German elites as a political instrument and a stabilizing factor in East–West relations.[130] Further, the normative implications of lifting the sanctions were not missed. As *Die Welt* commented, "Some good, however, has come out of this struggle in the Western alliance over the past months because there is now a clearer definition of a common and coordinated policy regarding trade with the East."[131] This view that the incident had clarified and reaffirmed community policy on the allocation of competence to prescribe and to apply norms of economic behavior during peacetime was also evident among the other European allies. The French foreign trade minister, Michel Jobert, echoed this theme: "We are urging the United States to regard us as partners, to see that we are not part of a system controlled by its initiative."[132] Moreover, French reaction to the lifting of the sanctions highlighted substantive differences within the Alliance on the trade issue. France simply did not share the security objectives of U.S. embargo policies,[133] refusing even to be party to the "informal agreement" among the allies through which the Reagan administration sought to save face in lifting the sanctions.[134]

Great Britain also refused to take part in the "informal agreement." Foreign Secretary Francis Pym emphasized that the sanctions policy and the decision to end it were unilateral actions of the United States.[135] Britain, however, was more conciliatory than any other European ally toward the United States on the issue of East–West security principles.[136] The British acknowledged that the Alliance could not

---

129. *Press Discusses Lifting of U.S. Pipeline Embargo,* Foreign Broadcast Information Service [hereinafter cited as FBIS] (W. Eur.), Nov. 16, 1982, at J1.

130. *Genscher on Trade After Shultz USSR Meeting,* FBIS (W. Eur.), Nov. 16, 1982, at 53.

131. *Press Discusses Lifting of US Pipeline Embargo, supra* note 129, at J1.

132. *Jobert Comments on Lifting of Sanctions,* FBIS (W. Eur.), Nov. 18, 1982, at K2.

133. *Le Monde Views Decision,* FBIS (W. Eur.), Nov. 17, 1982, at K2.

134. *Leaders Comment on Lifting of U.S. Sanctions,* FBIS (W. Eur.), Nov. 17, 1982, at K1.

135. *Pym on East Bloc Trade After Sanctions Lifted,* FBIS (W. Eur.), Nov. 15, 1982, at Q1.

136. *Id.* at Q2.

trade in ways that gave the Soviets strategic or military advantages.[137] However, the British acknowledgement of shared security interests did not extend to trade in commercial goods with less direct military applications.

At the other end of the world, the Japanese were also applauding the lifting of the pipeline sanctions, since this would enable them to resume fully their oil and gas projects with the Soviets.[138] The Japanese had protested strongly[139] the imposition of the sanctions, asserting that "the United States need[ed] to listen to the voices of its Western allies."[140] In addition, elite reaction in Japan welcomed the lifting of the pipeline sanctions because, like the Western Europeans, the Japanese wanted orders to alleviate a recession in the steel sector.[141]

The allies generally maintained a uniform position regarding both the sanctions policy and its withdrawal.[142] They wanted no part of either. So far as the allies were concerned, the United States was expecting too much of the Alliance in extending obligations for Western security broadly to the economic area.[143] The ability to trade with minimum interference was considered by Europeans to be an aspect of political independence that the United States had to respect.[144]

137. *Id.*
138. *MITI Lauds Lifting of U.S. Pipeline Sanctions*, FBIS (Japan), Nov. 16, 1982, at C5.
139. *Abe Confirms Protest*, FBIS (Japan), July 20, 1982, at C1.
140. *Trade Minister Criticizes U.S. Economic Policy*, FBIS (Japan), July 8, 1982, at C1.
141. *USSR Seeking Japanese Credits for Pipeline Equipment*, FBIS (Japan), Oct. 19, 1982, at C1.
142. Italy maintained a low profile during the entire incident. However, Prime Minister Giovanni Spandolini, in appraising the lifting of the sanctions, emphasized the consistency of Italian policy during this incident in reserving its right to freedom of action in trade contracts. *See Spandolini Interviewed on Economy, U.S. Embargo*, FBIS (W. Eur.), Nov. 17, 1982, at L5.
143. Soames, *America and Europe: Can This Partnership Be Saved?* 20 ATLANTIC COMMUNITY 331, 332 (1982).
144. *Id.* at 333. The utility of the sanctions was questioned even by Americans doing business in Europe. Tittman, *Extraterritorial Application of United States Export Control Laws to Foreign Subsidiaries of United States Corporations: An American Lawyer's View from Europe*, 16 INT'L LAW. 730 (1982). Soviet commentators naturally also stressed as unnecessary and futile the U.S. attempt to restrict its allies' commercial transactions. *See* Gorsky, *EEC-USA: The Transatlantic Duel*, INT'L AFF. (MOSCOW), Oct. 1982, at 24.

AUTHOR'S APPRAISAL

The informal agreement reached on November 13, 1982, by the United States and its European allies did nothing to impede completion of the pipeline project. The pipeline was duly completed and is in operation.[145] As noted above, the agreement has also had little effect on the trade policies of the allies. The ban on new natural gas contracts did not affect the long-term arrangements previously concluded by the Western Europeans and by the Soviet Union. No further restrictions on sales contracts were contemplated by the agreement, and its recommendations for stronger controls on strategic items have not been implemented. Yet, despite the failure of the agreement to alter the behavior of the Europeans, no new crisis over East–West industrial technology sales has occurred within the Alliance.[146] Rather, the agreement seems to represent a recognition by all parties of an emerging norm that the scope of politico-military alliances does not automatically extend to the peacetime trade of commercial goods.[147] The outcome of the pipe-

145. See *Chronology 1984, supra* note 1.

146. Hoffman, *Western Europe: Wait and Worry*, 63 FOREIGN AFF. 632 (1985).

147. The applicability of this norm to other alliances will vary according to the relative dominance of the state apparatus (as a concept distinct from society) in attempting to implement alliance policy. A key factor in establishing this dominance is the degree to which societal pressures condition state policies. See Katzenstein, *supra* note 6, at 16–18. As a predictive matter, it is likely that when private interests are influential in economic matters, it will be more difficult for the state to impose alliance policies that run counter to those interests. There is also reason to believe, however, that the norm proposing freedom of peacetime commercial transactions would be supported even within alliances in which the power of the dominant state to enforce a strategy of trade denial is relatively unrestrained by internal pressures. See Bunce, *The Empire Strikes Back: The Transformation of the Eastern Bloc from a Soviet Asset to a Soviet Liability*, 39 INT'L ORG. 1 (1985). The rapid expansion of East–West trade during the 1970s brought "a nine-fold increase from 1970 to 1981 of Western exports to the [Soviet] bloc, and an eight-fold increase in the same period of Western imports from the Soviet bloc." *Id.* at 36. This expansion resulted in Eastern Europe becoming more dependent on both the West and the Soviet Union for markets and capital. *Id.* at 3. Bunce argues that the pressures East–West trade placed on the command economies of Eastern Europe, the need for Western banks to recycle petrodollars in Eastern Europe in the 1970s, and the global recessions of 1973–1974 and 1979–1982 all served to limit, rather than to expand, Soviet power over the Eastern Alliance *Id.* at 44. This thesis suggests that it would be difficult for the Soviet Union to mobilize its alliance partners to deny economic power to the West. In fact, because of diminishing returns from its empire, the Soviet Union may be quite content to limit its control over state sovereignty to political and military affairs.

line incident suggests that delegation of duties within the Alliance, especially in regard to the wealth process, is to be determined by consultation, not imposition. Alliance duties are to be carefully defined in order to respect the autonomy of each state. Although the United States might invoke alliance responsibilities in the name of collective security or, alternatively, issue unilateral export regulations on grounds of its own national security, mere assertions of foreign policy objectives will not justify extensions of U.S. sanctions to its allies.

The norm embodied in the informal agreement represents a crystallization of expectations that developed over time in response to repeated attempts by the United States to implement trade restrictions. The Europeans have acted, and will continue to act, in accordance with these expectations. For a period following the pipeline incident, the United States also had begun to act in conformity with these expectations, with the result that economic autonomy in commercial transactions was accorded much more weight in the crafting of export control policy. However, on May 1, 1985, the Reagan administration tried once again to get its allies to cooperate in a trade embargo to counter a "security" threat posed by Nicaragua.[148] Although this attempt to extend politico-military responsibilities into the economic issue area seems to have been unsuccessful,[149] the Nicaragua "incident" offers an opportunity to test the viability of the norm proposed here.

The new norm manifests a preference by most members of the Atlantic Alliance that each state be free to engage in peacetime commercial transactions, even at the risk of transferring power through the wealth process to an adversarial alliance. The ability of these members to prevail suggests, in a larger sense, that spheres of influence promoted by the framework of collective security have their limits. Collective security arrangements exist to safeguard the public order goal of national autonomy.[150] These collective arrangements are thus a means of achieving a public order goal and are not an end in themselves. The clear lesson of the pipeline incident is that Alliance members will strenuously take issue with policies that they perceive as a threat to the very goals that the Alliance exists to promote.

148. Weinraub, *Reagan Declaring 'Threat,' Forbids Nicaraguan Trade and Cuts Air and Sea Links,* N.Y. Times, May 2, 1982, at A1, col. 6.
149. Oakes, *Reagan's Brezhnev Doctrine,* N.Y. Times, May 20, 1985, at A19, col. 2.
150. *See supra* note 7 and accompanying text.

THE ARGENTINE INVASION OF THE
FALKLANDS: International Norms of Signaling

6 MICHAEL P. SOCARRAS

States communicate by exchanging "signals."[1] This chapter is a study of an international incident in which signaling led to a serious misunderstanding and eventually war. From 1965 to 1982, the United Kingdom and the Republic of Argentina exchanged signals about the legal status of the Falkland Islands.[2] Argentina interpreted this exchange to mean that Britain was willing to recognize Argentine sovereignty over the islands, and that an Argentine invasion of the Falklands would not lead to an uncompromising British reaction and international ostracism of Argentina. The Argentine estimate of British intentions proved incorrect, and the result was a costly war and the fall of the Argentine government.[3]

1. "There are many ways other than verbal declarations by which states may communicate their intentions." G. Snyder, DETERRENCE AND DEFENSE: TOWARD A THEORY OF NATIONAL SECURITY 252 (1961). Signals are "statements or actions the meanings of which are established by tacit or explicit understandings among the actors." R. Jervis, THE LOGIC OF IMAGES IN INTERNATIONAL RELATIONS 18 (1970). Examples of signals include "diplomatic notes, military maneuvers, extending or breaking diplomatic relations, and choosing the shape of a negotiating table." Id.
2. As Professor Reisman notes in the introductory chapter, Spanish speakers generally refer to the Falkland Islands as Las Malvinas. The use of the English name here does not signal support for the British claim to the islands. See Reisman, *The Struggle for the Falklands*, 93 Yale L.J. 287, 287 n. 1 (1983).
3. According to published opinions, international courts and arbitrators have often

The purpose of this study is to determine what those events indicate about signals and international norms for their interpretation. The incident confirms that a complex system of tacit communication among states is in an advanced stage of development. It also reveals specific signaling norms. According to these, certain actions signal a state's willingness to give up sovereignty over disputed territory in spite of formal statements to the contrary. The incident also discloses a strong norm requiring caution in the interpretation of those signals. When a powerful Western state signals willingness to cede territory, the international community does not interpret the signals to mean that the sender would accept a military solution to the territorial dispute.

FACTS

The United Kingdom and Argentina have disputed sovereignty over the Falkland Islands[4] since at least 1833, when British warships evicted Ar-

---

relied on signals to decide territorial disputes. A scholar taking a traditional approach to international law might well invoke these precedents to determine whether Britain or Argentina should exercise sovereign control of the Falklands. The aim of this study, however, is not to judge what British and Argentine officials should have done on the basis of all the relevant case authorities, but rather to determine empirically what expectations the signals they exchanged caused them to have in early 1982.

It may be helpful nevertheless to refer to those decisions to establish the legal pedigree of signals. One international case holds, for example, that where two states claim sovereignty over disputed territory and one of them fails to object to a multilateral agreement explicitly referring to the territory in dispute as belonging to the other state, the first state has acquiesced to a display of authority by the second state over the disputed area. Legal Status of Eastern Greenland (Den. v. Nor.), 1933 P.C.I.J., ser. A/B, No. 53, at 68–69 (Judgment of Apr. 4, 1933). Cf. Islands of Palmas Case (U.S. v. Neth.), 2 R. Int'l Arb. Awards 829 (1928) (Dutch displays of authority over an island and effective Spanish acquiescence in such displays established Dutch title, weakening a claim of the United States as pretended successor to Spain). Similarly, British failure to object to United Nations General Assembly Resolution 2065, which urged Anglo-Argentine negotiations over the Falklands after identifying the islands as territories in the process of decolonization, could reasonably be seen as a British signal of acquiescence in the evolution of Argentine title to the Falklands. G.A. Res. 2065, 20 U.N. GAOR Supp. (No. 14) at 57, U.N. Doc. A/6014 (1965). See L. SCHOPEN, H. NEWCOMBE, C. YOUNG & J. WERT, NATIONS ON RECORD: UNITED NATIONS GENERAL ASSEMBLY ROLL-CALL VOTES (1946–1973), at 200, 442 (1975) (United Kingdom abstaining from General Assembly Resolution 2065). There is no evidence, however, that anyone interpreted British actions in that way because of what these decisions hold.

4. The Falkland Islands lie in the South Atlantic, some 772 kilometers northeast of

gentine settlers and lowered the Argentine flag.[5] The latest in a long-running series of attempts to resolve that dispute failed a month before the war began. As late as February 27, 1982, Argentine and British diplomats met in New York to negotiate the future of the archipelago but emerged without satisfactory results.[6] In March, British intelligence repeatedly warned Prime Minister Margaret Thatcher that some military confrontation appeared unavoidable in the wake of that diplomatic failure.[7]

Those intelligence assessments were vindicated on April 2, 1982, when Argentine forces occupied the islands and established military control over them.[8] They also seized the island of South Georgia and the South Sandwich Islands, all dependencies of the Falklands.

On April 3 the prime minister faced an emergency session of the House of Commons ringing with demands for the resignation of key ministers.[9] She asserted "that the Falklands Islands and their dependencies remain British territory," defended the "democratic rights of the islanders" to remain under British rule, and pledged "to see that the islands are freed from occupation and are returned to British adminis-

---

Cape Horn. They comprise 200 islands and cover a total land area of 11,961 square kilometers. There are two large islands, East Falkland and West Falkland. Apart from a number of small islands, the Dependencies consist of South Georgia, 1287 kilometers east-south-east of the Falkland Islands, and the uninhabited South Sandwich Islands, some 756 kilometers southeast of South Georgia. Report of the Special Committee on the Situation with Regard to the Implementation of the Declaration on the Granting of Independence to Colonial Countries and Peoples, 4 U.N. GAOR Supp. (No. 23) at 20, U.N. Doc. A/33/23 Rev. 1 (1980) [hereinafter cited as Report of the Special Committee]. The population of the Falklands and Dependencies is mainly of British origin, and numbered less than 2,000 in April 1982. N.Y. Times, Apr. 3, 1982, at A6, col. 4. They are governed by a governor appointed by the British government, a six-member Executive Council, and an eight-member Legislative Council comprised of six locally elected members and two appointed by the governor. Id.

5. M. HASTINGS & S. JENKINS, THE BATTLE FOR THE FALKLANDS 5–6 (1983); C. SEGRETI, TRES ARCHIPELAGOS ARGENTINOS 108–110 (1983).

6. SUNDAY TIMES OF LONDON INSIGHT TEAM, WAR IN THE FALKLANDS 21–30 (1982) [hereinafter cited as WAR IN FALKLANDS].

7. Id. at 71 ("British [intelligence] officials concluded that . . . Argentina was preparing to invade. They even predicted the exact date of the invasion").

8. HOUSE OF COMMONS, THE FALKLANDS CAMPAIGN 4 (1982) [hereinafter cited as FALKLANDS CAMPAIGN].

9. N.Y. Times, Apr. 4, 1982, at A1, col. 6. In the view of certain members of Parliament in the prime minister's own party, the invasion placed in question the prime minister's survival in office. Id. at A18, col. 3.

tration at the earliest possible moment."[10] To pursue that objective she announced that a large Royal Navy task force would leave for the Falklands in two days.[11] Within 24 hours she had accepted the resignations of the Foreign and Commonwealth Secretary, Lord Carrington, and his two principal assistants on Falklands matters.[12]

In Argentina, the events of April 2 were received with public jubilation and general support for the governing military council led by President Leopoldo Galtieri.[13] Although Argentina's foreign minister, Nicanor Costa Méndez, had envisioned the attack as a "short coup" to create a diplomatic crisis and accelerate the process of decolonization,[14] President Galtieri declared to cheering crowds that "not one meter would ever be given back to the invaders."[15]

Military operations proceeded rapidly. British forces seized South Georgia on April 25. British task force aircraft bombed the airstrip at the Falklands capital, Stanley, on May 1. The sinking of a large Argentine cruiser on May 2 with the accompanying heavy loss of life confirmed that a diplomatic crisis had become a war. Heavy land, sea, and air warfare continued until Argentine forces surrendered on June 14.

CONFLICTING CLAIMS

Neither side publicly accused the other of breaching an understanding reached through signals.[16] The lack of formal claims about signals, however, is no obstacle. The objective of this study is not the adjudi-

10. FALKLANDS CAMPAIGN, *supra* note 8, at 5.

11. *Id.* at 7–8.

12. WAR IN FALKLANDS, *supra* note 6, at 100–101.

13. M. HASTINGS & S. JENKINS, *supra* note 5, at 75. Only a few days earlier, serious civil disturbances in Buenos Aires, under a labor slogan of "Peace, Bread, and Jobs," led to four hundred arrests. La Prensa (Buenos Aires), Mar. 31, 1982, at 1, cols. 5, 8.

14. Interview with the Honorable Nicanor Costa Méndez, foreign minister of Argentina, in New Haven (Apr. 27, 1984) (notes on file with the *Yale Journal of International Law*) ("Argentina's plan was not to fight a war with Britain, nor was it Argentina's decision to take over and maintain the islands, but to have a very short coup to call attention from the Secretary General or big powers to intervene").

15. WAR IN FALKLANDS, *supra* note 6, at 122 (quoting senior official's account of Galtieri's speech). According to the *Sunday Times* of London, a senior Argentine official revealed to them that Costa Méndez "wanted to resign" when he heard Galtieri's balcony bravado. *Id.* Galtieri reportedly told Costa Méndez: "Don't worry, we can't lose!" *Id.*

16. Foreign Minister Costa Méndez made no signaling claim on April 3, 1982, during his speech to the United Nations Security Council. *See infra* note 55.

cation of a dispute. Rather, it is to use this incident to determine whether a system of norms of tacit communication exists, and to understand what some of those norms might be. One can impute claims to the parties concerning the meaning of their signals, and determine whether the parties' expectations, as revealed by their behavior, were consistent with those claims.

The Argentine claim can be constructed as follows:

> The signals long preceding our decision to invade the Malvinas tell us that Britain was not really serious about its sovereignty claim, is prepared to acquiesce to displays of increasingly sovereign Argentine authority over the islands, and is indeed pursuing a policy of abandonment with respect to its sovereignty claim. In departing from its tacitly communicated policy, Britain violated international norms of tacit communication or "signaling."[17]

Constructing the British claim is a somewhat more delicate task. The British government probably would not concede any merit in the Argentine claim set out above.[18] On the other hand it would be neither necessary nor, as will be shown, persuasive for Britain to deny all of the Argentine claim. Therefore the British claim may be constructed as follows:

> Perhaps Argentina was justified in interpreting our previous lack of resolve on behalf of our official sovereignty position as an indi-

17. Foreign Minister Costa Méndez told the author that Argentina invaded in part because "we had signals that Britain would not send the Fleet because it would be very expensive, would affect the commitment to NATO, and even if sent the results were not all for sure." Interview with the Honorable Nicanor Costa Méndez, *supra* note 14. He also stated that those signals from Britain "were rather confusing. They wanted to have the cake and eat it too. They wanted to spend nothing, didn't protest the Argentine takeover of the Sandwich Islands and did not protest in the case of the Russian fishing boats. The Foreign Office and the British Government were divided. But we knew that even if the signals were confusing the negotiations had no future." *Id. See also* M. HASTINGS & S. JENKINS, *supra* note 5, at 60 ("Costa Mendez also continued in his firm view that the diplomatic consequences could be contained and no military reoccupation by Britain would be attempted. In his defense, it should be said that there were sound empirical grounds for his view"). The Argentine Foreign Ministry may also have counted on Soviet support at the United Nations. *Id.* at 48–49.

18. Prime Minister Thatcher declared to the House of Commons on April 3, 1982, that the Argentine invasion "has not a shred of justification and not a scrap of legality." FALKLANDS CAMPAIGN, *supra* note 8, at 4.

cation of our willingness to allow some weakening of our title, but Argentina went too far in concluding that those precedents would permit it to invade the Falklands openly without a stern British response.[19]

Britain might also counterclaim that the Argentine claim is a rationalization, and that the junta had decided to invade as a result of domestic unrest unrelated to any theories of right or perceptions of British signals. This potential counterclaim, accusing the Argentines of hypocrisy, will not be treated here. Even if the junta decided to invade for domestic political reasons, to be rational its decision had to be premised on some expectation of success. The key gamble depended on the strength of British and international reaction as gauged from various signals.[20]

19. Shortly after her "not a scrap of legality" remark on April 3, 1982, *id.*, the prime minister more soberly noted that "[t]here had, of course, been previous incidents affecting sovereignty before the one in South Georgia. . . . In December 1976 the Argentines illegally set up a scientific station on one of the dependencies within the Falklands group—Southern Thule. The Labour Government attempted to solve the matter through diplomatic exchanges, but without success. The Argentines remained there and are still there. . . ." *Id.* at 5. The prime minister's remarks hint at a recognition that Britain had acquiesced in the Argentine seizure of Falklands territory on prior occasions, but her remarks were drowned out by protest before she could clearly distinguish between those earlier Argentine derogations of the British claim and the one at issue on April 3, 1982.

20. There could be other British responses to the Argentine claim. First, Britain could accuse the Argentines of being the ones who violated the norms of signaling. The official British investigation considered such a counterclaim when it stated that "Argentina had previously made threatening noises, accompanied by bellicose press comment, and indeed backed up its threats with aggressive actions, without the dispute developing into a serious confrontation." THE RT. HON. THE LORD FRANKS, CHAIRMAN, FALKLANDS ISLANDS REVIEW—REPORT OF A COMMITTEE OF PRIVY COUNSELLORS, para. 296 (1983) [hereinafter cited as FRANKS REPORT]. This allegation suggests that Argentina signaled to the United Kingdom that it would not invade the Falklands, regardless of apparent Argentine bellicosity.

The *Franks Report* dismissed this counterclaim. The report noted that this view of Argentine intentions was unfounded and exerted an undue influence on British policymaking. *Id.* Indeed, almost each case of Argentine saber rattling at official levels was followed up by some sort of material affront to British sovereignty. The severity of these affronts increased over time.

Another possible British counterclaim could be that the British strategy of "understated response" was a rational policy not intended to signal acquiescence to Argentine aggression, but meant instead to reduce the risk of armed conflict. This theory lacks merit

The credibility of the claims imputed to Argentina and Britain must be ascertained through careful examination of the pattern of signals in the years before the war. One starting point is the 1965 United Nations resolution that first classified the Falklands as territories in the process of decolonization.

Operation Condor and Its Aftermath

United Nations General Assembly Resolution 2065 of December 16, 1965,[21] from which the United Kingdom abstained, linked the Falklands to the international effort to decolonize and invited British-Argentine negotiations on the subject. A year later, in September 1966, "Operation Condor" revealed the vulnerability of the Falklands and their isolation from British power. Operation Condor involved the hijacking by twenty armed Argentine civilians of an Argentine government DC-4 airplane to Port Stanley, the capital of the Falkland Islands. Massive demonstrations in Buenos Aires supported this apparently unofficial action.

Operation Condor was an unofficial Argentine signal that the Falklands were vulnerable to paramilitary incursions and that Argentina could back up its territorial claim with military force.[22] The British government had foreseen such a signal at least eighteen months before Operation Condor. A March 1965 British Joint Intelligence Committee report estimating the vulnerability of the islands singled out such adventurist, unofficial action as the type of incident most likely to induce a radical and rapid change in Argentine public opinion and official policy.[23] It remains unknown whether the Argentine government sent the Operation Condor signal, but it is at least the case that some

---

because the facts presented here show that the British elite knew at the highest levels how dangerously its actions were being interpreted in Argentina.

21. G.A. Res. 2065, *supra* note 3.

22. *See* FRANKS REPORT, *supra* note 20, para. 21. It makes little difference whether the operation was an act of official Argentine policy, planned with the knowledge and participation of the Foreign Ministry and the president, or whether prior knowledge of the operation was limited to lower functionaries or a small group elsewhere within the politico-military structure. The operation signaled to Britain the continued immediacy of the Argentine claim, and the British response signaled the remarkable weakness of Britain's commitment to its claim.

23. FRANKS REPORT, *supra* note 20, para. 19. For a description of the role and composition of the Joint Intelligence Committee, see *id.* Annex B paras. 13–15.

group in Argentina with access to weapons was clearly signaling a strong commitment to Argentine sovereignty over the Falklands.

The British government's actions in the wake of Operation Condor clearly indicate that it received the signal. The immediate British response was to increase the British military presence on the Falkland Islands from one officer and five men to a full platoon—a number that remained roughly constant until the 1982 invasion.[24] British diplomatic aquiescence, however, far overshadowed the signal sent by the increased military presence. Within six months of the incident, the British government proposed a "sovereignty freeze" for a minimum of thirty years, after which the Islanders would be free to choose between British and Argentine rule.[25]

Argentina rejected the British offer,[26] thereby reemphasizing the seriousness of its legal claim. The British government responded in March 1967 by telling Argentina for the first time that Her Majesty would immediately "cede sovereignty" of the Falklands under certain conditions.[27] Britain first stated to Argentina that it would condition its recognition of Argentina's sovereignty on the Falkland Islanders' "wishes."[28] Negotiations then stalled when the Falkland Islands Council alarmed the British Parliament with allegations of an impending cession of sovereignty, provoking widespread political opposition in Britain to any cession plan.[29] The British government finally reached an agreement with Argentina in August 1968 on a Memorandum of Understanding regarding the official conditions for the cession of British sovereignty. It expressed concern for the Islanders' "interests" instead of guaranteeing their "wishes."[30]

These events establish that the signal sent by Operation Condor sig-

24. FRANKS REPORT, *supra* note 20, para. 21. The number did not increase substantially before April 1982. M. HASTINGS & S. JENKINS, *supra* note 5, at 72.
25. FRANKS REPORT, *supra* note 20, para. 22. A report submitted to the British Defence and Overseas Policy Committee prior to these negotiations stated that Argentina could easily occupy the islands by force. *Id.*
26. *Id.*
27. *Id.*
28. *Id.*
29. *Id.*
30. *Id.* para. 23. Publication of the Memorandum of Understanding "was to be accompanied by a unilateral" British government statement that made conformity with the Islanders' wishes an absolute condition for recognizing Argentine sovereignty. *Id.* para. 24.

nificantly affected subsequent policy decisions at the highest levels of the British government. Argentina benefited relatively quickly from Operation Condor, even though the British public opposed diplomatic concessions on sovereignty. The British concessions in the months after Operation Condor amounted to a British signal that Argentine paramilitary affronts to British sovereignty would weaken the British claim to sovereignty, as well as the Islanders' claim to self-determination. On the other hand, these events indicate strong political support in Britain for continuing British control of the islands.

Deteriorating Relations

The new British policy of negotiating away Her Majesty's sovereignty over the Falklands encountered increasingly sharp political opposition and critical press coverage. Following a rebellion by backbenchers on December 11, 1968, the British Cabinet abandoned the Memorandum of Understanding as a basis for settlement of the dispute.[31]

According to the *Franks Report*, however, earlier in 1968 the British government had recognized that "failure to reach an understanding with Argentina carried the risks of increased harassment of the Islanders and the possibility of an attack. The Government therefore decided to endeavor to continue negotiations with Argentina while making clear the British attitude on sovereignty."[32] The foreign and Commonwealth secretary told Parliament on December 11, 1968, that Britain would continue to negotiate.[33]

The British government pursued this negotiation strategy from 1968 until 1974.[34] Discussions from 1969 to 1971 continued under a "sovereignty umbrella" and focused on improving communications and other ties between Argentina and the Falkland Islanders.[35] Argentina's

31. *Id.* para. 25. The Cabinet based its decision to abandon the Memorandum of Understanding on the refusal of the Argentine government to insert a clause in the memorandum making a British recognition of Argentine sovereignty subject to the "wishes" of the approximately 1,600 Islanders, or to link the memorandum to the British unilateral publication statement. *Id.*

32. *Id.*

33. OFFICIAL REPORT, HOUSE OF COMMONS, 11 Dec. 1968, cols. 424–34.

34. FRANKS REPORT, *supra* note 20, paras. 25–30.

35. *Id.* para. 26. For example, in December 1971 the two governments issued a joint statement establishing new patterns of cooperation between the Falklands and Argentina. *Id.*

policy during this period apparently was to cooperate with British efforts to tie the islands more closely to the Argentine mainland. The two governments reached accords on several issues, including the provision of scholarships for Falklanders wishing to study on the Argentine mainland, the construction of an airstrip to link Port Stanley to Argentina, the issuance of Argentine immigration documents to the Islanders, reciprocal exemptions, from duties and taxes, and an exemption for Islanders from Argentine military service.[36] British willingness to enter into these agreements supports the Argentine claim that the agreements indicated a British readiness to allow the Falklanders to become Argentine citizens.

Even as Argentina began to implement these cooperative ventures, it pressed for a resumption of talks on sovereignty and conditioned its willingness to discuss further ties with the Islanders on the British government's acceptance of sovereignty negotiations.[37] An impasse on the sovereignty issue led Argentina to seek and obtain the passage in 1973 of UN General Assembly Resolution 3160 urging renewed negotiations on sovereignty in 1973.[38]

At the end of that year, British intelligence reported for the first time that the government of Isabel Perón might be preparing contingency plans for the military occupation of the Falklands.[39] As a result of these developments, the British Defence Committee proposed exploring the idea of a British–Argentine condominium over the Falklands. The Falklands Council indicated that it would not object to the proposal.[40] Before Argentina could pursue this new initiative, the British told Argentina in August 1974 that the Islanders' refusal to attend the negotiations on condominium, even though the Falklanders did not object per se to their taking place, made such talks pointless.[41] The condominium episode supports the British claim because it indicated that the Foreign and Commonwealth Office would formally continue to follow the formula in the Memorandum of Understanding and safeguard Islander interests.

36. *Id.*
37. *Id.* para. 27.
38. *Id.* para. 129. *See* G.A. Res. 3160, 28 U.N. GAOR Supp. (No. 30) at 108, U.N. Doc. A/9030 (1973).
39. FRANKS REPORT, *supra* note 20, para. 32.
40. *Id.* paras. 29, 30.
41. *Id.* para. 30.

In December 1974 the Argentine newspaper *Crónica* mounted a campaign advocating an invasion of the Falklands.[42] In April 1975, the British ambassador to Buenos Aires delivered a warning to Argentine foreign minister Vignes that Britain would respond militarily to any Argentine invasion.[43] Argentina confirmed indications that its policy was moving from one of cooperation to a more confrontational posture in July 1975, when it rejected a British proposal for the joint economic development of the South Atlantic territories.[44] Foreign Minister Vignes suggested linking any such agreement to a transfer of sovereignty plus a leaseback to Britain for some years.[45] He also suggested that Argentina occupy South Georgia and the South Sandwich Islands. Britain found this unacceptable, and negotiations stalled.[46] These official exchanges offer some foundation for the British claim. They indicate a stiffening of the British government's attitude after the domestic public debate over condominium. The Argentine government should have interpreted such stiffening as a signal that the British sovereignty claim would not be abandoned, diplomatically or militarily, without Islander agreement.

The RSS Shackleton *Incident*

In October 1975, the United Kingdom announced its decision to commission a report, to be directed by Lord Shackleton, on the long-term economic potential of the Falklands.[47] This provoked a sharp response from Argentina's foreign minister, who warned British prime minister James Callaghan on January 2, 1976, that in the absence of further negotiations their countries would "rapidly mov[e] towards a head-on collision," and that "[the Argentine] government could accept no responsibility for such an outcome."[48] British attempts at conciliation failed to temper the aggressiveness of subsequent statements by the Argentine government and print media.[49]

42. *Id*. para. 31.
43. *Id*.
44. *Id*. para. 33.
45. *Id*.
46. *Id*.
47. *Id*. para. 34.
48. *Id*. para. 36.
49. *Id*. paras. 37, 39. This strong Argentine reaction can be seen as a response-in-kind to earlier British diplomatic warnings not to occupy territory unilaterally. Both sides had

INTERNATIONAL INCIDENTS

The situation worsened in February when an Argentine destroyer fired shots at the unarmed British research ship *Shackleton* seventy-eight miles south of Port Stanley.[50] British intelligence reported that the decision to attack RSS *Shackleton* had been made in Buenos Aires six weeks earlier, but that the Argentine armed forces were nevertheless opposed to a full-scale military invasion that might help President Isabel Perón stay in power. "The Joint Intelligence Committee assessed the purpose of the operation as being an assertion of Argentine sovereignty over the Falkland Islands and surrounding waters, in order to bring pressure to bear on the British Government to negotiate."[51]

The firing on the *Shackleton* came after Britain's decision to withdraw its only armed vessel in the South Atlantic, the ice patrol ship *Endurance*.[52] As a result of the shooting, Britain retained HMS *Endurance* on active service in the area, subject to annual and biannual renewal.[53] Prime Minister Callaghan also agreed to send a Royal Navy frigate to the South Atlantic.[54] The deployment of the frigate was the firmest response of any British government to an Argentine challenge during this period until, of course, the decision of Prime Minister Thatcher to retake the islands in 1982.[55]

previously signaled their opposition to unilateral actions in UN General Assembly Resolution 3160, adopted in 1973. *See supra* note 38.

50. FRANKS REPORT, *supra* note 20, para. 42. According to the *Franks Report* the presence of the *Shackleton* did not have any connection to the mission led by Lord Shackleton. *Id.*

51. *Id.* paras. 41, 42. British intelligence indicated that the Argentine decision to intercept the ship was made by the armed forces, not by the government, and that the commander in chief of the Argentine navy had authorized firing upon the ship without causing casualties or sinking it.

52. *Id.* para. 44. The decision resulted from the 1974 Defence Review. *Id.*

53. *Id.*

54. *Id.* para. 45.

55. The deployment was based on the continued view of British intelligence that the main Argentine threat was harassment. *Id.* para. 40. One frigate would not have been an adequate response or deterrent to Argentine military designs more serious than harassment. Nevertheless, this response was sufficiently firm to influence Argentine thinking regarding British policy in the South Atlantic. Costa Méndez dedicated four paragraphs of his Security Council speech of April 3, 1982, to his account of this incident. In it he described the British decision as an attempt at intimidation "which constituted a real threat to my country and to the continent. . . ." Provisional Verbatim Record of the Two Thousand Three Hundred and Fiftieth Meeting, U.N. Doc. S/PV. 2350 (1982). He also argued that the British deployments near the Falklands "justify and explain the actions taken of necessity by the Government of Argentina in defense of its rights." *Id.*

The events surrounding the firing on RSS *Shackleton* are a substantial source of support for the British signaling claim. Official Argentine use of armed force upon a symbol of Britain's sovereignty over the Falklands—a British vessel conducting an economic resources survey in the vicinity of the islands—met with a strong British military and diplomatic response, signaling a limit to British acquiescence.

The Southern Thule Incident

Britain's ability to send an effective signal depended in part on intelligence reports of the Argentine armed forces' unwillingness to take decisive action that might bolster President Perón's popularity. The British were well aware of their own strategic constraints: a British Chiefs of Staff paper issued in February 1976 warned that an Argentine invasion would probably succeed and that Britain could repulse it only by using all of the Royal Navy's amphibious resources as well as a sizable task force.[56] This bleak assessment of British military options led the Callaghan government to enter into a fresh round of discussions. In December 1976, General Assembly Resolution 49[57] thanked the government of Argentina for "facilitat[ing] the process of decolonization" and urged both sides to expedite negotiations.[58] The United Kingdom stood alone in opposing the resolution.[59]

Against this diplomatic background, on December 20, 1976, the British "discovered the existence of an Argentine military presence" on Southern Thule in the South Sandwich Islands.[60] After inquiries from London, Argentina responded on January 14, 1977, that its intent was to establish a station on Southern Thule for future scientific investigation "within the jurisdiction of Argentine sovereignty." Argentina also expressed the hope "that nothing would cloud the 'auspicious perspectives' for negotiations," hinting that the presence of Argentine nationals on Southern Thule would not be permanent.[61] Five days later, the British government formally protested the Argentine presence "as a violation of British sovereignty," stating that Britain was "entitled to ex-

56. FRANKS REPORT, *supra* note 20, paras. 46, 47.
57. *Id.* G.A. Res. 49, 31 U.N. GAOR Supp. (No. 39) at 122, U.N. Doc. A/31/39 at 122 (1976).
58. *Id.*
59. FRANKS REPORT, *supra* note 20, para. 51.
60. *Id.* para. 52.
61. *Id.* para. 53.

pect" prior consultation and expressing the "hope" that the Argentine "scientific programme was being terminated."[62]

Shortly thereafter, on February 2, 1977, the British government decided that "the time has come to consider both with the Islanders and the Argentine Government whether a climate exists for discussing the broad issues which bear on the future of the Falkland Islands, and the possibilities of cooperation between Britain and Argentina in the region of the South West Atlantic."[63] The British government emphasized that it still reserved its positions both on sovereignty and on the need for Islander approval of any agreement.[64] Within two months, the governments agreed to terms of reference for new formal discussions.[65]

The outcome of the Southern Thule incident issued an even stronger signal of British acquiescence to the Argentines. Although the British responded to the *Shackleton* incident with a firm diplomatic protest and a naval deployment against Argentina, their reaction to the Southern Thule landing communicated a lack of seriousness on both diplomatic and military levels. Although HMS *Endurance* reported the Argentine landing on December 20, 1976, it was only on January 5, 1977, that the Foreign Office sought an Argentine "explanation."[66] The British took no further action until the Argentines had proffered such an explanation, thereby delaying delivery of Britain's formal protest until January 19, a month after the landing.[67] At no time did the British government make public the Argentine landing,[68] nor did it attempt any formal protest through international channels. The Southern Thule incident therefore furnishes a strong foundation for the Argentine signaling claim. From Argentina's perspective, it had intimidated the British government into stating publicly that "the time ha[d] come" to negotiate on sovereignty.[69] The success of Argentine

---

62. *Id.*

63. *Id.* para. 58.

64. *Id.*

65. *Id.* para. 60. The Islanders agreed to those terms of reference, but only under a "sovereignty umbrella" and with promises of full consultation. *Id.*

66. *Id.* para. 52.

67. *Id.* para. 53. The *Franks Report* stated that "[t]he Argentine expectation had been that the British reaction would have been stronger." *Id.* para. 54.

68. *Id.* These events did not come to public notice until May 1978. *See* The Times (London), Apr. 3, 1981, at 3, col. 8.

69. *See supra* text accompanying note 63. British intelligence expected a hardening of the Argentine position in the forthcoming negotiations. Intelligence reports also indicated that the failure of Argentina to prevail in the papal arbitration of the Beagle Chan-

policy probably surpassed Argentine expectations and apparently failed to precipitate a full invasion only because Argentina anticipated little if any international support for such a step.[70]

The Soviet and Bulgarian Incidents

Before talks between Argentina and Great Britain resumed in New York, Argentine naval forces detained seven Soviet and two Bulgarian fishing vessels in Falklands waters during September and October 1977.[71] One Bulgarian sailor was wounded by Argentine fire.[72] Admiral Anaya, Argentine naval attaché in London and later commander in chief of the navy, warned the British Foreign Office that Argentine admiral Massera had orders to sink any of the Bulgarian vessels if necessary.[73]

This series of incidents during late September and early October 1977 indirectly involved British interests. The Argentine interdiction of foreign vessels in Falklands waters amounted to a legal claim of right that necessarily challenged the British sovereignty claim. The Argentine government warned the British through diplomatic channels of similar actions in the future against "any other flag carrier and at any other place."[74] The boldness of the Argentine move and the failure of the British government to express strong displeasure in any significant way must have reinforced the Argentine perception, clearly established by the Southern Thule incident, that the British position on sovereignty lacked seriousness.

The British Secret Naval Deployment of 1977

After the attack on the Bulgarian and Soviet vessels, the British government secretly decided to deploy two Royal Navy frigates a thousand miles from the Falkland Islands, and a nuclear-powered submarine in the "immediate vicinity" of the Falklands.[75] The *Franks Report* asserts that "Cabinet Committee papers show clearly that it was agreed that

---

nel dispute with Chile and the lack of progress with Brazil in their River Plate Basin dispute could only increase Argentine eagerness to press for success in the Falklands dispute. FRANKS REPORT, *supra* note 20, para. 62.

70. *Id.* paras. 54, 56.
71. *Id.* para. 62.
72. *Id.*
73. *Id.*
74. *Id.*
75. *Id.* para. 65.

the force should remain covert. We have found no evidence that the Argentine Government ever came to know of its existence."[76]

The decision to deploy the force covertly prevented the action from being a signal and thus from having any effect on Argentine perceptions. The deployment of two ships and a submarine could not have prevented an Argentine invasion.[77] Bringing it to the attention of the Argentine government, however, would have reinforced the signal of resolve sent as a response to the firing on the *Shackleton*.

The force was withdrawn once the British believed negotiations were going well.[78] During subsequent negotiations the British proposed joint scientific activities in the Dependencies, a step that "would have retrospectively legitimized the Argentine presence on Southern Thule."[79] While Islander opposition killed the proposal,[80] Argentina could reasonably claim that the proposal conveyed a signal of continued British acquiescence in Argentine displays of sovereign authority. An opportunity to reassert the British claim publicly became instead a signal of continued willingness to recognize Argentine rights in disputed territory.

Other Territorial Developments

In the *International Herald Tribune* of November 6, 1980, the Argentine State Petroleum Company, Yacimientos Petroleros Fiscales (YPF), invited bids for a contract to drill for oil in an off-shore area called Magallanes Este. This area straddled the British-declared boundary line

76. *Id.* para. 66. Then Prime Minister Callaghan "has said that he ensured that the [naval] unit's presence was made known through undisclosed channels to the Junta of the day." A. GAVSHON & D. RICE, THE SINKING OF THE BELGRANO 10 (1984). That signal was supposedly to have reached the Argentines through American intermediaries. *Id.* Gavshon and Rice prefer the *Franks Report*'s version, particularly since it is damaging to the report's own conclusion exonerating the Thatcher government for not foreseeing the 1982 invasion. *Id.*

77. British intelligence knew that much more was needed to prevent or defeat a determined Argentine effort to seize the Falklands. FRANKS REPORT, *supra* note 20, para. 47.

78. *Id.* para. 66.

79. *Id.* para. 68.

80. *Id.* para. 69. The Islanders' main objection was that, "unless restricted to Southern Thule, [such cooperation] would give Argentina a further foothold in the Dependencies, which would start a process leading to eventual loss of sovereignty over the Falkland Islands themselves." *Id.* It seems, therefore, that even the Islanders interpreted British signals to mean that Britain was moving toward giving up the Falklands.

between the Falklands and Tierra del Fuego.[81] On December 9, 1980, the British responded to Argentine plans to drill for oil in the disputed territory by registering an official protest.[82] Approximately five months later, the British government published a notice in the *International Herald Tribune* warning oil companies of the possibility of legal action if they drilled in the disputed area.[83]

Argentina's reaction at the diplomatic level was to declare the basis of the British protest of December 9, 1980, "flatly unacceptable."[84] The Argentine Foreign Office declared that "there does not exist any boundary in the area in question, for the simple reason that the whole area corresponds to Argentine sovereignty."[85] The Argentine government reaffirmed that assertion of sovereignty by signing an agreement with the Soviet Union that provided for joint exploration and exploitation of fishing resources "in Argentine waters south of 46 south latitude, in accord with Argentine legislation in effect."[86]

On June 30, 1981, the British Parliament approved the expiry, effective March 1982, of the commission of HMS *Endurance*, the only British armed ship stationed in the South Atlantic. Lord Carrington, the British Foreign Secretary, had argued against the decision, warning that the presence and hydrographic tasks of *Endurance* "were an important aspect of the maintainance of the British claim to sovereignty."[87] On July 27, 1981, the Argentine Ministry of Foreign Affairs issued a communiqué warning that the question of sovereignty could no longer be deferred.[88] Lack of British counter-response, especially in view of the decision to decommission *Endurance*, could clearly support

---

81. *See* 2 A. SILENZI DE STAGNI, LAS MALVINAS Y EL PETRÓLEO 141 (1983). *See also* Report of the Special Committee, *supra* note 4, paras. 31, 32. (The United Kingdom also carried out seismic exploration around the Falklands in search of oil. The RRS *Shackleton* may have been part of this British effort.) *But see supra* note 50 (indicating no connection beween the RRS *Shackleton* and Lord Shackleton's mission).

82. A. SILENZI DE STAGNI, *supra* note 81, at 136.

83. *Id.* at 141 (quoting Lord Carrington's statement on subject).

84. *Id.* at 142.

85. *Id.*

86. *Id.* at 163 (quoting text verbatim of Ley No. 22.481, Aug. 10, 1981, Protocolo de Entendimiento Entre la Secretaría de Estado de Intereses Marítimos del Ministerio de Economía de la República Argentina y el Ministerio de Pesca de la Unión de Repúblicas Socialistas Soviéticas Sobre la Colaboración en Materia Pesquera, art. 6).

87. FRANKS REPORT, *supra* note 20, para. 114.

88. *Id.* para. 97.

an Argentine claim that the British had signaled an *animus derelin-quendi* toward the Falklands.

The South Georgia Incident

In December 1981 an allegedly private party of Argentine scrap metal dealers landed without authorization on South Georgia, ostensibly to inspect a disused British whaling station for which they had signed an option contract with an Edinburgh-based firm.[89] The governor of the Falklands told the British Foreign Office on December 31 that the Argentine party on South Georgia was violating Dependencies legislation by its failure to obtain clearance.[90] The Foreign Office replied that the governor should not take action that "would risk provoking a most serious incident which could escalate and have an unforeseen outcome."[91] Any action or diplomatic protest would have to wait for further developments on South Georgia.[92]

Although the British ambassador in Buenos Aires approached the Argentine Foreign Ministry on January 6, 1982, he withheld a protest about events on South Georgia pending an Argentine investigation.[93] The protest was delivered on February 9, and Argentina rejected it nine days later.[94]

On March 20, the governor of the Falklands notified the British Foreign Office that a sizable Argentine party of civilian and military personnel had arrived on South Georgia aboard a different ship. Upon landing, they had fired shots, raised the Argentine flag, and defaced a posted warning against unauthorized landings.[95] The British ambassador in Buenos Aires then warned the Argentine Foreign Ministry that the incident was serious and that "the British Government would have to take whatever action seemed necessary."[96] The British government ordered HMS *Endurance* to sail to South Georgia. The Falklands gov-

89. *Id.* paras. 161–62.
90. *Id.* para. 163.
91. *Id.* para. 164.
92. *Id.*
93. *Id.* para. 165.
94. *Id.*
95. *Id.* para. 169; C. KANAF, LA BATALLA DE LAS MALVINAS 18 (1982). On March 22, Falkland Islanders vandalized the Argentine government airline's office in Port Stanley. *Id.*
96. FRANKS REPORT, *supra* note 20, para. 169.

ernor instructed the British base commander at Grytviken, South Georgia, to tell the Argentines to lower their flag and report to Grytviken.[97]

On March 21, while the Argentines remained at Leith Harbor on South Georgia, the Argentine Foreign Office officially responded without apology, but expressing the hope that the British would not "exaggerate" the significance of the incident.[98] The Argentine naval headquarters meanwhile congratulated the ship *Bahía Buen Suceso* (the *Good Incident Bay*) on "a successful operation."[99]

On March 23, the British Foreign Office canceled HMS *Endurance*'s orders to confront the Argentine party at Leith. Instead, hoping to avoid "provocation,"[100] the British ordered the *Endurance* to remain at Grytviken. Foreign Secretary Lord Carrington obtained his Argentine counterpart's agreement that removal of the party at Leith by an Argentine vessel was a "welcomed" suggestion, while Dr. Costa Méndez in turn assured Lord Carrington that he would try to obtain the necessary authorization to carry it out.[101]

Yet on March 25 the British received information that Argentine warships had been dispatched to ensure that HMS *Endurance* would not remove the Argentine party at Leith.[102] London also learned that a second Argentine ship, previously supposed to be an unarmed scientific vessel, had brought three military landing craft and a military helicopter to Leith Harbor.[103] The June 1981 decision to pull the *Endurance* out of service was not changed, but the ship remained temporarily at Grytviken.[104]

The Argentine commanders in chief met on March 26, and the next day Costa Méndez announced that a firm decision had been reached to give the Argentine men on South Georgia "all necessary protection."[105] That same day, the president and commander in chief of the army, General Galtieri, announced to an audience of local politicians in Buenos Aires that "this year is not the most propitious one to face

97. *Id.*
98. *Id.* para. 170. *See also* C. KANAF, *supra* note 95, at 98.
99. FRANKS REPORT, *supra* note 29, para. 175.
100. *Id.* para. 184.
101. *Id.* paras. 184–86.
102. *Id.* para. 193. *Cf.* C. KANAF, *supra* note 95, at 99–100.
103. FRANKS REPORT, *supra* note 20, para. 193.
104. *Id.* paras. 194, 204.
105. *Id.* para. 207. *See also* C. KANAF, *supra* note 95, at 100.

fundamental solutions to the political, economic, and social problems of the Nation."[106]

The absence of visible British resolve on behalf of its sovereignty claim must have confirmed the message of the Southern Thule incident to the Argentine ruling elite. British inaction also came in the context of the scheduled decommissioning of HMS *Endurance* in March, which the British government refused to delay for budgetary reasons despite events on South Georgia.[107] Moreover, the British Foreign Office itself was, or should have been, aware of the message that decommissioning the *Endurance* would send, since Lord Carrington had unsuccessfully argued that its retention on station was important to the credibility of the British sovereignty claim.[108]

The Falkland Islands Council shared this interpretation of the decision,[109] and that became public knowledge as part of the parliamentary debate on the 1981 Defence Review. All Argentine newspapers that reported the decision took it to mean that Britain was "abandoning the protection of the Falkland Islands."[110] Indeed, British intelligence knew that Argentina had interpreted the decision as a deliberate political gesture and not as an expedient measure.[111]

THE NORMS AT ISSUE

Incident studies may reveal that the participants in an international incident disagreed about the norms applicable to their dispute. In tradi-

106. La Prensa, Mar. 27, 1982, at 1, col. 1 ("El presidente habló a intendentes bonaerenses—Dijo que este año no es el más propicio para encarar soluciones de fondo para el problema político, económico y social de la Nación"). Widespread political unrest had created public speculation as to whether significant changes in domestic policy would take place. The unrest took increasingly violent form, including demonstrations in several Argentine cities.

107. *See* M. HASTINGS & S. JENKINS, *supra* note 5, at 53 ("Relations between departments in Mrs. Thatcher's government had, by spring of 1982, become utterly dominated by budgetary considerations").

108. FRANKS REPORT, *supra* note 20, para. 114.

109. *Id.* para. 115 ("The people of the Falkland Islands . . . express extreme concern that Britain appears to be abandoning its defence of British interests in the South Atlantic and Antarctic at a time when other powers are strengthening their position in these areas"). *See also supra* note 80.

110. *Id.* para. 116.

111. *Id.* ("[Argentines] did not see it as an inevitable economy in Britain's defence budget since the implications for the Islands . . . were fundamental").

tional legal terminology such a disagreement could imperfectly be called a choice-of-law problem. There was no such problem in this incident. Argentine and British policy makers ultimately reached conflicting interpretations of their exchange of signals, but there is no indication that they followed different conceptions of the signaling process. As Lord Carrington told his Cabinet colleagues, for example, the British were well aware that the final decision to decommission *Endurance* would weaken the British sovereignty claim. Implicit in that conclusion is of course the view that an international political language exists, and that in that language decommissioning *Endurance* would have the international meaning Lord Carrington predicted. There is every indication that Argentina agreed with Britain both on the existence of such a language, and on the meaning it gave to decommissioning *Endurance*.

On the other hand, no convincing evidence exists that Argentine and British policy makers disagreed at any point on the norms of the international signaling language. For both sides the Argentine firing on vessels of third parties within disputed Falklands waters, like the decommissioning of *Endurance*, meant a weakening of the British sovereignty claim.

The fact that there was substantial agreement between the parties about the meaning of their signals is itself a significant conclusion. It means that complex international norms for interpreting signals exist. One of these is that the maintenance of a naval force, however small, around distant island territories indicates the seriousness of a claim to sovereignty over those territories.[112] Conversely, the withdrawal of such a force communicates a willingness to abandon that sovereignty claim. The significance of such withdrawal may be given greater weight than mere words of diplomats reaffirming a desire to continue exercising sovereignty.

Another, closely related norm is that the failure to control access to lightly populated territory communicates the lack of seriousness of a claim to sovereign status over that territory. Britain did nothing to remove, if need be by force, the party of Argentine citizens on Southern Thule, and subsequently on South Georgia. Any contention that for-

112. *Cf.* N.Y. Times, July 6, 1987, at 2, col. 1 (Canadian government will buy and deploy a new Arctic fleet of nuclear attack submarines "to reinforce its claim to sovereignty over tens of thousands of square miles of Arctic Sea").

cible removal of the Argentines would have instead worsened tensions indicates either inability or unwillingness to defend a sovereignty claim. Such a failure to control access to disputed territory appears to carry greater weight than verbal assertions of sovereignty.

Similarly, the failure of one claimant to react to a treaty between the other claimant and a third party relating to disputed seas, such as Britain's lack of strong reaction to the Soviet–Argentine fishing treaty partially relating to Falklands fisheries, also appears to signal the passive state's willingness to accept foreign sovereignty over the disputed territory.

Other signaling norms revealed by this incident relate to the treatment of persons living on disputed territory. The United Kingdom negotiated with Argentina to exempt the Islanders from Argentine military service, and to permit Argentina to provide them educational, immigration, communication, and transportation benefits normally characteristic of the relationship between a state and the people over which it is sovereign. These negotiations communicated a British policy of gradual cession of sovereignty to Argentina.

Finally, underlying all of Britain's signals is the fact that in 1965 Britain did not object when the United Nations General Assembly included the Falkland Islands among territories in the process of decolonization. This incident indicates that such an action, like the others above, communicates a readiness to cede control and recognize another state's sovereignty over the territory involved.

OUTCOME AND INTERNATIONAL APPRAISAL

The outcome of the Falklands incident was a total British military victory and recapture of the Falkland Islands and the Dependencies. This military outcome overshadows all prior incidents in the area and brakes a generally constant line of signals indicating British acquiescence to the Argentine claim. It reveals that Argentina somehow misunderstood British signals and incorrectly imputed intentions to the British government.

There were few noteworthy international reactions to the exchange that took place between the United Kingdom and Argentina in the Southwest Atlantic from 1965 to 1981. As Argentina did not make a public claim that British signals permitted it to invade, the international community did not respond to Argentina on those terms. In a sense, therefore, there was no international appraisal of the Argentine signaling claim presented here.

There are indications, however, that the international community supported the British claim; namely, that whatever British signals may have indicated about an eventual recognition of Argentine sovereignty, they could not have communicated the British government's willingness to be humiliated and run out of office by an invasion of the Falklands. General Assembly Resolution 49, passed in 1976, purported to express the tone, intensity, and direction of international interest in the dispute between Britain and Argentina over the Falklands. In it the international community encouraged the United Kingdom to continue the process of turning the Falklands over to Argentina. The resolution thus clearly indicates that the international community expected Britain eventually to recognize Argentine sovereignty over the Falklands. Given the official British assertion of sovereignty, it is clear that the international community saw actual British intentions as inconsistent with that official position. To that extent the international community accepted the Argentine claim; British governments had signaled a willingness to recognize eventually Argentine sovereignty over the Falklands. Britain's claim acknowledges as much.

In spite of this, however, the international community's reaction to the invasion agrees with the crucial part of the British claim; whatever Britain signaled, Britain did not intend to permit Argentina to seize the Falklands by military force. On April 3, the day after the Argentine invasion, the United Nations Security Council adopted Resolution 502 demanding an immediate cessation of hostilities and withdrawal of all Argentine forces, and calling for a diplomatic resolution.[113] That position essentially restated Britain's demands to Argentina. Similarly, the European Economic Community agreed on April 9 to oppose the Argentine invasion, and recommended economic sanctions.[114] Its member states quickly banned all imports from Argentina.[115]

Among Britain's key allies, only the United States expressed substantial initial reluctance to support the United Kingdom. The stated American policy was to mediate a peaceful solution to the crisis. Secretary of State Alexander Haig took the initiative and engaged in shuttle

113. WAR IN FALKLANDS, *supra* note 6, at 112.
114. *Id.* at 120–21.
115. *Id.* at 121. *See also* C. KANAF, *supra* note 95, at 131.

diplomacy between April 8 and 29.[116] When that effort failed, President Reagan declared on April 30 that the United States would make military supplies available to Britain and impose economic sanctions on Argentina.[117]

Thus nearly all important nations, including the United States, aligned themselves behind Britain and against the Argentine invasion. This occurred in spite of the international community's understanding and support of Britain's signaled intent eventually to cede the Falklands to Argentina. The outcome of the incident therefore reveals a different signaling norm than the others examined above. In its narrowest construction, this norm is that signals of a powerful Western state indicating willingness to cede colonial territories cannot mean that the Western state would accept their seizure by military force against the wishes of the local population. As stated below, such use of force would throw the offended government into a domestic crisis from which it might survive only by responding with uncompromising defiance. If it responds in that manner, as is likely, allied governments are also likely to demand a complete return to the *status quo ante*.

Nothing in the incident suggests, however, that the British government no longer wishes to find some way to give up the Falklands. As a political matter, the invasion did not change whatever economic and military factors may have led Britain to signal its willingness to recognize Argentine sovereignty over the Falklands. As a legal matter, the incident reveals a strong international norm against Argentina's interpretation of British signals, but it does not weaken the signaling norms that long had justified Argentine and international expectation of *eventual* Argentine sovereignty. Because the strong British military presence currently on the Falklands may signal British opposition to a military transfer of sovereignty, rather than opposition to any negotiated cession, the incident offers no clear evidence that Britain has changed its mind on the possibility of eventual Argentine sovereignty.

AUTHOR'S APPRAISAL

The objective of the Argentine invasion is unclear. Foreign Minister Costa Méndez' position is that the invasion was to be a "short coup"

116. WAR IN FALKLANDS, *supra* note 6, at 135–43.
117. M. HASTINGS & S. JENKINS, *supra* note 5, at 141–42.

ARGENTINE INVASION

designed to improve Argentina's bargaining position, but not to lead immediately to permanent military occupation. It is clear that the Argentine government was not unanimously of that view. Once the invasion took place the junta's policy, as expressed by President Galtieri, was to seize the islands permanently by military force. Both views, however, presupposed that Britain would accept the invasion as the starting point for a future relationship. Costa Méndez' stated view assumed negotiations while Argentine forces occupied the Falklands. President Galtieri clearly assumed that British efforts to recapture the islands would fail, if ever mounted at all, and that subsequently Britain and its allies would accept the situation.

The Argentine error is understandable. From the Argentine point of view, successive British governments signaled almost consistently that the United Kingdom was not serious about keeping control of the disputed area. The British repeatedly acquiesced in specific Argentine assertions of authority, including the seizure of Dependencies territory in Southern Thule and South Georgia and the conclusion of a Soviet–Argentine economic cooperation treaty that implicitly recognized Argentine sovereignty over the Falklands. The British concluded agreements with the Argentines establishing a special relationship between the Islanders and Argentina, including an exemption for Islanders from Argentine military service. These exemptions would be meaningful only if the Islanders were to become Argentines. Similarly, the British weakened their ties to the islands by withdrawing HMS *Endurance* from South Atlantic service, despite the March 1982 Argentine occupation of South Georgia, and by enacting the 1981 Nationality Act that denied British nationality to many native Falklanders.[118] Therefore, considering the preceding discussion and the facts surrounding the dispute—including the lack of British opposition to UN Resolution 2065 classifying the Falkland Islands among territories in the process of decolonization—it is reasonable to conclude that Britain signaled to Argentina that Britain was willing to surrender its sovereignty claim.

The British counterclaim acknowledges that this analysis has some merit, but asserts that Britain never signaled its readiness to acquiesce to an Argentine military occupation of the entire Falklands archipelago. Since the counterclaim relies heavily on assertions about what

118. M. HASTINGS & S. JENKINS, *supra* note 5, at 43–44; A. GAVSHON & D. RICE, *supra* note 76, at 11–12.

Britain *intended* to signal, resort must be made to British intelligence assessments, now made public in the *Franks Report*, to infer what the British government actually knew. Knowing what the government intended would help in assessing the reasons for the failure to communicate it.

The *Franks Report* states that shortly after the Southern Thule landing was discovered, British intelligence reported that the commander in chief of the Argentine navy had probably approved the landing during the prior months.[119] Moreover, earlier that year the British Joint Intelligence Committee had reported that the new Argentine government was likely to have high expectations for the resolution of the Falklands dispute.[120] The British cannot credibly claim that they were uncertain whether the Argentines on Southern Thule were instruments of Argentine authorities or that the deterioration of the dispute was a surprise.[121]

On the other hand, there are indications that the British government still intended the eventual settlement of the dispute to be a peaceful one. After the Southern Thule incident, British policy was to retain sovereignty for as long as possible, while making piecemeal concessions to the Argentines on maritime resources and the Dependencies.[122] In that manner, the government hoped to buy time to persuade the British public to accept concessions on sovereignty.[123] Whitehall saw a joint leaseback alternative, linked to economic cooperation, as the most likely solution to the dispute.[124]

After the Thatcher government came to power, it decided at first to pursue the same policy. Its review of British options listed three possibilities: (1) "Fortress Falklands," (2) no concessions on sovereignty while negotiations dragged on, and (3) substantive negotiations of sov-

119. FRANKS REPORT, *supra* note 20, para. 52.
120. *Id.* para. 50.
121. British intelligence also had concluded that although the Argentine military had refrained earlier from carrying out adventurist acts that would increase President Perón's popularity, its seizure of power had freed it from that constraint. FRANKS REPORT, *supra* note 20, paras. 41, 49, 50. *See also id.* para. 75 (On October 12, 1979, Lord Carrington told the prime minister and other Defence Committee members that "continuing talks but without making any concessions on sovereignty . . . carried a serious threat of invasion").
122. *Id.* para. 61.
123. *Id.*
124. *Id.*

ereignty.[125] Lord Carrington persuaded the Defence Committee to explore the third option as the only one that could avert an Argentine military "invasion,"[126] but Islander objections derailed any renewed consideration of a leaseback option in early January 1981.[127] As a result, it appears that British policy reverted to option 2. The British pursued this course despite the knowledge—demonstrated in the Defence Committee's rationale for preferring option 3—that option 2 was not likely to avert an Argentine military response. British policy toward the Falklands in early 1982 risked Argentine military action, although it conceded nothing on sovereignty and provided inadequately for the islands' defense. At best, this was a confusing policy.

Complex reasons, including divided authority within the British government, occasional bureaucratic irrationality, and the inherent imprecision of tacit communication underlay the Cabinet's decision. First, the demands of the House of Commons that the Islanders' wishes be guaranteed before any transfer of sovereignty could take place conflicted with Foreign Office policy as expressed in Resolution 2065 and in subsequent British acquiescence to Argentine displays of sovereign authority.[128] The origins of this conflict between the Commons and the Cabinet can be traced to the government row over the Memorandum of Understanding. The memorandum's importance became evident in subsequent years. Britain seemed to follow two conflicting policies with regard to the Falklands dispute. After the Memorandum of Understanding was abandoned, the official position followed Commons' demands that Britain would transfer title only with Islander consent. Nevertheless, British actions unofficially signaled gradual withdrawal of British interests and a general British *animus derelinquendi* toward the territory and its inhabitants.

Who was speaking for Britain and under what authority? Again there are formal and informal approaches to the problem. The Cabinet formally charged the Foreign Office with Falklands policy and the Defence Ministry with their defense against armed threat. But the Commons exercised a practical check on the Cabinet's ability to speak for Britain. The distribution of political authority between Whitehall and

125. *Id.* para. 73.
126. *Id.* paras. 75, 80.
127. *Id.* para. 83 (Falklands Joint Council urged that "the British delegation should seek an agreement to freeze the dispute over sovereignty for a specified period of time").
128. *See supra* note 17.

Westminster depended on the factual circumstances in which authority would be exercised. On April 2, 1982, with the invasion of British-held territory causing a national crisis, the House of Commons forcefully demanded that the prime minister choose between action and resignation.[129]

A second cause of ambiguity is the irrationality common to bureaucracies. Relatively mundane bureaucratic decisions, such as taking an icebreaker out of service or permitting a few Argentines to wave their flag over remote rocks, can be inconsistent with the complex national interests of a state. The overwhelming importance of cost cutting in the British bureaucracy during Sir Geoffrey Howe's tenure at the Exchequer made a rational decision about keeping HMS *Endurance* in service impossible at a crucial juncture in the dispute.[130] In context, Lord Carrington's view that decommissioning the *Endurance* could weaken the British sovereignty claim could have been seen as an argument of special interests against cost-cutting measures.

The budgetary pressures that led to the March 1982 decision to decommission the *Endurance* became totally irrelevant within a few days. The Argentine invasion abruptly reordered bureaucratic priorities; national interests that had been compromised earlier suddenly became the overriding national concern.

The expectations established by British signals in the South Atlantic probably would have supported other Argentine actions short of invading the Falklands. For example, it seems that Britain would have done nothing to prevent quiet Argentine exploitation of fishing resources in Falklands waters. Similarly, the dispute in 1980–1981 over oil exploration in Magallanes Este[131] was unlikely to provoke a serious British challenge to Argentine oil activity, as opposed to a challenge to private oil company drilling or production. The British probably would have lost much more in economic terms than they could have gained by destabilizing the military situation around the Falklands. The *Shackleton Report* noted that it would not have been realistic for Britain to develop Falklands oil or fishing resources without Argentine cooperation.

---

129. *See* WAR IN FALKLANDS, *supra* note 6, at 98 ("[t]here was only one way she could respond: by promising to get the islands back").

130. See M. HASTINGS & S. JENKINS, *supra* note 5, at 53.

131. A. SILENZI DE STAGNI, *supra* note 81, at 138–42. *See also* Report of the Special Committee, *supra* note 4, at 28–29.

In sum, the operative limitations on Argentina centered less on tactical particulars, such as whether Argentina could set up a base covertly in populated Falklands territories, than on the British government's fundamental need to avoid public humiliation. Britain's actions were irresponsible in that they communicated opportunities for Argentina but gave little hint of the limitations. Such limitations could have been signaled, for example, by a substantial strengthening of the British garrison on the Falkland Islands after the Southern Thule incident. The incident shows that the process of signaling requires communication of both opportunities and limits in order to avoid unintended and potentially dangerous misunderstandings.

THE WAR IN LEBANON: The Waxing and Waning of International Norms

7

D. BRIAN HUFFORD AND ROBERT MALLEY

PROBLEM

In June of 1982, the Israeli Defense Forces (IDF) began an invasion of Lebanon that lasted over three months, resulted in heavy civilian casualties, and extended over the entire territory of Lebanon, including the occupation of the presidential palace and the capture of Beirut. The purpose of the invasion, according to Israel, was to protect the security of its borders and the security of the state itself, by destroying the bases of the Palestine Liberation Organization (PLO) and restructuring the political power in Lebanon to favor a treaty with Israel. To justify this extensive invasion Israel invoked the norm governing the use of force by a state against an opposition group (whether it is called "terrorist" or one of "national liberation") and against the neighboring country from which that group operates.

The asserted norm of anticipatory self-defense is said to be governed by standards of necessity and proportionality that are widely accepted in the international community.[1] The critical actors in this incident

---

1. See, e.g., M. McDougal & F. Feliciano, Law and Minimum World Public Order: The Legal Regulation of International Coercion (1961). See also M. McDougal & M. Reisman, International Law in Contemporary Perspective: The Public Order of the World Community Part IV (1981).

presumably held certain expectations concerning the proper coercive response by a nation (in this instance, Israel) to the coercive actions or political changes it deemed to be a threat (the PLO).[2] This study explores how those expectations—including the concepts of necessity and proportionality—were affected by the Israeli invasion of Lebanon, premised on the right of self-defense, and the international reaction to those actions and claims.

To study this norm, the factual context of the invasion is presented first, followed by an analysis of the conflicting claims of the actors in the incident. The ultimate outcome of the invasion is then described, to be evaluated in terms of the interactions of the relevant actors and the international appraisal of the lawfulness of the Israeli actions.

FACTS

Israel and the PLO reached what amounted to a de facto ceasefire in June of 1981.[3] Negotiated by the American and Saudi Arabian governments, it was an attempt to end hostilities between the Jewish State and the Palestinian organization. By the time of the ceasefire, the PLO had developed into a virtual state within a state in southern Lebanon, basing its politico-military infrastructure on Lebanon's soil.[4] The precise implications and extent of the ceasefire were never made clear,

2. Because this study's purpose is not to evaluate the political merits of the larger issue of the status of the parties, it pays less attention to the political claims of the Palestinians that reject the very legitimacy of the Israeli state. The PLO, for example, would object to the assumption that Israel has any right to a claim of self-defense against Palestinian activities, let alone against the Lebanese entity. Rather, the purpose of this essay is to weigh as objectively as possible in what manner international perceptions, discourses, and actions have and will influence attitudes taken by elites who find themselves in a situation similar to the Israelis'. As the Israelis have tended to depict the case in terms of a self-defensive move against the PLO threats, the only norm that they may deem relevant—i.e., the only norm that any elite seeking to judge or check Israeli actions had to address—is the norm defining limitations on the use of self-defensive force against outside-based, nonstate, violent actors. As such, this norm is the one most appropriate for our purposes.

3. Two quasi-exhaustive chronologies, compiled from information found through reviewing over eighty publications—American, European, Israeli, Arab, and French—have been especially useful in preparing this section. The first, by Collins, appeared in 44/45 *Journal of Palestine Studies* (Summer/Fall 1982). The second was published in *Revue d'Etudes Palestiniennes* (Aug. 1982) [hereinafter cited as CHRONOLOGY].

4. Congressional Research Service, *Lebanon: Israeli-Palestinian Confrontation*, 32 Issue Brief IB81O9O (Aug. 10, 1982).

however, and on May 13, 1982, Prime Minister Menachem Begin declared that the accumulation of PLO violations made it null and void—a declaration that followed shortly after the Israeli air strike on PLO positions in Lebanon on May 9. Then, on June 4, 1982, Israeli fighters flew over Beruit and in one hour bombed the Palestinian camps of Sabra, Chatila, and the Cite Sportive, acting in apparent retaliation for the assassination attempt on the life of the Israeli ambassador to the United Kingdom, Shlomo Argov, the previous day. The death toll of the bombing was estimated to be near 100, with some 250 wounded. The PLO responded to the Israeli attack by shelling northern Galilee, as well as the enclave held by long-time Israeli ally, Commandant Saad Haddad. The shelling prompted further actions by Israel; on the following day, it bombed southern Lebanon, essentially attacking three zones: to the north, Damour; in the center, Zahrani; and to the south, Rachidey. This led to a heavy artillery barrage by the PLO in northern Israel.[5]

The real "peace for Galilee" operation, as Israel called it, began on Sunday, June 6. Entering Lebanon through three axes—the coastal road toward Tyr, the central sector through Haddad's enclave, and the eastern border from Chebaa to the Litani River—with over 250 tanks and thousands of infantrymen, the IDF initiated the invasion of Lebanon, assisted by air raids, and ignoring the presence of United Nations troops.[6] At the time, however, the ultimate goal of the operation remained unclear: the announced aim of the action was the protection of the population of northern Israel, with the express objective of establishing a forty-kilometer (twenty-five mile) *cordon sanitaire* on the Lebanese border, a demilitarized zone to protect Israel from PLO incursions and bombings. But within only a few days the forty-kilometer line had been surpassed and the Israelis had engaged in brief, decisive battles with Syrian forces, which led to the destruction of the Syrian ground-to-air defense system and of one quarter of the Syrian air force.

By June 9, the extent of the invasion became clear, with Israel then in charge of 2,500 square kilometers—a quarter of Lebanon. To the west, the Israeli forces had reached Saadiyat, to the north, the limit was defined by the Saadiyat/Ain Dara line, just a few kilometers south of

5. CHRONOLOGY, *supra* note 3, at 86.
6. For a full account of the initial stages of the war, see ZE'EV SCHIFF & EHUD YA'ARI, ISRAEL'S LEBANON WAR 109, 113 (1984). *See also* G. BALL, ERROR AND BETRAYAL IN LEBANON 139 (1984).

the Beirut–Damascus road in the Chouf region. The strategy—whether preceding the invasion or arrived at progressively[7]—was to entrap the PLO, not simply to push north. By the end of the day, Beirut was only four kilometers away, and the local population was being asked to protect the *fedayeen* of the PLO no longer. Israeli and Lebanese phalangist forces had linked up in Beirut by June 14, thus beseiging the PLO forces.

At this time, the invasion had essentially become a showdown between the IDF and the PLO, since on June 11 a ceasefire had been concluded with Syria, with informal understandings also reached between Israel and what remained of the Lebanese political power base.[8] While Lebanon's capital was being encircled, which occurred as soon as June 13, so was its political headquarters. Baabda, the location of the presidential palace, was taken by the IDF and placed under the direct control of Israeli defense minister and mastermind of the invasion, Ariel Sharon. According to Israeli correspondents, Ze'ev Schiff and Ehud Ya'ari, the aims of the invasion at this point were "(1) eliminating the PLO as an independent political factor . . . ; (2) cutting Syria down to size and neutralizing the threat it posed to Israel; [and] (3) installing an allied regime in rehabilitating Lebanon under the rule of [Phalangist leader] Bashir Gemayel."[9]

CONFLICTING CLAIMS AND CONCEPTIONS OF LAWFULNESS

Little can be said about the Israeli invasion that is not adamantly denied by one of the parties. In certain conditions of warfare, where politics require that neither side explicitly recognize the legal right to exist of the other and where one key actor, operating within the borders of

7. Schiff and Ya'ari provide a provocative discussion of the disputes and infighting that tore the Israeli Cabinet over the extent of the war. This situation adds a new, complex dimension to the invasion; it remains unclear whether key members of the government were aware of the aims of the operation. SCHIFF & YA'ARI, *supra* note 6, at 56, 301–304.

8. Renewed confrontation between the Israeli and Syrian forces did occur, however.

9. SCHIFF & YA'ARI, *supra* note 6, at 34. The authors also added a fourth goal: "heightening cooperation with the U.S. while further supplanting Soviet influence in the Middle East." However, this motive was not apparent from Israel's actual military moves. The authors also emphasize that these were the goals of Ariel Sharon, the minister of defense, and not those of the entire Cabinet. In any event, the war did seem to revolve around these objectives.

another state, is a guerrilla organization—albeit using many tools of conventional warfare and being recognized by many nations as the lawful representative of a people—conflicting claims and counterclaims abound. To understand these claims, the perspectives of each party must be properly considered. As the International Commission—a private group of international experts chaired by Sean McBride, inquiring into reported violations of international law by Israel during its invasion of Lebanon—explained: "[B]y the very nature of international society, with its decentralized process of decision-making and the absence of international machinery for assessing the claim and counter-claim automatically, it becomes necessary to turn to a state's reasons."[10]

The perspectives of the parties in the incident differ in fundamental ways. Israel's perspective is shaped by the perception of Arab hostility to Israel's existence as a state. In this context, Israel views the PLO as a terrorist group, trying to suppress a race of people, rather than a liberation force, struggling for lost rights; thus, by its very existence, the PLO is a threat to the state of Israel. In contrast, the PLO sees itself as a valid, internationally recognized liberation organization, representing a people dispossessed of their land by Israel. The conflicting visions of Lebanon are also relevant. Because, in the view of Israel, Lebanon's status as an independent country—free to implement autonomous policies—is doubtful, given its dual Palestinian and Syrian occupations, Tel Aviv authorities view their role as a self-defending, even liberating force for Lebanon. The PLO is seen as using the impotence of Lebanon as a protective shield and base of operations for its war on Israel. Conversely, the conflict for the PLO revolves around whether Israel had the right to go to war with it at all, since it sees itself

10. INTERNATIONAL COMMISSION, ISRAEL IN LEBANON 1 (1983). The chairman of the International Commission, Sean MacBride, explained its formation: "[A] small group of concerned and influential persons in the United Kingdom came together in July 1982 and decided to constitute and invite an International Commission to enquire into reported violations of International Law by Israel during its invasion of Lebanon. . . . I [MacBride] agreed to accept this assignment [as chairman] on the strict understanding that the Commission to be appointed would consist of independent and qualified persons of standing and that there would be no attempt to interfere, in any way, with the Commission in the course of its work." *Id.*, at vii. The International Commission consisted of: MacBride, president of the International Peace Bureau; Richard Falk, of Princeton University (appointed vice-chairman of the commission); Kadar Asmul, of Trinity College, Dublin; Brian Bercusson, of Queens College, University of London; Geraud de la Pradelle, of the University of Paris; and Stefan Wild, of the University of Bonn.

as a legitimate political organization, actively participating in Lebanon because Palestinians have been expelled from their land.

Many of the conflicting claims of necessity and proportionality grow out of these basic conflicts in perspective.

Conflicting Claims of Necessity

As noted above, the Israeli position assumes that the nature of the PLO itself is sufficient ground for attempting to eliminate it. Thus, although the PLO may well barricade itself behind the impotent Lebanese state, the Israelis argue that the organization cannot thereby compel Israel to exercise more than the level of restraint it has consistently shown throughout the years. The legal basis for this contention is therefore the law regarding the harboring of violent, terrorist organizations, and a nation's right to self-defense.

One element of this claim of self-defense is necessity: the military action must be vital to protecting the security of the invading state. What is "necessary" of course depends on where one looks for justification. Israel's claims of necessity were based upon its perception that the PLO is an inherent threat to Israeli security, that Lebanon was unable or unwilling to carry out its responsibility to control that threat, and that the claimed PLO actions prior to the invasion constituted precipitating events necessitating armed response.

In justifying its actions as a necessary response to the inherent threat of the PLO, the historical context is critical. Richard Falk raises this point when discussing the 1968 retaliatory Israeli raid on the Beirut airport. Considering only the PLO attack on the El Al passenger plane, which preceded the bombing, the Israeli justification for its reaction, in his view, "turns out to be weak." But, if the justification is based on "the connection between a Lebanese-based liberation movement operating with government knowledge and approval, and the Beirut attack calculated to alter this course of policy," the argument "is far stronger."[11] Similarly, by reviewing the activities of the PLO over the months preceding the 1982 invasion, it may be virtually impossible to justify the necessity of the broad military action that followed. However, Israel's claimed justification for its decision to push forward for

11. Falk, *The Beirut Raid and the International Law of Retaliation* (1969), *reprinted in* Moore, THE ARAB-ISRAELI CONFLICT, VOL. II: READINGS 221, 239 (1975).

the destruction of the PLO was based upon the context of the entire mideast conflict and the ongoing aim of the PLO with respect to Israel. This perspective can be seen in William O'Brien's defense of the Israeli actions when he said: "Israel's war with the PLO . . . in Lebanon is the continuation of a war of legitimate self-defense that has in fact been in progress since the formation of the PLO in 1965."[12] Hence, the view develops that Israeli responses are not mere "reprisals" but are "incidents or phases of the ongoing war."[13] O'Brien adds: "[I]t seems clear that a pattern of continuous terrorist and guerilla attacks emanating from a neighboring state that is under a legal obligation to prevent hostile acts from being launched from its territory will engender self-defense rights."[14] This virtual "state of war" would therefore permit Israel to implement a strategy designed to protect itself in the overall conflict, rather than having to respond only to the most immediate provocation.

Furthermore, Israeli action was necessary because Lebanon had taken no action to deter PLO attacks. The threat to Israel's national security was, according to the Israeli position, the responsibility of Lebanon, justifying steps to be taken in self-defense. Following the Israeli bombing of PLO targets in Beirut in July of 1981, reportedly killing hundreds of civilians, the Permanent Representative of Israel to the United Nations defended the actions to the Security Council, stating that "if a State is unwilling or unable to prevent the use of its territory to attack another State, that latter State is entitled to take all necessary measures in its own defense," and thus, the bombings simply represented Israel's exercise of its "inherent right of self-defense enjoyed by every sovereign state, a right also preserved under Article 51 of the United Nations Charter."[15]

12. O'Brien, *Israel in Lebanon*, MIDDLE E. REV., at 5 (Fall/Winter 1982–83).
13. *Id.* at 6. O'Brien explains: "The reactive, retaliatory character of many Israeli actions was more a matter of assuring domestic morale and providing tactical justifications for measures that were bound to displease a critical international opinion. In essence, however, they were measures of military necessity, usually planned well ahead of their implementation, with a view to the long term strategic goals of the war." *Id.*
14. *Id.* at 9. *See also id.* at 5 (The "long war with the PLO, 1965–1982, is justified as an exercise of the inherent right to self-defense recognized in Article 51 of the U.N. Charter.").
15. 36 U.N. SCOR (2292d plen. mtg.) 21, U.N. Doc. S/PV. 2292 (1981), *cited in* Levenfeld, *Israel's Counter-Fedayeen Tactics in Lebanon: Self Defense and Reprisals under International Law*, 21 COLUM. J. TRANSNAT'L L. 1, 5 (1982).

Beyond this, of course, lies the question of timing in which precipitating events take on their meaning. Israel's claims regarding this issue arise from the framework in which Israel perceives the PLO—as a menace, not as a legitimate organization. The three dimensions of this menace—a direct threat to the Israeli border regions, a threat to the very existence of the state, and a threat to Jews worldwide—were seen to have coalesced in the days preceding the invasion. When Argov was shot by a Palestinian terrorist on June 3, the initial action occurred. The Israelis viewed this as a violation of the July 1981 ceasefire. In response to PLO claims that the perpetrator of the act belonged to a renegade group, one analysis summed up what was probably the feeling in Tel Aviv: The PLO "claims to represent all Palestinians, but . . . tends to be selective about accepting responsibility for acts of Palestinian violence."[16]

When the PLO shelled northern Galilee in retaliation for the Israeli bombing, Israel proceeded with the invasion of Lebanon. The Israeli embassy in Paris explained the rationale behind the action:

> The operation led by the Israeli defense forces against terrorist concentrations in Southern Lebanon is destined to put an end to the continuous and increasing threats on the lives and security of the Israeli population in Galilee. . . .
>
> . . . The terrorist threat against Israel and its population has become imminent because of the numerous and serious violations of the cease fire, including the bombing of towns and villages of northern Galilee, terrorist infiltrations, the smuggling of explosives into Israeli villages and the attempts against the lives of Jews and Israelis abroad.
>
> . . . The terrorist groups have taken advantage of the cease fire [since July 1981] to widen and strengthen their bases and fortifications in Lebanon. . . . They have installed an offensive infrastructure that includes roads, arsenals, missile launching bases, all with a single aim: to be used against the civilian Israeli population.
>
> . . . The central objective of the action undertaken by the IDF is to repel the terrorist artillery out of reach of the cities and villages of Galilee. . . .[17]

16. Wash. Post, June 7, 1982. Upon hearing this objection, Chief of Staff Rafael Eitan reportedly exclaimed: "Abu Nidal, Abu Schmidal!" SCHIFF & YA'ARI, *supra* note 6, at 98.

17. *See* CHRONOLOGY, *supra* note 3, at 93.

In essence, the criteria governing the timing factor were the fact that, according to the Israeli government, the PLO had violated the ceasefire some 150 times between July 1981 and 1982[18] and the Israeli belief that it had become essential to take some kind of action, since "the PLO had been engaged, since 1978, in a frantic process of transformation from a disorderly and lightly equipped guerilla force into something approaching a structured conventional army."[19] Thus, Avner Yaniv concluded, "the longer Israel waited until the showdown, the more difficult and the more costly the task of dislodging the PLO would become."[20]

What Israel may have unofficially viewed simply as timing, the PLO saw in terms of pretexts for an illegal invasion. The PLO based its claims of Israeli illegality upon its own status as a legitimate nationalist organization. By presenting itself as an at least equal partner in its un-official "dialogue" with Tel Aviv, the PLO initiated the debate and fo-cused its claims on who broke the cease-fire first, a perspective Israel gave only limited consideration. In supporting its contention, the PLO argued that if either side had broken the cease-fire, it was the Israelis: by sinking Lebanese fishing boats in 1982, by conducting training ex-ercises in the south, and by violating Lebanese airspace 2,125 times and its territorial waters 652 times.[21] The PLO claimed the definitive

18. Immediately before the invasion, on June 5, Israel's ambassador to the United Nations, Yehuda Blum, mentioned the "150 acts of terrorism instigated by the PLO, originating in Lebanon, against Israelis and Jews in Israel and elsewhere: in Athens, Vienna, Paris, and Mondon." INTERNATIONAL COMMISSION, *supra* note 10, at 2. The office of the UN General Secretary numbered some 47 acts of violence caused by PLO/leftist forces between June 16, 1981, and June 3, 1982. S/14789, at 9–13, S/15194, at 9–11, *quoted in* H. COBBAN, THE PLO, PEOPLE, POWER AND POLITICS 112 (1984).

19. N.Y. Times, Oct. 12, 1982. Schiff & Ya'ari provide details of the PLO's details in this area. SCHIFF & YA'ARI, *supra* note 6, at 83–84.

20. SCHIFF & YA'ARI, *supra* note 6, at 83–84. *See* Yaniv, *Moral Fervor vs. Strategic Logic: A Note on the Rationale of the Israeli Invasion of Lebanon*, MIDDLE E. REV. (Spring/Summer 1983).

21. Christian Sci. Monitor, Mar. 18, 1982. *See also* COBBAN, *supra* note 18, at 112. The Report of the Secretary General of the United Nations Interim Force in Lebanon reported:

There were violations of Lebanese air space by Israeli aircraft and of Lebanese waters by Israeli naval vessels. UNIFIL observed 130 air violations and 62 sea violations in December 1981, 285 air violations and 53 sea violations in January 1982, 121 air violations and 54 sea violations in February, 187 air violations and 97 sea violations in March, 368 air violations and 59 sea violations in April, and 302 air violations and 59 sea violations in May.

breaking of the truce to be the Israeli bombing of a PLO center in the coastal area south of Beirut, apparently in retaliation for the death of one Israeli soldier from a land mine.[22] This bombing was followed, on May 9, by the Israeli bombing of Lebanon in response to the discovery of land mines in Israel and the destruction of a bus in Jerusalem. The PLO reacted to this attack by shelling Israel with rockets and artillery.[23] Soon after, however, the PLO asserted that it attempted to return to the cease-fire, by "reaffirming its commitment to stop all military operations across the Lebanese border,"[24] but Israel did not accept the reaffirmation and proceeded with plans for the invasion.

Controversy also surrounds the assassination attempt of the Israeli ambassador, which Tel Aviv singled out as the most immediate reason for the bombing preceding the invasion. The PLO vehemently denied responsibility. This position was supported when British prime minister Margaret Thatcher revealed that many PLO leaders were found to be on the hit list of the terrorist who attacked the ambassador. Evidence indicated that the assassin worked for Abu Nidal, a PLO renegade excluded from the organization and condemned to death. Yet when Israel retaliated, it bombed in areas where Abu Nidal had no likelihood of being located.

The PLO argued, then, that the "precipitating events" Israel claimed as necessitating the invasion were a mere pretext. Rather, the timing of the invasion, according to the PLO, had little to do with the increased

---

During the period under review, various UNIFIL positions and personnel came under close fire by IDF. Seventeen such incidents were reported. Those incidents as well as the repeated violations of Lebanese territory were strongly opposed.

Doc. 5/15194, 10 June 1982, at 11, para. 45.

22. J. RANDALL, GOING ALL THE WAY: CHRISTIAN WARLORDS, ISRAELI ADVENTURERS AND THE WAR IN LEBANON 3 (1984). Randall summed up the events, stating: "The first Israeli cease-fire violations—in which Israeli warplanes on April 21 killed twenty persons and wounded more than sixty—was carried out in reprisal for the death of an Israeli officer whose jeep blew up on a mine in territory outside Haddad's lines and under nominal U.N. control. In theory, at least, no Israeli should have been in either place. The PLO did not respond."

23. See SCHIFF & YA'ARI, supra note 6, at 55, for a detailed account of these actions and reactions. They stress the fact that Israel deliberately provoked the PLO and claim that when the PLO responded on May 9, "[these] misses were not a display of Palestinian incompetence but a clearly framed message that artillery could be aimed where the terrorists chose. . . ." Id.

24. See Provisional Verbatim Record of the 2,375th Security Council Meeting, at 3. See also SCHIFF & YA'ARI, supra note 6, at 107–108, 116.

threat and much more to do with the political prospects of Palestinian gains and the opportunity for Israel to strike with the least resistance. In this context, the precipitating events were actually the state of inertia in which the Arab world found itself—paralyzed by Camp David, the Iraq/Iran war, the division between Syria and Libya on the one side and Jordan and Iraq on the other, and the diplomatic offensive of the PLO tending toward a mutual recognition policy. Uri Avineri, an Israeli publisher and journalist, claims that Issam Sartaoui was scheduled to announce this policy shift on June 14, but the events apparently stopped such plans, if indeed they existed.[25] An Israeli historian Yehoshua Porath explains: "The decision of the government flowed from the very fact that the cease-fire had been observed."[26] From the Palestinian perspective, there was nothing that Begin feared more than a moderate Palestinian leadership capable of accepting the minimal objective of West Bank and Gaza autonomy in a confederation with the Hashemite kingdom of Jordan. For if the Palestinians were to take a moderate stance toward the Middle East conflict, Israel would be forced either to recognize the need to deal with them or to appear to the international community as the sole cause of the problems in the area. Moreover, the invasion coincided with the establishment of an increasing number of Israeli settlements in the occupied territories, which pointed to a link between Israel's northern and eastern border security concerns and overall security strategy.

To Israel, the PLO was a menace to its security, justifying the initial drive into Lebanon. Moreover, given the lack of independence of the Lebanese political system, something had to be done to eradicate the threat permanently. In contrast, the PLO sees the survival of its people at stake, as well as the sovereignty and independence of Lebanon. The PLO thus rejected the Israeli claim that Lebanese sovereignty was violated both by the PLO and by Syria. In the PLO's view, its presence on Lebanese soil was legitimized and regulated by the 1969 Cairo agreements, which were subsequently reaffirmed. As for the Syrian pres-

---

25. See CHRONOLOGY, supra note 3, at 177.

26. Ha'aretz, June 25, 1982. On the same matter, the International Commission found that the "cease-fire had the effort of enhancing the legitimacy of the PLO as a responsible political body. The dynamics of such a development could well have brought on world-wide pressure at some future date for negotiations between Israel and the PLO on the future of the Occupied Territories." INTERNATIONAL COMMISSION, supra note 10, at 9.

ence, it was agreed upon in the wake of the 1976 civil war at the Riyadh Arab summit, with Lebanon's consent. The mandate of the peace-keeping force—essentially Syrian—was to expire three weeks after the invasion began, on July 27, 1982.[27] From this perspective, the Israeli march into Beirut was perceived by the PLO as being part of a long-term political strategy to exterminate a people and complete the balkan-ization of the region into states neutralized by Israel's military and po-litical might.[28]

The conflicting claims of the necessity of Israel's initial decision to undertake the invasion are typical of those presented in an incident involving anticipatory self-defense. Their resolution tends to be based on a choice between conflicting characterizations of the facts of the incident—did the PLO constitute a serious threat to the security of Is-rael? Was that threat immediate enough to justify armed response? The standards of necessity upon which the parties in this incident based their claims may not have exerted unusual pressures on the norm of self-defense.

Conflicting Claims of Proportionality

In order to evaluate the claims of proportionality, it is necessary to eval-uate the actual extent of the invasion. Initially, Israel presented the operation as a strictly limited self-defensive move, destined to "place all the civilian population of the Galilee beyond the range of the terrorists' fire."[29] This objective was equated with the symbolic forty-kilometer line. However, when Israeli forces went beyond the line shortly after the invasion began, the limited nature of the exercise became suspect, and it soon became clear that the Israeli invasion was going beyond a punctual, "surgical" operation on Israel's borders.

The justification for the extent of the actions tended to translate "proportionality" into "effectiveness," as Israel had to extend the con-cept of proportionality in order to justify its actions—pressuring for ex-tension of the acceptable extent, duration, and essential nature of an-ticipatory self-defense. The proportionality of the invasion was not

27. *See* SALLY V. MALLISON & W. THOMAS MALLISON, ARMED CONFLICT IN LEBANON, 1982: HUMANITARIAN LAW IN A REAL WORLD SETTING 4 (1983).

28. Some have suggested that Israel was pursuing economic goals in Lebanon as well, in an attempt to dislocate the Lebanese economy. For a summary of this argument, *see* INTERNATIONAL COMMISSION, *supra* note 10, at 11–12.

29. INTERNATIONAL COMMISSION, *supra* note 10, at 2.

linked to past Palestinian attacks or to imminent threats but rather to a potential, long-range danger represented by the PLO and the politico-military situation in its entirety. Thus, the Israeli action gradually shifted from the forty-kilometer line to an all-out attack against the PLO, Syrian forces in Lebanon, and the existing Lebanese political structure. Without this extension of the operation in Lebanon, it would have amounted to a minimal action incapable of preventing renewed activity against Israel, either from a reemerging PLO taking advantage of the Lebanese state's weaknesses, or under the umbrella of an over-whelming Syrian presence. Each phase could only be completed effec-tively with the actual implementation of its two complements. Accord-ing to Schiff and Ya'ari, Sharon gave a complete description of the war objective months before the invasion was initiated:

> I am talking about an action that will mean destroying the terrorist organizations in Lebanon in such a way that they will not be able to rebuild their military and political base. It is impossible to do this without running into the Syrians. . . . It is possible to achieve [a long-lasting change] on condition that a legitimate regime emerges in Lebanon, not a puppet government, that it sign a peace treaty with Israel.[30]

30. SCHIFF & YA'ARI, *supra* note 6, at 42. The express aim of Israel with regard to the PLO began to become more explicit soon after the 1981 bombing, turning from efforts to deter further violence against Israel to actual efforts to destroy the Palestinian infra-structure in Lebanon. Then prime minister Menachem Begin stated in 1981:

We will not intentionally direct our fire against the civilian population. We shall, however, continue to attack terrorist bases and headquarters, even if they are pur-posely located in the vicinity of or within civilian concentrations.
  Responsibility shall fall on those who seek immunity for themselves by knowingly endangering civilians.

N.Y. Times, July 19, 1981, at 1, Col. 3. This conclusion is also demonstrated by the fact that on June 10 Moshe Arens said that Israel might withdraw from Lebanon within a few months if a new Lebanese regime was set up, although on June 24, Sharon ac-knowledged that the twenty-five-mile or forty-kilometer security zone was the minimal goal of the invasion. The inconsistency may be explained in part by the fact that Sharon's intentions were not necessarily understood by other members of the Israeli Cabinet. Ac-cording to Schiff, "Ariel Sharon coordinated a very subtle coup whereby the cabinet's decision-making powers were unilaterally assumed by the defense ministry." More pre-cisely, he contended that at a Cabinet meeting on June 10 and 11, four days after the invasion, Sharon told the government that the army would not proceed into Beirut,

The logic of Israel's aim was clear to Vice-Premier David Levy, who explained on July 9: "Everybody realizes today that Beirut is the center and the headquarters of the PLO's military operations. The government, having decided on the 5th to destroy the military infrastructure of the PLO in Lebanon, it is obvious it had to reach Beirut."[31] Summarizing the evolution of the Israeli thought on the invasion, Jonathan Randall wrote:

> Simply to seize the area between the two rivers meant perpetual occupation; if the Israeli army were withdrawn, the PLO would come back in again, within rocket and artillery range of the Galilee. Every successive Palestinian target led farther north to yet another. So, from the very beginning, the only practical military solution was to destroy the PLO headquarters and infrastructure in Beirut.[32]

Significantly, Sharon explained that "[w]hen we mentioned the security belt, we never said we were going to leave the terrorists behind it."[33] Moreover, according to the argument of Tel Aviv, the elimination of the PLO could lead to the conclusion of peace treaties with all Arab states and to a semi-autonomy for the inhabitants of the occupied territories. In this context, Sharon's June 18 statement, when he described his aim as being to "establish in the very next few days, contacts with moderate political elements in the West Bank in order to form a Palestinian leadership accepting the principle of autonomy as Israel understands it," takes on additional meaning.[34] He alluded to this goal even earlier, stating on June 3: "We must act for the definitive destruction [of the PLO], and only that will permit the conclusion of the proc-

---

although he had reached a contrary decision on the morning of June 10. See N.Y. Times, Mar. 6, 1984, with extracts from SCHIFF & YA'ARI, supra note 6.

31. See CHRONOLOGY, supra note 3, at 160.

32. RANDALL, supra note 22, at 3. As the International Commission explained it: "[T]he Israeli view is that the right to self-defense goes beyond the idea of protecting borders implicit in Article 51 of the [U.N.] Charter and permits a state to take action, given the decentralized nature of international society, against the 'center of terrorism.'" INTERNATIONAL COMMISISON, supra note 10, at 4.

33. INTERNATIONAL COMMISSION, supra note 10, at 4.

34. CHRONOLOGY, supra note 3, at 118. Sharon also said: "The bigger the blow and the more we damage the PLO's infrastructure, the more the Arabs in Judea and Samaria and Gaza will be ready to negotiate with us and establish co-existence." The Times (London), Aug. 5, 1982, 1, 8, at col 3.

ess engaged at Camp David, as well as the signing of other agreements with Israel's remaining neighbors."[35]

With the goal of the war extending to the entire territory of Lebanon, the political makeup of the nation inevitably became a critical factor.[36] The threat to Israel could be said to have its roots in the weaknesses of the Lebanese state—if such a thing still existed—in its unwillingness or incapacity to control the activities of the PLO forces stationed in the country. The military dimensions of this realization implied the occupation of vast regions of the territory and the attempt to make the Lebanese civilian population exert enough moral pressure on the government to incite it to remove the PLO. More importantly, the political dimension of the operation required changing the political map of the country to the advantage of the only faction willing to cooperate with Israel and expel Arafat and his men: the Phalange of Bechir Gemayel. The extent of the war was therefore determined to a significant degree by the desire to tip the balance of power in a highly divided country in favor of one group.[37]

The Israeli strategy in Lebanon illuminates the evolution in military doctrine caused by the changing political environment. Prior to the invasion, Israeli efforts had focused on retaliatory responses seeking to deter foreign governments from harboring or assisting the PLO. But, as Yanin explains, "to apply this approach to Lebanon was . . . more complicated because of the absence of a government capable of re-

35. CHRONOLOGY, *supra* note 3, at 86.

36. Blum declared on June 6: "As long as these non-Lebanese elements are allowed to operate within and from Lebanon, no real progress will be achieved towards a return of the effective authority of the government of Lebanon throughout the length and breadth of the country." INTERNATIONAL COMMISSION, *supra* note 10, at 2.

37. Evidence that all three aspects of the invasion were in the minds of the war strategists is given in Schiff & Ya'ari. In particular, it is claimed that the general staff meeting of May 13, 1982—only three days after the Cabinet meeting that reportedly espoused the forty-kilometer version—made this explicit. SCHIFF & YA'ARI, note 6, at 53. Decisions taken early on in the war illuminate this point. On Sunday, June 6, the choice was made that "called for a division to make its way up the central axis through the Shouf Mountains to the Beirut–Damascus highway and then turn East. . . . The corollary of this decision was incontestable: it meant war with the Syrians. . . ." *Id.* at 112. Moreover, "[f]rom the outset the division climbing up the Shouf Mountains was aiming farther than the forty-kilometers." *Id.* at 113. By the second day of the war, on June 7, voluntary clashes with Syrian forces were "the first signal to Damascus that Israel did not intend to limit its military operation to South Lebanon." *Id.* at 155.

straining the PLO."[38] With neither the Lebanese government nor the Christian Phalangist militia able to deport the PLO, limited actions were fruitless in the long run. And the strategies employed earlier in Egypt, Jordan, and Syria were simply unworkable in Lebanon.[39]

The rationale of the Israelis thus derived from their own view of their "presence" in a country they considered to be occupied both by Syria and the Palestinians. From Israel's perspective, the Syrian troops, under the guise of Arab Deterrent Forces, and the PLO, under the mask of Arab solidarity, made a mockery of Lebanese sovereignty. Hence, the Israelis argued, opposition against an Israeli invasion of a country that has not known freedom for a number of years would appear weak and hypocritical.[40]

Tel Aviv, then, presented a picture of itself as a "liberation" army, with no territorial ambitions, merely seeking the security of its own state while ridding its neighbor of occupying forces. On June 13, Joseph Rom—Likud deputy and member of the commission on security and foreign relations in the Knesset—explained the Israeli plan: "We will stay in Lebanon as long as a political solution . . . is not found."[41] The ultimate aim of this plan was described by Israel's embassy in Paris as follows: "Israel continues to aspire to a peace treaty with an independent Lebanese State, while preserving its integrity."[42]

The Israeli position was based on a concept of proportionality that looked beyond the immediate events justifying armed force to a broader concept of threat. According to the Israeli theory of proportionality, if a terrorist organization has so undermined the sovereignty of its "host" country and poses a continual threat to the very existence of a nation, proportionality is not measured in terms of retaliation of act for act, but requires action that effectively removes the threat entirely. To justify this goal, Israel had to redefine anticipatory self-defense to include not

38. Yaniv, *supra* note 20.

39. The Israelis point to the 1978 Litani operation as a precedent. Essentially limited to southern Lebanon, it failed to remove the threat posed to the inhabitants of Galilee, in northern Israel.

40. An Israeli spokesman referred to a "war of aggression [which] has been waged by the PLO and Syria in Lebanon since 1975, a war which has wreaked destruction in that state and undermined the normal functioning of its government." INTERNATIONAL COMMISSION, *supra* note 10, at 4.

41. CHRONOLOGY, *supra* note 3, at 104.

42. *Id.* at 93.

merely actions designed to limit a state of war but also actions designed to structure political situations to achieve peace.[43]

In responding to Israel's position that the only effective action that would provide security to its people was the total elimination of the PLO and the restructuring of Lebanon, the PLO focused on the immediate actions of both parties as the proper measure of proportionality. The Palestinians insisted that the total number of Israelis killed during fifteen years of cross-border raids had been 106, compared to the 200 killed by the Israelis in the most recent bombing raids, demonstrating the disproportionate impact of the Israeli actions in comparison to those of the PLO.[44] The PLO's position had its roots in what appeared to it to be the very premise of the ceasefire: indirectly, it had given the two belligerents equal status, and both were thus to be measured by the same standards.[45] Further, the PLO focused on the relative strength of the parties to demonstrate the disproportionate nature of Israel's actions. The "military threat" to Israel caused by the PLO, though at times played up by the Palestinian media, has been denied in private and official communications. Although Prime Minister Begin continued to speak of fifteen Palestinian brigades, or five divisions, for example, Schiff and Ya'ari, relying on official Israeli statistics, write that "the quantity of men and material represented the power of about one infantry division with enough weapons to equip another force of approximately the same size."[46]

By focusing on the comparison of a minimal immediate PLO threat with the extensive military reaction by Israel, the PLO argued for the application of more traditional standards of proportionality.[47]

43. See text accompanying notes 34–35, *supra*.

44. The International Commission noted this argument, concluding that Israel's "reactions have always been overwhelming, premeditated and all out of proportion to any initial 'wrong.' " INTERNATIONAL COMMISSION, *supra* note 10, at 18.

45. In many ways the very existence of the cease-fire was a moral victory for the PLO, because indirectly it had to give the two belligerents equal status in order for an effective "agreement" to be reached between the parties. By the same token, however, once the cease-fire was broken, Israel quickly retreated into a position from which it may fundamentally never have departed, that of refusing to consider demands by a group dedicated to its destruction.

46. SCHIFF & YA'ARI, *supra* note 6, at 135. *See also* CHRONOLOGY, *supra* note 3, at 172.

47. For a more complete view of the standard requirement of proportionality as applied in this case, see MALLISON & MALLISON, *supra* note 27, at 27–29.

OUTCOME

Soon after Israeli forces entered Lebanon, they moved on Beirut, with continuous shelling of West Beirut from early on and a total blockade initiated on July 3.[48] Two days later, Israel began a total economic and military seige of the Lebanese capital. Throughout the period, Israel was pushing for the removal of Syrian and PLO forces from Lebanon. As early as June 16, Sharon had reported that a final agreement on the withdrawal of Israeli forces would have to include an agreement for all foreign forces to leave. By July 1, Saeb Salam declared that the PLO would leave Beirut, and on August 8, after lengthy behind-the-scene negotiations, Arafat publicly announced that an agreement had been reached between PLO and Lebanese officials on a Palestinian evacuation to Syria, Jordan, Egypt, and Iraq. Finally, the kinks were worked out of the plan, and on August 20 Israeli forces withdrew from the Beirut port. The following day, as Israel pulled back from the "Green Line"—separating East from West Beirut—the PLO fighters began to evacuate, and French troops arrived as the first of the multinational peace-keeping force (MNF) to oversee the evacuation. Syrian forces followed the PLO out of Lebanon on August 30 and 31, with the final PLO fighters departing for Syria on September 1.

This result did not occur without significant influence from the international community. A major part of the negotiations over the Lebanese settlement revolved around the role of the United Nations in the evacuation. Arafat wanted some form of a multinational force to protect refugee camps and leftist Muslim groups remaining in Lebanon after the PLO soldiers departed. But Israel continued to oppose direct UN intervention, preventing its observers from entering Beirut on August 2 and again on August 5. By August 8, Israel was prepared to accept the MNF, but only after the PLO forces had departed. Subsequently, Israel agreed in principle to U.S. negotiator Phillip Habib's plan for the simultaneous departure of the PLO and the arrival of the MNF.

Instead of pulling back after the PLO and Syrian armies left, however, Israel saw a need to continue to exert its presence, bombing Beka'a on September 13. The next day, the Israelis received the justi-

---

48. In general, the information in this section was taken from the report of the International Commission, *supra* note 10, especially from the Chronology of Events, Appendix III. Where appropriate, individual citations are provided.

fication to move in again. President-elect Bashir Gemayel—the head of the Israeli-supported Phalangist faction, who had risen to power with the help of the Israelis—was assassinated, along with over fifty Phalangists. On September 15, the Israeli Defense Forces entered West Beirut for the first time, claiming a need to prevent serious incidents following the assassination. Near total occupation of West Beirut began the following day, with Palestinian camps encircled. Christian militia were allowed to enter Sabra and Chatila and the infamous massacre of Palestinian refugees began, continuing until September 18.

The IDF began to withdraw on September 20, and by September 23 the first units of the MNF, including marines from the United States, returned to West Beirut, professing a desire to help Amin Gemayel, who had been elected president two days earlier. The IDF pulled completely out of West Beirut on September 26, three and one-half months after it entered Lebanon.

The initial results of the invasion seemed to achieve what Israel had intended: the Syrians had been beaten, minimizing for the moment their influence in Lebanon; the Lebanese leftist and Moslem parties were suppressed and disarmed by the Israeli army surrounding Beirut, giving President Gemayel the occasion to assert control; and the PLO guerrillas were removed from Lebanon, appearing to offer the opportunity that Israel perceived as key to peace in the Middle East, a unified Lebanon, and a peace treaty with Israel. But it did not work out. Deeprooted problems between Moslem and Christian factions in Lebanon persisted. And as a senior Christian Lebanese banking official was quoted as saying, the United States never recognized "that a Phalangist president had been imposed on the country by the Israeli invasion and that that could cause problems later on."[49]

Soon after Amin Gemayel took over, the Lebanese government and army became identified with the United States, but Lebanese unity did not grow with the power of the military over the country. Instead, Gemayel used the army to reinforce his own power, creating antipathy to the American presence. For months negotiations between Israel and Lebanon continued over troop withdrawal, with little success. It was not until May 17, 1983, that an accord was finally reached. But the negotiations had taken so long that the Syrian influence had built back

49. Friedman, *American's Failure in Lebanon*, N.Y. Times Magazine 32, 37 (Apr. 8, 1984).

up, preventing the success of Israel's efforts. Thomas Friedman explains:

> In the view of the Lebanese opposition, [the May 17 accord] was far too favorable to Israel, and took so long to negotiate that by the time it was ratified, Syria had recovered from its 1982 defeat and was in a strong position to scuttle the accord.
> With Moscow's help, Syria had been able to rebuild its entire army and air-defense system during the seven and ½ months it took for the accord to be negotiated. More important, the Syrians had discovered that the policies of the Gemayel Government had created a substantial opposition coalition within Lebanon through which they could work to undermine the agreement.[50]

Israel eventually decided that the casualties occurring during the policing of the Shuf Mountains were too high, and saw the difficulty, if not impossibility, of Gemayel working out an understanding with the Druse and Shiite opposition. The Israelis thus withdrew from the Shuf and the area around Beirut on August 31, 1983. Friedman describes the import of this decision:

> In retrospect, the American military officials say, what the Israelis were essentially doing was giving up on their wider political ambitions for Lebanon—ambitions that the United States had indulged and worked for—and focusing entirely on their security considerations.
> "The Israelis retreated to the south," commented an official American source close to the situation, "and left us holding the bag."[51]

Ultimately, the aims of the war were to deal the PLO a crippling blow, to remove a Syrian presence in Lebanon, and to bring about a more favorable political order in Lebanon. On each of these dimensions, the results were at best ambiguous, and on the whole could be viewed as total failures. The PLO has arguably suffered immensely from the loss of its last effective front-line base. Militarily it now lacks its former credibility. More indirectly, the war also led to divisions within the PLO while deepening those between Palestinians and Syri-

50. *Id.*, at 40.
51. *Id.*, at 42.

ans. However, the essential and central political issue is as burning as ever; the PLO's purpose and, more important, its support, remain. Schiff and Ya'ari concluded: "The Lebanon war has in no way tempered the virulence of the Palestinian problem—which is hardly surprising, inasmuch as the roots of that problem do not lie in Lebanon."[52]

In the initial stage, Syria did retreat to a more discrete position on the Lebanese scene. But as events unfolded and as Israel realized the futility of its attempts to control Lebanese developments, Syria quickly reacquired its role as power broker in Beirut and, by some accounts, eventually strengthened its influence. As for Lebanon itself, not only was the May 17 agreement eventually repudiated, but also the political scene was soon dominated by Damascus-backed Shiite forces, with the Christians increasingly relying on Assad's protection. As the results of the invasion came clearer, it began to seem as if "close to 600 Israelis and 250 Americans lives had been lost in Lebanon just to bring the situation full circle."[53]

INTERNATIONAL APPRAISAL

The Israeli invasion of Lebanon was a highly visible international incident, generating ideological, economic, diplomatic and military responses from around the world. In appraising the incident, the world was divided roughly into two "camps": those who understood the conflict in terms of self-defense (whether or not they accepted the Israeli view of the conflict), and those rejecting this construct. Among the former group, reaction shifted from partial and implicit acquiescence to outright condemnation and tentative control as the Israeli action extended further into Lebanon. The perceptions of the latter group consistently condemned the Israeli action but took few controlling actions to deter it.

This section will examine first the reactions of these two groups to the initial decision to invade and the effect of that reaction upon the necessity standard of the norm of anticipatory self-defense. The shift in reaction that occurred as the invasion continued will then be explored, along with its effects upon the standards of proportionality.

52. SCHIFF & YA'ARI, *supra* note 6, at 306.
53. *Id.* at 299. One should not forget, of course, that Americans and Israelis were not the only victims, nor did they have the greatest number of casualties.

International Appraisal of the Decision to Invade:
The Necessity Standard

The observers that reject the characterization of this incident as engaging the norm of self-defense include the Soviet Union, the Arab states, and of course the Palestinians themselves. Among those nations viewing the incident as potentially engaging the self-defense norm, the decision to invade was initially supported (as by the United States) or somewhat tolerated (as by the European community).

Nations Rejecting a Self-Defense Characterization. Fundamentally, the perceptions of the USSR and the Arab nations, in their refusal to consider any aspect of the Israeli justification, can be seen as having set the precedence of national struggle over state security needs. However, by deliberately placing themselves outside of any framework acceptable to the Israelis, these actors have, in effect, forfeited their claim to authoritative influence upon Israeli expectations. The only way in which the declamatory disapproval of these nations could be translated into effective opposition (i.e., an opposition having long-lasting effects on the evolution of international law) is through forceful actions. We must see, then, whether these actors that reject the Israeli framework took that forceful action necessary to create expectations of a control intention.

To understand the Soviet response it is important to explore its predispositions. As expressed in the government-controlled Soviet media, the PLO is a "national liberation organization"—rather than a terrorist force—struggling against a local manifestation of imperialism. Thus, "any attack against [the PLO] is both an 'international crime' and an offensive against the people [it] represents."[54] The journal *Komsomolskaya Pravda* clearly expressed the Soviet view: "The raids by Palestinian partisans [from Lebanon] on the territory occupied by Israel have never been proscribed by the U.N. Security Council, while Israel's actions against the Arab people of Palestine have been described as aggression on several occasions, . . . and so, counteractions by Palestinian people may with every justification be regarded as the exercising of their legitimate right of self-defense."[55] The situation is then viewed

54. *See* Spulber, *Israel's War in Lebanon through the Soviet Looking Glass*, MIDDLE E. REV. (Spring/Summer 1983).
55. Pravda, Aug. 12, 1982.

as one in which the Palestinians are the threatened party, not Israel. And in Lebanon, "Israel is perpetrating a criminal act of genocide."[56] Following the 1982 invasion, however, there was a problem in delivering on this policy.

Generally, Moscow limited itself to issuing "stern warnings" to Israel, to the United States, and to the Arabs. Israel was reminded that the "Middle East is an area in close proximity to the Soviet Union," and the United States was warned not to send marines into Lebanon.[57] As for the Arabs, they were blamed for watching the destruction "with feebleness and apathy."[58] Although there is clear ideological commitment to these protestations, the gap between action and rhetoric brings into doubt the Soviet intention to enforce its appraisal. This Soviet inaction provided an important signal to the Israelis that actual enforcement of the Soviet view would be delegated to the Arab states.

The main purpose of the Soviet response, then, was to indicate that, though it condemned the Israeli actions, it would not take strong action against Israel as long as the United States also left direct enforcement to nations within the region. One important factor that influenced Soviet reaction was its continuing perception that despite the strategic importance of the Middle East, its main value to the Soviet Union lies in its weight in the U.S.–USSR confrontation. Accordingly, the ultimate target of Moscow's communications—and the final barrier on Soviet actions—was and is Washington. The Soviet Union sought to avoid a superpower conflict over its treaty with Syria more than it desired to punish the Israelis. Since the Syrians also wanted to avoid an "all-out-war" with Israel, Galila Golan noted, "[i]n the present war, these Soviet preferences presumably caused little difficulties between Moscow and Damascus."[59]

Overall, the underlying message of the Soviets to the Americans concerned the risks of an Israeli/Syrian confrontation growing out of a war they disapproved of but could do little or nothing to prevent. As Golan writes: "The noteworthy point was that although Brezhnev underlined Moscow's concern by referring to its interest in a conflict located in close proximity to its southern border, he did not include anything

56. *Id.*, June 15, 1982.
57. *Id.*, June 14, 1982.
58. *Id.*, June 15, 1982.
59. Golan, *The Soviet Union and Israeli Action in Lebanon*, INT. AFF. 7 (Jan. 1983).

which might be construed as an ultimatum or operative steps should the demand for a halt to hostilities and Israeli withdrawal be ignored."[60] The Israelis knew to what audience the Soviets' message was aimed and what ultimate concern motivated it. Thus, those actions the Soviet Union did take had little effect. For example, when the Soviet Union told radical Palestinian PFLP leader George Habbash that it was considering reinforcing its Mediterranean fleet, implying the move was in response to the invasion, the United States explained that this military action was not unusual activity. In sum, through an entirely symbolic act designed to placate Arab demands, the Soviets were telling the Israelis and the Americans that they were, in effect, doing nothing. In this case, the Soviet actions were especially significant when compared to the dramatic airlifts of the Yom Kippur War. Other gestures also require reexamination. Though Moscow dispatched General Yevgeniy Yurasov, deputy commander of the Soviet air defense forces, to Damascus, this diplomatic strategy was clearly not a strong step. Golan explains: "[I]f Moscow wanted to signal its intention of guaranteeing Syria's air defense, it would have done so more blatantly and officially."[61] It is also noteworthy that the Soviets made little reference to the Israeli/Syrian skirmishes, thus de-dramatizing them. Though officially depicted by the Soviets as an unjustifiable genocidal act, the Israeli war effort was not the real concern of the USSR, which "seemed to be limiting its commitment quite clearly to Syria proper."[62] The emphasis of the Soviet responses, then, did not revolve around Lebanon or the PLO, an organization with which the Soviet Union has had ambiguous relations,[63] but rather was determined by the global politics of superpower relations and by the Soviet relationship with Syria, the only reliable asset for the USSR in the region.

The best illustration of the ultimate concern of the Soviets in pre-

60. *Id.* at 8.
61. *Id.*
62. *Id.* at 9.
63. The Palestinians, however much they needed Moscow's diplomatic and material support, grew increasingly suspicious of Soviet intentions. Aby Iyad, one of the top PLO leaders, stated that from "the first hour, we wanted the Soviet position to be more radical, but our Soviet brothers have their own way of acting." Radio Monte Carlo, June 11, 1982. Nawef Hawatmeh, head of the DFLP, complained that the result of the Soviet deeds was "limited, if not zero." Reuter, June 26, 1982. As for the letter Brezhnev sent to Arafat, Abu Iyad commented that it "contained pretty words, but they have no bases on the ground." Radio Monte Carlo, June 26, 1982.

venting outside action, especially by the United States, came in the final stages of the conflict. As the PLO was being beseiged in West Beirut, and no concrete Soviet response was forthcoming, only the possibility of the introduction of U.S. marines in the area seemed to (mildly) alter the Soviet attitude. "The July 8 warning" about this impending move, according to Golan, "did not even mention Israeli withdrawal from Lebanon, an omission designed perhaps to lower the price necessary for American agreement to desist from sending troops, a move obviously considered more threatening to Soviet interests than the continued presence of the Israeli army in Lebanon."[64] The Soviet Union also initially opposed the presence of a French contingent in Beirut, while Arafat had pressed for it. This again demonstrates that the Soviets were more concerned with their rhetorical battle with the West than with supporting the PLO.

Although ideologically supporting the PLO position, the Soviet Union viewed the conflict in a global, geopolitical framework in which the Israeli invasion was seen as a peripheral concern. A further factor in Soviet inaction might be that the invasion may have even presented some advantages for the Soviets by further polarizing the region, reinforcing the Soviet–Syrian alliance, and deepening American involvement in a "dirty" war that could embitter the United States' relations with moderate Arab states. In sum, the Soviet appraisal of Israel's actions consisted of weak protests against the Israelis and an apparent delegation of enforcement to the Arabs.

The Arabs, however, may also have seen some advantages in crippling the PLO. This was particularly true for Syria, both because of Assad's strained relations with Arafat and because of the continuing Syrian ambition to hold all the Arab cards in the region. Convinced that in the long run the Syrian influence in Lebanese politics could only survive and even be strengthened, Assad may very well have considered that by the elimination of the independent Palestinian organization, Syrian power would be enhanced and the existing PLO power structure could be replaced with leaders more subservient to Syrian influence. This is evidenced by the early Syrian cease-fire with Israel, on June 11, which left the PLO isolated to face the IDF.

Despite the presence of 30,000 Syrian troops in Lebanon on June 5, when Israel began its initial raids into Lebanon leading up to the in-

64. Golan, *supra* note 59, at 14.

vasion, Syria took no action against Israel and, very significantly, no aircraft engaged the Israeli jets invading Lebanese airspace. The only direct Syrian reaction came when they were directly confronted by Israeli forces on the days following. Any "lesson" presented by this reaction could only be to encourage bolder Israeli moves. This conclusion is reinforced by the fact that early on Syria began to move its troops from the Beirut area toward the Beka'a Valley, closer to Syrian security needs and away from any negative influence on Israel.[65] The Syrian response thus tended to mirror that of the Soviets.

The Arab states were often very violent in their denunciation of the Israeli action. By June 4, Lebanese premier Chafiq al-Wazzan called for an emergency meeting of the UN Security Council to deal with the Israeli bombing raids, thus formally rejecting Israel's rationale that its troops were a "liberation" force. In addition, the invasion was the catalyst for the strongest language emanating from Cairo since Anwar Sadat's trip to Israel. On June 6, President Hosni Mubarek denounced the Israeli "invasion," contrasting sharply with Sadat's reaction to the 1978 Israeli offensive. These reactions should not be underestimated; they demonstrate the continuing promotion of a policy condemning the use of force by Israel. Yet, beyond the language, evidence pointed toward Arab paralysis when confronted with the invasion. And it is this type of reaction that could have the effect of encouraging, or at least not discouraging, future uses of force in similar circumstances in which states weigh control intentions more heavily in decisions to act than authority signals. Despite repeated Lebanese demands, the Arab states were incapable—or unwilling—to organize an Arab League meeting early in the crisis. In all, the Arab states seemed to demonstrate that they expected U.S. pressure to achieve results, and were unwilling or, because of division, unable to exert their own influence.

The behavior of those who did not directly confront the norm—i.e., the right of a state to use force against a group it perceives as a threat, in the name of self-defense—did nothing of real substance to influence

65. After the initial Israeli attacks on Syrian forces, Schiff & Ya'ari point out: "[F]ive new batteries of SAM-6 missiles were brought into Lebanon. . . . Yet even while reinforcing their missile system in the Bekaa, the Syrians continued to signal that they did not want war. The new batteries were not transferred from the Syrian heartland but came from the Golan Heights—a definite indication that Damascus was not interested in exacerbating the hostilities and running the risk that the fighting would spread to the Golan or, worse yet, points east." SCHIFF & YA'ARI, *supra* note 6, at 159.

or enhance the effectiveness of the norm to control state actions. Theirs seemed to be a fatalistic attitude, almost accepting the inevitability of an action whose very justification they denounced and rejected. Hence, they relied on constant appeals to the enemy's principal and essential ally, the United States, in the vain hope that the invasion could be stopped at the very source of its conception.

Groups Accepting the Self-Defense Characterization. This fatalist approach was not singular to the Arab nations. Indeed, it seemed to a large extent to have shaped the attitudes and behavior of elites who accepted, in its general contours, the self-defense motive as a potentially valid reason for Israel's actions in the context of the invasion. Thus, although the United States or other Western nations may not have agreed with the military rationale behind the initially forecast Israeli decision to move to the forty-kilometer line, they deemed it acceptable or at least inevitable, given the circumstances of a Lebanon that could not realistically be said to be independent and considering the disproportionality between the potential risks of trying to stop Israel compared to the relatively benign results of another minor Israeli excursion into Lebanon against the PLO.

This experience is actually an example of the Israelis' skill in promoting their views about what constitutes lawful actions while blunting control intentions by presenting actions as inevitable. As Randall notes: "Israel telegraphed its invasion of Lebanon the way bad prize-fighters telegraph punches . . . 'Don't be surprised,' Bechir Gemayel confided to Lebanese newspaper editors in March, 'if you stick your necks out of the office windows and see Israeli tanks in the streets.' "[66] Randall adds:

> The Israelis, virtually from the minute they agreed to the ceasefire in July '81, began to make a case for the invasion of Lebanon by complaining vociferously that the Palestinians there were violating the ceasefire provisions. [Thus, there is created a] sense of inevitability [as] the world becomes so accustomed to Israeli military operations in Lebanon, that even the . . . concerned governments took them for granted.[67]

Judging by reactions expressed in the initial Security Council meetings, key Western powers did condemn Israeli military activity. On

66. RANDALL, *supra* note 22, at 3.
67. *Id.*, at 245.

June 5, the council unanimously called on all parties in the conflict to "cease immediately and simultaneously all military activities within Lebanon and across the Lebanon/Israel border."[68] Moreover, on the following day, the council unanimously adopted a resolution demanding that Israel withdraw its forces "forthwith and unconditionally" from Lebanon.[69]

During a meeting in Versailles on June 6, the industrialized nations renewed their call for an end to military hostilities in the area. France was the most explicit, with French President François Mitterrand stating that "France does not hesitate to condemn the Israeli invasion."[70] The French position was emphasized on June 8, by Foreign Minister Claude Cheysson when he declared that "the condemnation by France of the Israeli invasion is absolute," adding that "it is time to condemn unequivocally the Israeli invasion of Lebanon and to take sanctions against Israel."[71] France's lead was followed by the European Community when, on the following day, the foreign ministers "vigorously condemned the new Israeli invasion of Lebanon," and spoke of eventual "future action" in response to what was viewed as "a flagrant violation of international law."[72] On a more practical level, Paris decided to cancel a scheduled meeting of the mixed Franco-Israeli Commission. The Western press, which did not have the same political limitations on responses as did governments, contributed to the condemnation by adding extensive criticism of the Israeli actions to the environment in which the invasion was being appraised.[73]

68. U.N. Chronicle, Sept. 1982, at 14 (quoting Resolution 508).
69. *Id.* (quoting Resolution 509).
70. *See* CHRONOLOGY, *supra* note 3, at 90.
71. *Id.* at 96.
72. *Id.* at 98.
73. Separating itself from the American view, the *London Times* criticized the U.S. veto of the Security Council resolution for an immediate cease-fire by asking: "What is unbalanced about [the resolution]? Presumably the fact that Israel alone is condemned. But Israel was the only party to have refused compliance with the two previous resolutions, both of which had been passed unanimously. Does 'balance' require that one condemn equally those who comply and those who refuse, and if so, is there any point in passing resolutions at all? The fact is that Israel is the aggressor in this conflict." London Times, June 10, 1982. The *Daily Express* wrote that "the world has stood idly by while Israel has conquered southern Lebanon and besieged Beirut." One should stop Israeli gunfire, it added, and "if the Israelis cannot see this, then the U.S. should make them see." Daily Express, June 9, 1982. *Le Monde* agreed on the necessity for action, declaring: "No one has the right to remain silent." Le Monde, July 7, 1982. And *Le Soir* of

In spite of the condemnatory attitude, however, there remained the impression that most European countries, including France (which played the most visible role), also held to the belief that the Lebanese situation preceding the invasion was equally unacceptable. On June 9, Mitterrand explained what may have been the prevailing view: "We cannot speak [of Lebanese territorial integrity] as a reality but we can and we must speak of it as a will. Lebanon was occupied by two armies before being occupied by a third."[74] Prime Minister Pierre Mauroy added on June 18 that "France asks . . . not only for the withdrawal of Israeli forces . . . but also for the withdrawal of all foreign armies."[75] With France and other European nations condemning both the situation in Lebanon prior to the invasion and the attempt of Israel through the invasion to modify it, it would be difficult for the Israeli elites to develop an understanding of what exactly was expected of them in the future.

In reality, the main source of Israeli support was the United States. Because of its moral, political, and military leverage, it was the single most important actor and communicator watching and appraising the invasion, and by its ultimate inaction, it became Israel's most decisive ally. In evaluating the U.S. reaction, whatever was said or done has to be weighed against what could have been said or done.[76]

Given the potential for action by the United States, and the general frame of mind of policy makers—viewing the PLO as a Soviet proxy and Syria as a (perhaps temporary) foe—U.S. reactions to the invasion appear to have been limited. More important, the message conveyed in the weeks preceding the invasion indicated a generally positive posture vis-à-vis Israeli intentions. Schiff, as military correspondent for *Ha'aretz*, wrote two months before the operation:

> The aim of such intervention would be two-fold: not only to damage Syrian forces, but to destroy the PLO infrastructure in Lebanon, especially in all the territory south of Beirut. Success of such

---

Brussels tried to unmask the ideological double standard of the European states: "Imagine that under some pretext an Arab country had launched a 'reprisal' raid against Tel Aviv and that a hundred Israeli civilians had lost their lives from the bombing. . . . Today hundreds of Lebanese and Palestinian civilians are already dead and many others are threatened with the same fate." Le Soir, July 10, 1982.

74. CHRONOLOGY, *supra* note 3, at 99.
75. *Id.* at 119.
76. For a discussion of U.S. leverage, see BALL, *supra* note 6, chapters 17–21.

action could deal a mortal blow to the PLO. What is more, it is very possible that Israel would meet with understanding in the Reagan administration in this matter. Washington is seeking to check any Soviet clients, and why should it be against harming Moscow's more important clients—Syria and the PLO?[77]

A week later, David Shipler, *New York Times* correspondent to Jerusalem, noted "a basic change in the attitude of the United States toward Israeli military action in Lebanon [that] appears to have given a new flexibility to Israel's Army and Air Force, which have been busy recently with air strikes and ground assaults against Palestinian guerrilla bases in Lebanese territory."[78] This "message" from the United States did not go unnoticed by the rest of the world. As Sheila Ryan writes, although "Begin later insisted that 'sovereign Israel' had no need of a green light from Washington, and a U.S. State Department spokesman denied lamely that the Reagan administration had intended to flash such a signal . . . [T]he concert between the two capitals was nonetheless clear for all the world to see."[79]

During the months preceding the invasion the United States was acutely aware of the Israeli momentum toward attack. The overall effect of the actions taken by the Reagan administration during this period "can only be construed as giving strategic sanction to the attack, while offering tactical restraint."[80] As one example, just before the May 1982 visit by Sharon to the United States, the administration informally notified Congress of the sale of seventy-five additional F-16 fighters to Israel.[81]

With regard to the administration's knowledge of the invasion plans, George Ball concluded: "Not only did the Administration know that Israel planned to invade Lebanon, but it had clear notice well in ad-

77. Ha'aretz, April 10, 1982. Schiff and Ya'ari expanded on this aspect of the incident: "[I]t is clear that the Israeli government had grounds for believing that Washington had indeed bestowed its tacit approval on a limited military action in Lebanon. It was all part of a cagey dynamic prompted by Sharon in which ears strained to hear what was not said rather than what was." SCHIFF &YA'ARI, *supra* note 6, at 76. In this account, just as Sharon took on a pivotal role in Israel, so did Haig in the United States.

78. N.Y. Times, April 18, 1982.

79. Ryan, *Israel's Invasion of Lebanon: Background to the Crisis* 44/45 J. PALESTINIAN STUD. (Summer/Fall 1982), at 34.

80. *Id.* at 36.

81. New Statesman, June 18, 1982.

vance that the IDF would push as far as Lebanon's capital."[82] Schiff and Ya'ari referred to this process as an "illusion of collusion," in which a series of Israeli communications to the Americans—the exchange at Sadat's funeral between Begin and U.S. secretary of state Alexander Haig,[83] the visit by the director of Israel's military intelligence during which the southern suburbs of Lebanon were mentioned, and Sharon's presentation to the U.S. State Department[84]—that elicited little or no U.S. response led Israel to believe it had the "green light" from the United States.[85] As final evidence, Schiff and Ya'ari cite a May 28, 1982, letter Haig wrote to Begin, with the intention of clarifying the American stance. According to the author's analysis:

> [T]his crucial communication contained no hint of a threat or ul-
> timatum to Israel—a favored technique when Washington wished
> to head off an undesirable move on Israel's part. The unconven-
> tional step of Haig reporting directly to Begin, contrasted with the
> curiously bland style of the missive itself, encouraged reading be-
> tween the lines, and the Israelis came away with the impression
> that the letter represented a cautious diplomatic maneuver—the
> formal expression of a reservation by which the Americans in-
> tended to cover themselves against liability in case Israel got itself
> into deeper trouble than it could handle.[86]

Provided with ample forewarning and opportunity to convey its opposition, the inability or unwillingness of the American administration to
do so only strengthened Israeli convictions. What resulted was the
highly volatile mix of confused authority signals coupled with the denial of all control intent.

Any U.S. "condemnation" that may have followed the invasion was

82. BALL, *supra* note 6, at 34.
83. *See* A. HAIG, CAVEAT: REALISM, REAGAN AND FOREIGN POLICY 323 (1984). Begin told Haig "that Israel had begun planning a move into Lebanon and would not draw Syria into the conflict," to which the secretary of state responded: "Unless there is a major, internationally recognized provocation, the United States will not support such an action."
84. *See* HAIG, *Id.* at 335 ("General Sharon shocked a room full of State Department bureaucrats by sketching out two possible military campaigns: one that would pacify Southern Lebanon, and a second that would rewrite the political map in favor of the Christian Phalange").
85. *See* SCHIFF & YA'ARI, *supra* note 6, at 72–75.
86. *Id.* at 75.

correctly perceived by Israel as insignificant in comparison to what might have been done, and could well have given the impression of fundamental approval for the operation. Although some rhetoric may have been harsh, as it was aimed at an Arab audience, other U.S. actions belied its words. On the day of the invasion, Haig refused to condemn it on the grounds that the most important thing was to put an end to hostilities on both sides, thus placing both sides to the dispute on the same level. At the same time Henry Kissinger, who played an unofficial but influential role in American foreign policy, insisted that "one of the principle casualties of the Lebanese crisis has been the Western illusion . . . that the key to Middle East peace is to be found in a PLO–Israeli negotiation based on various formulae to 'moderate' the PLO. It was always a mirage. . . . Nor was it desirable. It would have given a veto on negotiations to the most intransigent element in the Arab world."[87] Jeane Kirkpatrick, then United States ambassador to the United Nations, indicated that "[i]t would be neither reasonable nor fair to accuse only one of the parties who has violated the U.N. resolution on the ceasefire in Southern Lebanon when, apparently, both of them have. . . . It would not be unreasonable that Israel has exercised its right of legitimate self-defense according to Article 51 of the U.N. Charter."[88]

The U.S. delegation to the United Nations, although supporting resolutions 508 and 509, the second demanding that Israel withdraw its forces "forthwith and unconditionally," cast its veto, the sole negative vote, against a June 8 draft resolution. It would have specifically condemned Israel and asked that "in the event of non-compliance [with 508 and 509] [the Security Council] meet again to consider practical ways and means in accordance with the Charter of the United Nations."[89] The veto was motivated by the fact that "the resolution not only . . . placed the entire blame for hostilities on Israel but also . . . sanctions were implied."[90] Haig also felt that "we don't need a public break with Israel,"[91] as he concluded: "[I]n this tragic situation lay the

87. Wash. Post, July 16, 1982.
88. CHRONOLOGY, *supra* note 3, at 93.
89. U.N. Chronicle, Sept. 1982, at 16.
90. HAIG, *supra* note 83, at 332. According to Haig, he convinced the President of the necessity of the veto at the last minute, against the will of most members of the administration.
91. *Id.* at 346.

great opportunity to make peace. Syria and the PLO, the two forces that had destroyed the authority of the Lebanese government and brought on the fighting, had been defeated."[92]

Overall, the international reaction to the decision to invade was a mix of strong verbal condemnation by the Soviet Union and the Arab states, varying degrees of condemnation and restrained acceptance by the European Community, and veiled support by the United States.

International Appraisal of the Extent and Duration of the Invasion: The Proportionality Standard

The United States continued to affirm the necessity of some Israeli action, even as Israel crossed the forty-kilometer line; however, appraisal of the proportionality of the invasion became increasingly negative. As Israel extended the attack into Lebanon, the United States demonstrated a reluctance to condemn the invasion without qualifications relating to the unacceptable situation that had existed in Lebanon.[93] This could be interpreted as an affirmation of the goals of the Israeli actions. But U.S. reactions began to shift as the war dragged on over several months, and the Reagan administration's invocation of its inability to intervene lost credibility. Secretary of State Haig reportedly "resigned" over these shifts in policy on June 25 as Reagan was trying to "save [his] credibility in the conservative Arab world. . . . The United States had at first gone along with the war, but now opposed any extension of the conflict to the rest of Lebanon, much less to Syria."[94]

This did not prevent the United States from vetoing a June 26 UN resolution demanding the withdrawal of Israeli forces engaged around Beirut "as a first step towards the complete withdrawal of Israeli forces from Lebanon, and the simultaneous withdrawal of the Palestinian armed forces from Beirut, which shall retire to the existing camps."[95] The reason for the veto appeared to be the fact that the resolution left too vague the issue of Palestinian presence in Beirut and elsewhere. That same day, the United States joined Israel in the sole negative votes in the General Assembly against a resolution condemning Israel for its noncompliance with resolutions 508 and 509 and threatening to im-

92. *Id.* at 342.
93. *See* text accompanying notes 87–92, *supra.*
94. RANDALL, *supra* note 22, at 261.
95. U.N. Chronicle, Sept. 1982, at 18.

pose sanctions.[96] The most explicit explanation for the American re-action was given by President Ronald Reagan in an interview with *Le Figaro*:

> There is no doubt that Israel's reaction has been disproportionate. However, it is equally true that, in many cases, perhaps even in most, it is the PLO that violated the ceasefire. Then came the Israeli response and, I repeat it, it was out of proportion. I ask myself whether the PLO was not trying to provoke Israel. . . . The Israelis entered Lebanon to respond to artillery shots and missiles from the other side of the border. The villages of Galilee have suffered losses of human lives and material damages—and this is why the Israelis contend, justifiably, that their advance was defensive. Their initial objective was to advance far enough to prevent the shelling from reaching Israel, but their soldiers face attacks. So, what could they have done? Stay where they were and die? . . . Hence, the Israelis advanced further, again and again."[97]

On August 1, however, the Israeli aviation conducted its fiercest bombing of Beirut to date, leading the United States to vote for the unanimously accepted Security Council Resolution 516, which de-manded an "immediate ceasefire." As Israel moved the IDF into West Beirut, Reagan called the Israeli action "a disproportionate one," add-ing that it "raised questions about whether Israel was using American weapons for legitimate self-defense."[98] Furthermore, the U.S. delega-tion to the United Nations abstained on Resolution 517, which "cen-sured" Israel for the West Beirut bombing. After the intense bombing and artillery barrage against West Beirut on August 12, Reagan ex-pressed his "outrage" to Begin.[99] This occurred in part because of the dilemma occurring in the Middle East in response to the attacks, as Randall explained:

96. CHRONOLOGY, *supra* note 3, at 18–19.
97. Le Figaro, Aug. 9, 1982, *quoted in* CHRONOLOGY, *supra* note 3, at 211.
98. BALL, *supra* note 6, at 46.
99. *Id.* According to Schiff & Ya'ari, U.S. pressure on Israel increased steadily until the PLO withdrew: "[T]he Pentagon had relayed orders to two of the Sixth Fleet's ships anchored outside Beirut harbor to enter the port and escort the Greek ships and its Pal-estinian passengers and if the IDF opened fire to fire right back! . . . Relations between Israel and the U.S. reached a potentially disastrous nadir." SCHIFF & YA'ARI, *supra* note 6, at 228.

177

[U.S. Policy in the Middle East] risked coming apart when Israel inflicted such humiliation, embarrassment, and pain that the conservative Arabs felt obliged to denounce their would-be American protectors. Whatever misgivings the Saudi, Kuwait, and other oil sheiks felt about the future existence of an independent Palestinian state, they could not afford to stand by as Americans acquiesced in Israel's blatant destruction of an Arab capital.[100]

Despite the European Community's condemnation of the Israeli advances toward Beirut, the gap between will and capability restrained the Europeans from any kind of forceful action, especially since they lacked the maneuvering power that a flexible response strategy might have given them. Because they accepted the Israeli claim to secure borders and were restrained in their support for Palestinian rights, the Europeans had to choose an intermediary position between total support for Israel and total denunciation, but the means at their disposal were not sufficient for implementing such a compromise position. Israel thus felt nothing but moral pressure, which, it could be argued, ultimately had an effect by discouraging total occupation of the capital.

The fact that Europe went as far as it did may have resulted from their concern for another audience—the Arab states. Hans Dietrich Genscher, the West German foreign minister, said that he "had never seen King Hussein of Jordan so despairing"; the Dutch foreign minister added that the "moderate, pro-Western States were increasingly alarmed at the upsurge of anti-Western feeling in their countries."[101] In spite of these fears, the threat of Arab retaliation would probably have had to have been much greater for it to have had a drastic effect on European policies.

Some action was taken in that the EEC refused to sign a new financial protocol with Israel, and Great Britain decreed an embargo on arms sales to Israel, but such measures were at best symbolic. The more pro-Palestinian members of the EEC went further. The Papandreou government in Greece called on the EEC to recognize the PLO formally, comparing, as Bruno Kreisky of Austria had, Begin with the Nazis or fascists. Although not nearly this extreme, the French and Italians distinguished the issue of Israeli security from that of the legitimacy of the PLO, which they came close to recognizing. More signif-

100. RANDALL, *supra* note 22, at 252.
101. Int'l Herald Tribune, June 16, 1982; Time, June 15, 1982.

icantly, on August 16 France cast its vote in favor of a Soviet resolution calling for a military embargo against Israel, a move that clearly surprised and outraged Jerusalem.[102]

In general, as has been discussed, European votes in the United Nations reflected this condemnation—calling for aid to civilians in the conflict area, asking Israel to lift its blockade of Beirut and to withdraw from battle zones in West Beirut, and supporting sending UN observers into the area.[103] These and other actions might be interpreted to signify a rejection of the lawfulness of the proportionality of the Israeli invasion. Although not determinative, this again allows for seeing, at least on the surface, that the philosophical, or at least political, position was against the extent both spatial and temporal, of the Israeli invasion. When the international community was finally prompted to action, with the sending of the MNF, the message may have been given that Israel was going too far in attempting to take over the Lebanese capital and physically exterminate the PLO. To this extent, the peace-keeping force also served as an indication of the international recognition of the need to put limits on what might have been seen as the ultimate aims of the invasion.[104]

The insistence on the forty-kilometer security belt—not only by world opinion, but also, at least initially, by the Israeli Cabinet itself—made it clear that a norm of proportionality is embodied in elite expectations. Confusion within the Israeli government and antagonism be-

102. In this vote, it should be noted that Great Britain abstained. CHRONOLOGY, *supra* note 3, at 204.

103. France also took the political initiative of proposing a resolution with Egypt that, although calling for a withdrawal from Lebanon of all foreign forces, also laid the grounds for a peaceful solution to the Palestinian problem, including self-determination and a degree of PLO representation. By putting the Lebanese crisis into its larger Middle East context, France was making a clear political statement.

104. The MNF was originally sent in to watch over the withdrawal of the PLO from Lebanon. After the task was completed, the MNF departed, only to return following the massacre. "[W]hat brought the peacekeeping troops to Beirut a second time," according to Friedman, "was not some well-conceived plan to restore Lebanese sovereignty or rebuild the Lebanese Army—it was guilt." Friedman, *supra* note 49, at 36. Italian ambassador Franco Lucioli Ottieri explained: "We left the first time after the job of evacuating the PLO was complete. We came back under the pressure of public opinion." *Id.* An American source added: "We said publicly that we would help put the Lebanese Government back on its feet. It was understood privately, though, that we would protect the Lebanese Moslem and Palestinian living in West Beirut from Israelis and Phalangists." *Id..*

tween its civilian and military branches apparently stemmed from the will, expressed by many, to adhere to this "legitimate" limitation on self-defensive action.[105] The weight of moral pressure from Western public opinion in this respect, especially as conveyed by the press, also reinforced this norm.[106] Hence, it is fair to say that from the view of international elites, the Israeli invasion exceeded the generally recognized standards of proportionality. This view that a certain limit for self-defense had been crossed could be said to have reinforced the existence of a norm of proportionality, and thus to have clarified and affirmed that norm.

All of the European initiatives, however, called, to some degree, for Palestinian disengagement from Lebanon, thus granting de facto legitimacy to Israeli security concerns—the justification for the initiation of the invasion and for the extent of it. By refusing a return to the situation preceding the war and by, more specifically, demanding a PLO withdrawal, the message to Israel became ambiguous. In a sense, it served to justify Tel Aviv's operation, not only to the forty-kilometer security belt but possibly even to the much more extensive march to Beirut. Even the MNF-sponsored evacuation of the PLO could be viewed as international recognition of the need to remove the threat to Israel from Lebanon, justifying in part the aims of the invasion.

The necessity of the Israeli invasion was, to some extent, legitimated, first by an absence of concrete measures to stop the invasion, then by the implicit acceptance of its rationale. Indeed, by espousing the view that the PLO and Syria were "occupying" forces, certain elites confirmed the necessity of some kind of action. In effect, Israel's presence was perceived as no more illegitimate than that of the two other parties, while possibly creating the opportunity to remove all foreign intervention. But although the need for the invasion was, at least implicitly, recognized, a limit on the extent of the invasion was activated through application of the norm of proportionality.

105. *See* Schiff & Ya'ari, *supra* note 6, at 105–06, 111–13.

106. See discussion of the reaction of the Western press, *supra* note 73. The humanitarian side of the war, the heavy casualty rate among civilians, and the alleged violation of the Geneva Convention on the treatment of prisoners of war were the criteria that prompted the media to criticize Israel. Generally, this perspective—as had the European states when they chose to act—focused on the disproportionality of the Israeli actions, with the level of opposition rising as the invading forces went beyond the forty-kilometer line and began the Beirut phase of the operation.

THE GULF OF SIDRA INCIDENT
OF 1981: The Lawfulness of
Peacetime Aerial Engagements

8

STEVEN R. RATNER

PROBLEM

On August 19, 1981, U.S. F-14 fighter aircraft engaged in combat with two Libyan Sukhoi-22 fighters above the Gulf of Sidra, approximately sixty miles off the coast of Libya.[1] By the end of the encounter, both Libyan planes had been destroyed. According to Libyan assertions, one of its fighters destroyed one of the F-14s, but the United States denied this contention. Although Libyan aircraft had on previous occasions fired upon U.S. military planes,[2] the Gulf of Sidra incident marked the first time that U.S. aircraft returned fire.

The Gulf of Sidra incident demonstrates that aerial rules of engagement formulated by individual states are subject to an identifiable and widely accepted norm. This norm requires that, in peacetime, military aircraft attempt to avoid the first use of force during potentially hostile

---

1. The F-14, or Tomcat, is one of the United States' main tactical fighter aircraft. It can reach a maximum speed of mach 2.4 (approximately 1,840 miles per hour). The SU-22, or Fitter, is the export version of the Soviet SU-17 fighter. It can reach a maximum speed of mach 2.17 (approximately 1,660 miles per hour). *Le F-14 et le SU-22: Deux avions à flèche variable*, Le Monde, Aug. 21, 1981, at 4, col. 1.

2. *See infra* notes 6–10 and accompanying text.

181

encounters with the aircraft of another state. The norm permits a first use of force only when necessary for immediate unit or national self-defense, and then usually only after giving warning.

Rules of engagement (ROE) is the general term used to describe the "directives that a government may establish to delineate the circumstances and limitations under which its own naval, ground, and air forces will initiate and/or continue combat engagement with enemy forces."[3] With respect to the particular form of ROE to be discussed in this study, the practice followed by most states appears generally to consist in ordering the intruder to identify itself and to turn back or land at a prescribed place, and, only as a last resort, failing compliance with such orders, attacking.[4] Although ROE are formulated by individual states to govern their own military operations, it may be assumed that national ROE are derived with reference to international expectations regarding appropriate behavior.[5]

As will be seen in the following discussion of the Gulf of Sidra incident, the tacit acceptance by international elites of the U.S. application of its aerial ROE, coupled with an apparent refusal to support the ROE

3. Roach, *Rules of Engagement*, NAVAL WAR C. REV., Jan.-Feb. 1983, at 46 (quoting DEPARTMENT OF DEFENSE DICTIONARY OF MILITARY AND ASSOCIATED TERMS 298 (1978)). Roach also notes that ROE reflect the influence of military, political, and diplomatic factors. *Id.* at 46–49.

4. M. MCDOUGAL, H. LASSWELL, & I. VLASIC, LAW AND PUBLIC ORDER IN SPACE 272 (1963). Yet, as the authors caution, "[t]he practice of states is not, however, uniform and the lack of an unequivocal community policy affords states a very considerable discretion with respect to intruders." *Id.*

5. See, e.g., Lissitzyn, *The Treatment of Aerial Intruders in Recent Practice and International Law*, 47 AM. J. INT'L L. 559 (1953). Lissitzyn identifies "certain standards of international law with respect to the treatment of intruding aircraft [into a state's territory] which may be regarded as established or in the process of being established." *Id.* at 586. These standards include the following:

(1) Intruding aircraft must obey all reasonable orders of the territorial sovereign, including orders to land, to turn back, or to fly on a certain course. . . .

(2) The territorial sovereign must not expose the aircraft and its occupants to unnecessary or unreasonably great danger—unreasonably great, that is, in relation to the reasonably apprehended harmfulness of the intrusion. . . . In times of peace, intruding aircraft whose intentions are known to be harmless must not be attacked even if they disobey orders to land, to turn back, or to fly on a certain course. . . . In cases where there is reason to believe that the intruder's intentions may be hostile or illicit, a warning or order to land should normally be first given and the intruder may be attacked if it disobeys. *Id.* at 586–89.

demonstrated by the Libyans, resulted in a reinforcement of international normative expectations concerning the appropriate use of force during peacetime aerial encounters.

FACTS

The 1981 incident over the Gulf of Sidra was not the first time that Libyan and U.S. military aircraft had confronted one another in the airspace near or above the Gulf. On March 21, 1973, Libyan interceptors fired missiles at a C-130 cargo plane after the latter flew inside a "restricted area" that Libya had created within a one-hundred-mile radius of Tripoli.[6] (See map, p. 184.) Some seven years later, on September 16, 1980, Libyan planes attacked a U.S. reconnaissance aircraft.[7] In neither of these cases did the Libyan missiles hit their apparent targets, and in neither case did the U.S. aircraft return fire.[8] In addition, the Libyan government has documented numerous instances of what it termed "[a]ir-space violations and American terror and spying missions."[9] In none of these claimed instances, however, did either side resort to the use of force.[10]

Although Libya and the United States disagree over many of the facts regarding the August 19, 1981, incident,[11] a rough reconstruction of the events that preceded the aerial engagement can be drawn from those facts agreed upon by both sides. On August 12 and 14, the United States issued warnings to mariners and pilots that it would hold naval maneuvers and missile tests in the Gulf of Sidra on August 18

6. The United States had previously communicated its objections to Libya over the creation of this zone. *See* Letter Dated 18 June 1973 from the Permanent Representative of the United States of America to the United Nations Addressed to the President of the Security Council, June 20, 1973, U.N. Doc. S/10956 (citing protests made in November 1972 and February and April 1973). *See also* Dig. U.S. Prac. Int'l L. 302–303 (1973).

7. *Libyan Fighters Suspected of Firing on U.S. Aircraft*, Wash. Post, Sept. 18, 1980, at A17, col. 1. *See also* Safire, *Looking for Trouble*, N.Y. Times, Sept. 25, 1980, at A27, col. 1.

8. *See supra* notes 6–7.

9. Letter Dated 1 Aug. 1980 from the Chargé d'Affaires A.I. of the Permanent Mission of the Libyan Arab Jamahiriya to the United Nations Addressed to the President of the Security Council, Aug. 6, 1980, U.N. Doc. S/14094 Annex, at 3–4.

10. *Id.*

11. *See infra* text accompanying notes 38–48.

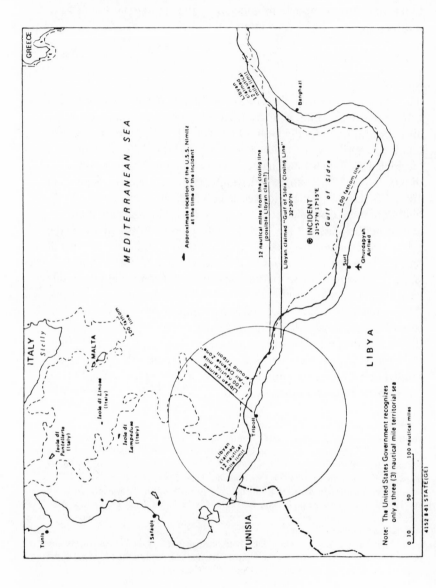

The Coast of Libya at the Time of the August 19, 1981, Incident

and 19.[12] The Gulf had been claimed by Libya since 1973 as territorial waters, a claim that the United States had expressly refused, and continues to refuse, to recognize.[13]

The maneuvers took place in a hexagonal region, the lower portion of which crossed the line that Libya claims as the beginning of its territorial waters (the 32 degrees 30 minutes line of latitude—demarcating the area where the Gulf meets the Mediterranean—plus a twelve-mile band of territorial sea).[14] The military vessels assigned to participate in the maneuvers were a powerful force, comprising the aircraft carriers *Nimitz* and *Forrestal,* four cruisers, four frigates, four destroyers, and two destroyer escorts.[15] During the first day of the maneuvers, Libyan planes conducted a number of sorties[16] to observe the area of the exercises. In each case, carrier-based U.S. aircraft intercepted the Libyan fighters, which then turned away.[17] The United States and Libya have characterized virtually all subsequent events during this incident in sharply contrasting ways.

CONFLICTING CLAIMS

Libya and the United States adopted conflicting versions of the actual engagement. Moreover, the two states differed in their perception of the factual background out of which the incident arose. The two prerequisite or background disputes involved the following issues: (1) the legitimacy of Libya's claim to sovereignty over the Gulf of Sidra and (2) the purpose and lawfulness of U.S. maneuvers conducted in the Gulf of Sidra. A brief discussion of each is necessary for a complete

12. These announcements were made through the official channels of the International Hydrographic Organization and International Maritime Organization and broadcast over a designated frequency from Madrid in English and Spanish. Telephone interview with U.S. Department of Defense Official C (Mar. 29, 1984) (notes on file with the *Yale Journal of International Law*).

13. *See infra* notes 20–21 and accompanying text.

14. *See supra* map.

15. *To the Shores of Tripoli,* NEWSWEEK, Aug. 31, 1981, at 14, 15 [hereinafter cited as *To the Shores*].

16. Offical and unofficial estimates vary. *See* Crowell, *45 Libya Incidents Detailed by Navy,* N.Y. Times, Aug. 25, 1981, at A1, col. 3 (45 sorties); *To the Shores, supra* note 15, at 16 (72 sorties).

17. *To the Shores, supra* note 15, at 16.

understanding of each side's factual and legal claims underlying its use of force in response to actions taken by the other.[18]

Dispute over the Sovereignty of the Gulf of Sidra

In October 1973, representatives of the Libyan Arab Republic[19] submitted notes to the United Nations and to the United States and other nations officially declaring, for the first time in any international forum, that the Gulf of Sidra formed "an integral part" of Libyan territory and was therefore completely subject to Libyan sovereignty as "internal waters."[20] The U.S. government responded to the Libyan claim in February 1974. The United States found Libya's claim "unacceptable as a violation of international law" and declared that it "re-

18. The Gulf of Sidra incident thus involved norms concerning not only aerial engagements but also territorial waters, the law of the sea, and naval maneuvers. Such an agglomeration of expectations of appropriate behavior will occur in many studies of incidents. Since space will not allow full treatment of each of these norms, however, this study confines its analysis to the rules of aerial engagement.

19. On March 2, 1977, the Libyan government issued the Declaration on the Establishment of the Authority of the People, which changed the name of the state to the Socialist People's Libyan Arab Jamahiriya.

20. The complete text of the Libyan declaration reads as follows:

> The Gulf of Surt located within the territory of the Libyan Arab Republic and surrounded by land boundaries on its East, South, and West sides, and extending North offshore to Latitude 32 degrees 30 minutes, constitutes an integral part of the Libyan Arab Republic and is under its complete sovereignty.
>
> As the Gulf penetrates Libyan territory and forms a part thereof, it constitutes internal waters, beyond which the territorial waters of the Libyan Arab Republic start.
>
> Through history and without any dispute, the Libyan Arab Republic has exercised its sovereignty over the Gulf. Because of the Gulf's geographical location commanding a view of the Southern part of the country, it is, therefore, crucial to the security of the Libyan Arab Republic. Consequently, complete surveillance over its area is necessary to insure the security and safety of the State.
>
> In view of the aforementioned facts, the Libyan Arab Republic declares that the Gulf of Surt, defined within the borders stated above, is under its complete national sovereignty and jurisdiction in regard to legislative, judicial, administrative and other aspects related to ships and persons that may be present within its limits.
>
> Private and public foreign ships are not allowed to enter the Gulf without prior permission from the authorities of the Libyan Arab Republic and in accordance with the regulations established by it in this regard.
>
> The Libyan Arab Republic reserves the sovereign rights over the Gulf for its nationals.
>
> In general, the Libyan Arab Republic exercises complete rights of sovereignty over the Gulf of Surt as it does over any part of the territory of the State.

serve[d] its rights and the rights of its nationals in the area of the Gulf of [Sidra]."[21]

If the Gulf were internal waters, Libya would be able, under international law, to forbid the conduct of naval maneuvers.[22] On the other hand if, as the United States claimed, the Gulf were international waters, international law would permit overflight and the exercise of other high seas freedoms, as long as they were carried out "with reasonable regard to the interests of other states."[23]

Dispute over the Legitimacy and Purpose of U.S. Maneuvers in the Gulf

Among the rights that the United States asserted in accordance with its rejection of the Libyan claim of sovereignty over the Gulf was the right of its military vessels to enter the area and, in particular, to conduct naval maneuvers there. For several decades, the Sixth Fleet had sailed in and out of the Gulf.[24] According to a State Department official, the United States had also conducted naval maneuvers and missile tests in the Gulf for many years.[25] Between 1977 and 1981, the U.S. Navy conducted eight large-scale maneuvers there.[26]

After the August 1981 incident, the United States justified its use of the Gulf for maneuvers on two principal grounds. First, it noted that international law permits states to use the high seas to conduct naval

21. 1974 DIG. U.S. PRAC. INT'L L. 293–94 (quoting U.S. reply, dated Feb. 11, 1974).

22. Indeed, if this were the case, Libya could, under international law, deny even innocent passage to vessels sailing in the Gulf. See United Nations Convention on the Law of the Sea, Dec. 10, 1982, arts. 17–19, U.N. Doc. A/CONF. 62/122 and Corr. 1–11, reprinted in 21 I.L.M. 1261, 1273–74 (1982) [hereinafter cited as 1982 Law of the Sea Treaty].

23. Convention on the High Seas, Apr. 29, 1958, art. 2, 13 U.S.T. 2312, 2314, T.I.A.S. No. 5200, at 10, 450 U.N.T.S. 82, 84. [hereinafter cited as 1958 High Seas Treaty]. The 1982 Law of the Sea Treaty, supra note 22, still in negotiation at the time of the incident, has a similar provision in Article 87 for high seas freedoms. In a statement made on the day of the incident, the State Department explicitly relied on these freedoms in asserting: "The oceans beyond the territorial sea are high seas on which all nations enjoy freedom of navigation and overflight, including the right to engage in naval maneuvers such as those recently concluded in the Mediterranean." Department Statement, Aug. 19, 1981, DEP'T ST. BULL., Oct. 1981, at 59.

24. Telephone interview with U.S. Department of State Official A (Mar. 27, 1984) (notes on file with the Yale Journal of International Law).

25. Id.

26. Neutze, The Gulf of Sidra Incident: A Legal Perspective, 108 PROC. U.S. NAVAL INST. 26, 29 (1982).

maneuvers.[27] Second, U.S. officials defended the maneuvers as "routine" and thus implicitly legitimate. Exercises had been conducted in the Gulf many times in the past,[28] and, American officials claimed, the Gulf was selected primarily on the basis of logistical factors.[29]

Other circumstances, however, cast doubt on the purportedly routine, nonpolitical nature of the 1981 Gulf exercises. The presence of U.S. vessels in the Gulf is consistent with longstanding U.S. policy of directly challenging territorial waters claims that the United States refuses to recognize by sailing American military ships into the claimed areas.[30] Moreover, the decision in the summer of 1981 to conduct maneuvers sixty miles off the Libyan coast was also consistent with the openly anti-Qadhafi policy of the Reagan administration.[31] President Ronald Reagan had been quoted in the press on the need to demonstrate U.S. military might to potential "trouble makers,"[32] and Secretary of State Alexander Haig had made clear that any proposal by the President to "get tough" with Qadhafi would meet with great favor at the State Department.[33]

Furthermore, the United States' characterization of the maneuvers as

27. See *supra* note 23 and accompanying text.

28. U.S. Secretary of Defense Caspar Weinberger stated, "We've had naval and air exercises there before. This one was scheduled for some time, and the notification went out in the perfectly normal fashion . . . and the exercises took place as scheduled." U.S. Planes Attacked by Libyan Aircraft: News Briefing, Aug. 16, 1981, DEP'T ST. BULL., Oct. 1981, at 58.

29. According to U.S. officials, the low level of civilian air traffic over the Gulf made it "an ideal location for safe conduct of such an exercise in the Mediterranean." Neutze, *supra* note 26, at 26.

30. This policy was formalized in the late 1970s as the Freedom of Navigation Program. Telephone interview with U.S. Department of State Official A, *supra* note 24. *See also Those Maritime Exercises,* Letter to the Editor, Wash. Post, Aug. 4, 1984, at A22, col. 3 (stating that "U.S. Freedom of Navigation Program is nothing more than a routine exercise of generally accepted maritime rights"; also, referring to Libya's claim to the Gulf of Sidra as "one of the most egregious maritime claims existing in the world today") (written by Hugh O'Neill, representative for ocean policy affairs, Office of the Secretary of Defense).

31. In spring 1981, the Reagan administration ordered the closure of the Libyan embassy in Washington. *U.S. Expels Libyans and Closes Mission, Charging Terrorism,* N.Y. Times, May 7, 1981, at A1, col. 3.

32. *Transcript of Remarks by President and Laingen at White House,* N.Y. Times, Jan. 28, 1981, at A14, col. 3 (promising "swift and effective retribution to those who violate the rules of international behavior").

33. *See U.S. Pledges to Aid Countries in Africa That Resist Libyans,* N.Y. Times, June 3, 1981, at A1, col. 4, A4, col. 4.

strictly routine is belied by the circumstances under which the decision to hold them was made. Although such exercises were conducted in the Gulf by the United States in years past, all maneuvers in that area had been suspended by President Jimmy Carter during the Iranian hostage crisis, in an effort to avoid provoking a military response from Libya.[34] Although the exercises may once have been routine, the choice to reinitiate them after this hiatus was not. The Reagan administration itself treated the resumption of the maneuvers as a matter of great political sensitivity, with final approval of the exercises given by the President himself.[35] After the 1981 incident, the Libyans challenged the American assertions that the maneuvers were routine. Libya characterized the exercises as a manifestation by the United States of its "aggressive intentions against the people of the Libyan Arab Jamahiriya."[36] Furthermore, Libya linked the U.S. maneuvers to Egyptian war games allegedly being held along the Libyan–Egyptian border.[37]

Dispute over the Events of August 19

According to the United States, on the morning of August 19, the USS *Nimitz* was sailing outside the Gulf of Sidra. At the same time, and as

34. See *U.S. Downs Libyan Fighters Over Mediterranean In Latest Round of Political and Military Hostility*, Wall St. J., Aug. 20, 1981, at 3, col. 1. *See also Shootout over the Med*, TIME, Aug. 31, 1981, at 24, 25 (noting that in December 1979, one month after the hostages were taken in Iran, a Libyan mob attacked and burned the U.S. embassy in Tripoli) [hereinafter cited as *Shootout*].

35. The proposal to reinstitute maneuvers in the Gulf was brought to the National Security Council (NSC) by Defense Secretary Caspar Weinberger in June 1981. The NSC discussed the implications of the maneuvers and strongly recommended their approval to the President. *See* Winchester, *Why Reagan Set the Tomcats on "The World's Dangerous Man,"* Sunday Times (London), Aug. 23, 1981, at 6, col. 2. For normal maneuvers, the final authorization would come from the director of the State Department's Bureau of Politico-Military Affairs and the Defense Department's undersecretary of defense for policy. Interview with U.S. Department of State Official A, *supra* note 24.

36. Letter Dated 20 August 1981 from the Chargé d'Affaires A.I. of the Permanent Mission of the Libyan Arab Jamahiriya to the United Nations Addressed to the President of the Security Council, Aug. 20, 1981, U.N. Doc. S/14646 Annex, at 1 [hereinafter cited as August 20 Libyan letter]. *See also* Interview with Mr. Rajab Azzarouk, minister plenipotentiary and legal advisor, Libyan Mission to the United Nations (Apr. 3, 1984) (noting that, if the U.S. had intended only to conduct routine maneuvers, it could easily have chosen a less sensitive location) (notes on file with the *Yale Journal of International Law*).

37. Kifner, *Tripoli in a Protest Note Accuses U.S. of "International Terrorism,"* N.Y. Times, Aug. 20, 1981, at A12, col. 1.

they had done the previous day, two American destroyers cruised below the 32 degrees 30 minutes line—i.e., within the disputed waters of the Gulf—to patrol the southern perimeter of the missile testing area. As in previous sorties, two Libyan SU-22s took off from their land base and set course toward the testing area. Two American F-14s, already in the air, proceeded due south and met the Libyan planes, then approaching due north, at a point approximately sixty miles from the Libyan coast.[38]

At this point, one Libyan SU-22, heading directly toward one of the F-14s, fired a heat-seeking missile that, according to U.S. reports of the incident, missed its target. The two F-14s, after being shot at, maneuvered behind the SU-22s and fired their AIM-9 sidewinder missiles at the Libyan planes.[39] Both Libyan planes were destroyed.[40] The entire encounter lasted about one minute. Immediately thereafter, the F-14s returned to the carrier *Nimitz*. The maneuvers ended as scheduled at 5:00 P.M. G.M.T. on August 19, without further incident.[41]

According to Libya, the events of August 19 constituted part of a pattern of foreign military threats that had recently been made against it. Libya claimed that United States and Egyptian aircraft had conducted extensive troop exercises near the Libyan border on the days immediately prior to the incident.[42] On the day of the incident itself:

> [f]rom the very early hours of the morning, the Libyan Air Force discovered an unusual density of aircraft in the air space just in the vicinity of the Libyan Arab Jamahiriya. These appeared to be 36 planes in the operational zone of Tripoli. Another 36 planes were flying in the operational area of Benghazi. A further 12 aircraft were flying over Libyan territorial waters, right in front of the Gulf of Syrte. These were no farther than 100 kms. from the city of Syrte.[43]

38. *See id.*; Neutze, *supra* note 26, at 27.

39. *See* Department Statement, Aug. 19, 1981, DEP'T ST. BULL., Oct. 1981, at 58.

40. According to U.S. reports, one of the two Libyan pilots was killed in the encounter. *See To the Shores, supra* note 15, at 17. The United States government stated that it incurred no loss of life during the encounter. *See* U.S. Planes Attacked by Libyan Aircraft, News Briefing, DEP'T ST. BULL., Oct. 1981, at 58.

41. *To the Shores, supra* note 15, at 18.

42. Kifner, *Tripoli in a Protest Note Accuses U.S. of "International Terrorism,"* N.Y. Times, Aug. 20, 1981, at A12, col. 1.

43. S. YUSSEF, ARAB-AMERICAN CONFRONTATION OVER SIRT GULF 198 (1982) (distributed by Libyan Mission to the United Nations).

Libya thus rejected the U.S. claim that the F-14s were performing a routine intercept, claiming instead that they were part of a large force of aircraft on a mission of aggression against Libyan territory.

Libya's account of the facts of the aerial incident diverges sharply from that of the United States. According to the most complete Libyan account available,[44] events unfolded as follows. At 7 A.M. on August 19, two Libyan fighters were sent to intercept a formation of eight U.S. aircraft headed for the Libyan city of Sidra. The Libyan planes encountered two planes from the U.S. formation "at a relatively close distance from the city of Syrte."[45] The Libyan pilots were surprised to find the U.S. aircraft "fully prepared for an attack."[46] After these aircraft attempted to maneuver behind the Libyan fighters, one Libyan pilot fired a missile that succeeded in destroying one of the U.S. planes.[47] Then, finding themselves surrounded by the six other aircraft of the U.S. formation, the Libyan pilots ejected.[48]

Later that day, the United States filed a protest with the United Nations Security Council, claiming that the incident constituted an unprovoked attack by Libya upon aircraft participating in previously announced exercises in international airspace.[49] Libya formally responded on August 20, claiming that the U.S. attack on Libyan aircraft, which it said had been conducting reconnaissance duties in Libyan airspace, was a "provocative terrorist act."[50]

CONFLICTING CONCEPTIONS OF LAWFULNESS

Both the Libyan and American governments justified the actions of their pilots in terms comporting with norms pertaining to the appropriate use of force in peacetime aerial encounters. Each side characterized its pilots' actions as defensive. The United States claimed that its use of

44. *See generally id.*

45. *Id.* at 199–200.

46. *Id.* at 200.

47. The Libyan government claimed that the U.S. fighter crashed about ten miles west of Poisano, Sardinia. *See* Downed U.S. F-14 Reportedly Fell Near Sardinia, Foreign Broadcast Information Service [hereinafter cited as FBIS] (No. Africa), Aug. 26, 1981, at Q1 (text from Tripoli, Voice of the Arab Homeland).

48. Libya asserted that both its pilots survived. S. YUSSEF, *supra* note 43, at 200–201.

49. Letter Dated 19 August 1981 from the Acting Representative of the United States of America to the United Nations Addressed to the President of the Security Council, Aug. 19, 1981, U.N. Doc. S/14632.

50. August 20 Libyan letter, *supra* note 36, at 1.

force was a justified response to being fired upon.[51] Libya at first asserted that its pilot fired only as a matter of unit self-defense after first being fired upon by the U.S. planes.[52] Later, Libya claimed that its pilots' initiation of force was a necessary act of national self-defense against a clear threat to Libyan territory.[53] While each side sought to characterize its own actions as purely defensive and therefore lawful, each labeled the actions of the other as unlawful aggression.

The conflicting conceptions of lawfulness demonstrated in the Gulf of Sidra incident do not then appear to have involved a dispute over the general content of the international norms that govern the ROE practiced by individual states. Rather, the legal dispute seems to have centered on what behavior constitutes a communication of hostile intent sufficient to justify a defensive use of force.

American Conceptions of the Right of Peacetime Self-Defense

The specific content of American ROE for peacetime aerial encounters is classified; nevertheless, its general contours may be ascertained from known practice. The appropriate initial response for a U.S. fighter encountering a foreign aircraft on an apparently hostile mission would be to approach the aircraft, ask it to identify itself, and order it to leave the area. The U.S. plane would then wiggle its wings in an international signal to move off. If, after receiving the warning, the foreign craft did not comply, and if its apparent mission threatened a U.S. target, the U.S. plane would be authorized to shoot the foreign craft down. U.S. peacetime ROE thus contemplate a first use of force against an apparently hostile foreign aircraft that refuses, after being warned, to turn away from a U.S. target.[54]

51. See U.S. Planes Attacked by Libyan Aircraft, News Briefing, *supra* note 40, at 57–58.

52. *Shootout*, *supra* note 34, at 25.

53. *Le colonel Kadhafi reconnait que les avions libyens ont tiré les premiers*, Le Monde, Aug. 25, 1981, at 4, col. 1 [hereinafter cited as *Le colonel Kadhafi*]. This article also reported the Libyan leader's statement that a warning was given before the Libyan pilot fired. This prior warning claim was not, however, repeated in later Libyan accounts. *See, e.g.*, S. YUSSEF, *supra* note 43, at 199–201.

54. Roach, *supra* note 3, at 49. In formulating its current ROE, the United States may also have relied on normative expectations derived from the practice followed in previous encounters with Soviet or Eastern European fighters. For example, during the early 1950s, Soviet or Eastern European military aircraft shot at U.S. fighters at least six times. See Lissitzyn, *supra* note 5, at 574–85. The United States claimed in each in-

The ROE used during the Gulf incident would therefore have included provisions allowing the initiation of the use of force when attempts at peaceful communications had failed to eliminate an imminent physical threat to U.S. vessels. Furthermore, under American ROE, if a foreign aircraft fires at a U.S. aircraft, U.S. pilots may be authorized to return fire and take the measures necessary to eliminate the immediate threat posed, including destroying the attacking aircraft.[55] In other circumstances U.S. officials could have instructed their pilots to follow an "escape at all costs" rule. Although such an instruction would have decreased the possibility of a combat encounter between Libyan and American forces, U.S. officials believed that a refusal to allow forcible unit self-defense would have signaled acquiescence in Qadhafi's claims over the Gulf.[56]

Thus, in justifying the behavior of its military personnel during the incident, the United States relied upon its conception of a peacetime self-defense norm that would allow pilots flying over international

---

stance that its aircraft had not violated Warsaw Pact airspace and that the planes had been attacked for no reason. The Soviet Union, on the other hand, claimed that U.S. aircraft had entered Warsaw Pact airspace. Most important, the Soviets always claimed that the U.S. pilots had fired first: "The striking fact is that the Soviet Government has in no case claimed the right to open fire on a intruding aircraft without warning, but alleged in most of these cases that the intruders had been the first to open fire. In some cases where this was not alleged, the Soviet fighter was said to have opened fire *by way of warning only.* The Soviet Government, moreover, has sought to emphasize its contention that the instructions to Soviet airmen on the treatment of intruders are similar to those in force in other countries." *Id.* at 580 (emphasis added). Although the frequency of hostile encounters between Soviet and U.S. aircraft has greatly decreased since that time, the basic norms against firing first appear to have endured. Thus, Soviet and American military pilots today habitually observe one another over certain areas above the high seas, following a peculiar form of etiquette to ensure the other side that its intentions are not hostile. *See* Honan, *The Games Pilots Play Over the Mediterranean,* N.Y. Times, Aug. 23, 1981, at D2, col. 3. *See also* Agreement on the Prevention of Incidents On and Over the High Seas, May 25, 1972, United States–U.S.S.R., 23 U.S.T. 1168, T.I.A.S. No. 7379 (1972) (requiring noninterference by aircraft of one state with naval maneuvers conducted by the other).

55. In addition to the self-defense requirement, U.S. peacetime ROE is further moderated by requirements that any use of force in a peacetime military encounter be governed by the principles of necessity and proportionality. Necessity implies the use of force only when other methods cannot defuse a threat; proportionality requires a military decision maker to respond with no more than that amount of force needed to eliminate the threat. *See* Roach, *supra* note 3, at 49.

56. Telephone interview with U.S. Department of State Official A, *supra* note 24.

waters to fire when fired upon by aircraft from a potentially hostile state. U.S. officials also appeared to acknowledge implicitly the potential force of a claim that the presence of their naval forces in the Gulf may not have comported with international norms of nonaggression. In their statements after the incident, U.S. officials were careful to emphasize the routine nature of the maneuvers, to state that they were held in international waters, and to omit reference to political motivations or an intent to make a symbolic demonstration of force. In other words, the U.S. officials sought to say nothing that might lend credence to a Libyan assertion that the presence of American air and naval vessels presented a real threat to Libyan sovereign territory.

The United States, both in its actions during the incident and in its later justifications, indicated its conception of an international norm of self-defense relating to peacetime aerial encounters that would allow the use of force only as a response to the actual use of force by the other side or to a threat of imminent attack, but not as a response, particularly if made without warning, to a symbolic threat.

Libyan Conceptions of the Right of Peacetime Self-Defense

After studying the incident, many U.S. officials came to believe that the firing of the first shot by the Libyan pilot was the result of simple pilot error, rather than a manifestation of Libyan ROE.[57] Nonetheless, the Libyans themselves refused to characterize the attack upon the U.S. aircraft as a mistake and consistently justified the event as necessary for national self-defense. Therefore, no matter what the actual motivations of the Libyan pilot may have been, the official justifications given for

57. The "pilot error" theory is based on three facts. First, the Libyans had not fired during previous sorties. Second, the SU-22, an old Soviet warplane, is not Libya's ideal interceptor aircraft. Had the Libyan high command intended to shoot down an F-14, it should have sent a more sophisticated craft, such as a MIG-23, to perform the mission. Finally, if the Libyans had instructed their pilot to shoot down the U.S. plane, he must have been grossly incompetent, since the missile was fired from the wrong direction. The missile fired from the Libyan plane was a heat-seeking missile, which must be directed toward the rear of an aircraft in order to home in on the plane's heat source, its exhaust. Thus, the pilot's firing at the front of an aircraft would seem to indicate either tactical incompetence, or that the shot was fired in panic or through some other error. Telephone interview with Department of Defense Official B (Mar. 30, 1984) (notes on file with the *Yale Journal of International Law*). *But see* Winchester, *supra* note 35, at 6, col. 5 (concluding that the pilot's firing in the wrong direction indicated not pilot error but rather that the U.S. planes had lured the Libyans into a trap).

his action may be evaluated as assertions by Libya of a right of self-defense under the circumstances as Libya believed them to be.

One of the self-defense claims advanced by Libya derived from its claim of sovereignty over the Gulf,[58] and thus implied an assertion that the right of first use of force may be triggered by any breach of territorial space by foreign craft. According to an American military authority, however, Libya had no right under international law to use force without first attempting to escort the intruding forces from claimed territory or requesting the United Nations Security Council to effect such removal.[59]

Libya did not, however, rely exclusively on the claim of territorial breach as justification for its first use of force, but rather used that argument primarily as support for its larger claim that the U.S. fleet and planes were in position for an imminent raid upon the northern parts of the country.[60] With this assertion, Libya could justify any failure to use warning maneuvers[61] to escort U.S. craft out of claimed areas, or to apply to the Security Council for their removal, on the basis of the need to act immediately to defend its territory against an impending attack.

According to the most detailed Libyan account available of the incident, their belief that U.S. forces were prepared for immediate attack was based on the American forces having breached a predetermined Libyan "Line of Engagement," set at the boundary of Libya's claimed territorial waters.[62] Once foreign forces entered this area, they would be warned to proceed no further. Should the warning not be heeded, the local military commander would be authorized to shoot down the intruder. In addition, should the foreign craft proceed within the Gulf and enter a zone designated as the "Confrontation Area," military personnel would be required to act immediately to destroy the intruder.

58. See *supra* note 20 and accompanying text.

59. See Neutze, *supra* note 26, at 30. According to a U.S. military source, Algeria once escorted U.S. warships out of claimed Algerian waters and the U.S. did not resist. Telephone interview with U.S. Department of State Official A, *supra* note 24.

60. See *supra* text accompanying notes 42–48.

61. Some earlier Libya accounts did contend that a warning was given before firing. *See, e.g., Le colonel Kadhafi, supra* note 53, at 4, col. 1. However, the United States disputes this contention, which was omitted from later accounts. *See* U.S. Planes Attacked by Libyan Aircraft: News Briefing, *supra* note 40 (no warning given); S. YUSSEF, *supra* note 43, at 199–201.

62. S. YUSSEF, *supra* note 43, at 189–90.

The "Confrontation Area" concept appears to be based on the belief that once this point was reached, Libya's national security would require the presumption that any intruding aircraft was on an attack mission, since it would be traveling so quickly that any delay—including attempts to ascertain intent or to warn off the aircraft peaceably—would allow a hostile craft to reach and destroy its target unhindered.[63]

INTERNATIONAL APPRAISAL

The international community responded quickly to the Gulf of Sidra aerial incident. A number of international commentators criticized the U.S. presence in the area, characterizing the maneuvers and exercises as a dangerously provocative show of strength.[64] On the whole, how-

63. *Id.* at 197. Such predetermined security lines, located within a specified distance of a country's shores, are used by a number of states, including the United States and the Soviet Union. However, unlike Libya, these states give notice to the international community of the existence of a threat to its security. *See, e.g.*, Security Control of Air Traffic, 14 C.F.R. § 99 (1987) (describing U.S. air defense zones); Jet Navigation Chart J.N.C.–5 (Defense Mapping Agency, 1973) (showing Soviet Union's "Asian Coastal Buffer Zone"). The general practice of states appears to be to warn foreign forces of the intent that will be attributed to their actions should they breach these lines.

64. With respect to the legitimacy of the U.S. exercises, most international commentators took the view that the United States acted unwisely in provoking the incident. *See, e.g.*, *FRG: Papers View Effects of U.S. Libyan Air Clash*, FBIS (W. Eur.), Aug. 21, 1981, at J3 (text from the Frankfurter Rundschau) ("One can surely contest [unreasonable claims over international waters] without hesitation. It is more than questionable, however, whether it must be done as [the United States] did [by holding] maneuvers off Libya's coast"); Rattner, *Western Europeans Expressing Favor and Unease*, N.Y. Times, Aug. 21, 1981, at A10, cols. 1–3 (officials in the United Kingdom, France, Germany, and Italy expressing the belief that the United States had deliberately invited the incident); *Turkey: Press Reaction to U.S.-Libyan Incident*, FBIS (No. Africa), Aug. 28, 1981, at T5 (asking how the U.S. would react to Soviet exercises in the Gulf of Mexico). Many Third World states also strongly condemned the U.S. *See Daily Report: Middle East and South Asia Review, Libyan-U.S. Clash*, FBIS (Mid-East), Aug. 24, 1981, at 1 (Organization of African Unity denounced U.S. for promoting the "policy of cowboys" in a "wanton act of aggression" constituting a "provocative act of undeclared war"); *Pravda Comments on Sidra Incident, Views Reaction*, FBIS (USSR), Aug. 26, 1981, at N6 (excerpted by Pravda from La Presse de Tunisie) (The Islamic Conference stated that "the U.S. 'muscle-flexing' policy jeopardiz[ed] peace . . . throughout the world," and was a policy based on disregard for the norms of international law.) No state other than Libya, however, *see supra* note 36, lodged any formal protest challenging the maneuvers' legality. A distinct minority of commentators unreservedly praised the U.S. show of force

ever, the international community deemed lawful the U.S. pilots' return of force during the incident itself, and most of those commentators who were critical of the maneuvers offered no criticism of the pilots' actions in firing back.[65] This international reaction indicates the separability of the norms relating to the option of a superpower to conduct naval maneuvers in or near the disputed territory of a hostile state and the norms regulating the defensive use of force by a military aircraft that is being fired upon. Furthermore, the international community generally supported neither Libya's claim to the Gulf as internal waters[66] nor its attempt to characterize its first-use position as a necessary defensive response to the situation.[67]

---

in the maneuvers. *See, e.g., U.K.: Telegraph Praises U.S. Response to Libyans*, FBIS (W. Eur.), Aug. 27, 1981, at Q1 (excerpt from the Daily Telegraph (London)).

65. *See, e.g.*, Rattner, *supra* note 64; *But see Libya's Larger Meaning*, Christian Sci. Monitor, Aug. 21, 1981, at 24 (editorial questioning whether the U.S. pilots could have taken evasive action, especially in light of previous nonviolent episodes); *FRG: Papers View Effects of U.S.-Libyan Air Clash*, FBIS (W. Eur.), Aug. 21, 1981, at 3 (text from Frankfurter Rundschau ("It is also feasible that the attacked American pilots fired their rockets too quickly to tell [the Libyan pilots] what is what in the American way"). A few commentators characterized the return of fire by the United States as unlawful. *See Bahrain: Paper Scorns Reagan Justification of Libyan Clash*, FBIS (No. Africa), Aug. 24, 1981, at C1 (describing the U.S. attack as indicating that "the only law Reagan respects is the law of the jungle and the law of the gun"); *Turkey: Press Reaction to U.S.-Libyan Incident*, FBIS (No. Africa), Aug. 28, 1981, at T5 (text from Hurriyet) ("it is impossible to justify the shooting down of planes"); *Pravda Comments on Sidra Incident, Views Reaction*, FBIS (USSR), Aug. 24, 1981, at N6 (denouncing the "U.S. Air Force's piratical attack on Libyan aircraft"). *See also* Letter to the Editor, PROC. U.S. NAVAL INST., May 1982, at 42 (written by Lieutenant Joseph R. McFaul, U.S. Coast Guard, arguing that even if the U.S. fleet was in international waters at the time of the incident, the United States may have violated international law by firing upon the Libyan planes: "The United States cannot claim self-defense if the Libyan attack had no chance of success. Considering [the technological superiority of the F-14s over the export version SU-22s] U.S. action was only retaliation, not self-defense. . . . [In addition, because this was] a peacetime incident, there [was] no justification for shooting down the second plane").

66. Only a few international actors supported Libya's claim to sovereignty over the Gulf. *See World Peace Council Denounces U.S. Aggression*, FBIS (No. Africa), Aug. 21, 1981, at A1 (text from Tripoli Domestic Service) (denouncing U.S. aggression against Libyan aircraft within Libyan airspace and territorial waters as part of an imperialist plot aimed against the Libyan Arab People); *Palestinian Reaction to U.S.-Libyan Dogfight: As-Sa'iquah Support*, FBIS (No. Africa), Aug. 21, 1981, at A2 (text from Tripoli JANA) (condemnation by Palestinian organization of U.S. actions against Libyan planes within Libyan airspace and territorial waters). The League of Arab States skirted the issue by noting only that the maneuvers occurred "near Libyan shores." News Release, League of

The failure of international elites to condemn the U.S. response constitutes an affirmation of American normative expectations concerning peacetime ROE. The failure to condemn Libya's attack directly does not, however, imply approval of the Libyan ROE. By accepting the outcome of the incident, international elites may be seen as expressing a consensus that the norms governing ROE include both the right to return fire if attacked and the duty to warn intruders before firing upon them.

OUTCOME

The decision of the international community was brief. There were no attempts to characterize the incident as an ongoing dispute in need of resolution, nor were efforts made to censure either actor or otherwise change behavior toward either party. Furthermore, after making their

---

Arab States, Office of Permanent Observer to the United Nations, Aug. 19, 1981. Comments by the Soviet government used similarly guarded language. *See, e.g. U.S. Naval Manuevers, Libyan Incident Condemned*, FBIS (USSR), Aug. 21, 1981 at H1 ("in the immediate vicinity of the Libyan coast"); *id.* at H2 ("according to Tripoli radio, this attack occurred in the airspace over Libyan territorial waters"); *Pravda Comments on Sidra Incident, Views Reaction*, FBIS (USSR), Aug. 26, 1981, at H6 ("on the approaches to Libya's shores"). *See also FRG: Papers View Effects of U.S.-Libyan Air Clash*, FBIS (W. Eur.), Aug. 21, 1981, at J3 (text from Frankfurter Rundschau) (noting that "most people did not take [Libya's 1973 claim of a 200-mile territorial waters zone along its coast] very seriously" since it "would include the Greek island of Crete as well as independent Malta").

67. Although many commentators criticized the maneuvers by the United States as unwise or instigatory, they did not argue that Libya was therefore justified in asserting as a necessary defensive measure an initiation of force in response to a symbolic show of strength. *But cf. Turkey: Press Reaction to U.S.-Libyan Incident*, FBIS (No. Africa), Aug. 28, 1981, at T4 (commenting that Libya was justified in considering the maneuvers to be provocative, implying that therefore the United States should not have been surprised at the Libyan response). *See also Palestinian Reaction to U.S.-Libyan Dogfight: Arafat Message*, FBIS (No. Africa), Aug. 21, 1981, at A1 (text from Tripoli Voice of Arab Homeland) (PLO leader praises shooting at "American forces, enemies of the people"). A few commentators directly condemned the Libyan resort to force as a violation of international law. *See Gunfight*, Wash. Post, Aug. 20, 1981, at A28, col. 1 (characterizing the act as typical of a lawless regime); *Daily Report: Middle East and South Asia Review, Libyan-U.S. Clash*, FBIS (No. Africa), Aug. 24, 1981, at 2 (Egyptian president Anwar el-Sadat criticizes Qadhafi for causing the incident, saying that the Libyan leader deserved to be executed for the "foolish act" in which heavy and unwieldy Sukhois took on the U.S. planes).

initial formal representations to the UN Security Council,[68] neither Libya nor the United States requested any further action.[69] The United States has continued to hold maneuvers in waters near the coasts of both friendly and hostile states and to challenge, through the presence of U.S. vessels or aircraft, other states' territorial claims to waters that it regards as international.[70]

In sum, the lack of further action implies that elites in the United States, Libya, and the international community decided that their public pronouncements, coupled with the actual outcome of the incident, were sufficient means of enforcing these norms. Resort to action may not have been possible or perceived as either necessary or productive under the circumstances.

Until 1986, it was unclear to what extent, if any, Libya had modified its ROE to redefine the point at which it would presume that its territory is in imminent danger of attack as to require the immediate defensive use of force. Libya had not attempted any similar actions against any aircraft flying over the Gulf of Sidra. On March 24, 1986, however, Libyan ground forces fired six SAM-2 and SAM-5 missiles at American aircraft on maneuvers in the Gulf. The United States responded with force, as U.S. aircraft fired Harpoon antiship missiles and HARM antiradiation missiles, destroying or damaging two Libyan ships and a coastal missile base. Later that day and early the next day, U.S. naval vessels and aircraft attacked two other ships and executed another attack on the coastal base.[71] This clash, whose magnitude well ex-

68. *See supra* notes 49–50.

69. The United States may have declined to do so both because of the probability of a Soviet veto and out of a desire to avoid a protracted discussion of U.S. military policy.

70. *See supra* note 30.

71. *See* Weinraub, *U.S., Citing Libyan Fire, Reports Attacking a Missile Site and Setting 2 Ships Ablaze*, N.Y. Times, Mar. 25, 1986, at A1, col. 6; Weinraub, *2 More Libyan Vessels Sunk and Base Hit Again, U.S. Says, Vowing to Keep up Patrols*, N.Y. Times, Mar. 26, 1986, at A1, col. 6 [hereinafter cited as *2 More Libyan Vessels Sunk*]. The United States apparently adopted ROE permitting an earlier use of force. After the first Libyan attacks, the United States stated that it would "now consider all approaching Libyan forces to have hostile intent." Gulf of Sidra Incident, Statement by the Principal Deputy Press Secretary, 22 WEEKLY COMP. PRES. DOC. 412 (Mar. 24, 1986). Indeed, the U.S. attack against the two Libyan ships on the second day of the encounter was precipitated not by any Libyan missile attack, but by Libyan forces having moved within a distance of the fleet that the U.S. considered too close. *2 More Libyan Vessels Sunk*, *supra*, at A8, cols. 1–2. A U.S. bombing raid on Libya on April 14, 1986, was, according to the United States, undertaken in response to Libyan support for terrorism, and was

ceeded the scope of the 1981 incident, clearly demonstrates both the unresolved nature of the dispute over the sovereignty of the Gulf and the continued reliance by Libya upon ROE that permit a first use of force based upon ill-defined threats to its territorial integrity.

AUTHOR'S APPRAISAL

The reinforcement by the United States and other international actors of existing norms governing the peacetime application of ROE for military aircraft, coupled with the apparent acquiescence of Libya, has important ramifications for the stability and predictability of peacetime military behavior. Thus, regardless of which side's version of the facts one adopts—both with respect to background facts and the facts of the incident itself—certain conclusions emerge.

The acceptance of a norm setting strict defensive limits upon the peacetime use of force against potentially hostile aircraft—and the inherent rejection of the Libyan conception of lawful behavior—promotes world public order by discouraging unwarranted employment of force. The reaction to the incident indicates both that the use of force will be seen as justifying a limited return of force and that states should be cautious about initiating defensive attacks against foreign aircraft—even if those aircraft are located over disputed waters over which a coastal state believes itself to have a strong claim.[72] The tacit reinforcement by international elites of the norms regarding the appropriate and inappropriate defensive uses of force in peacetime promotes the basic norms of both Articles 2(4)[73] and 51[74] of the United Nations Charter,

---

not directly related to any activities in the Gulf of Sidra. Security Council Considers U.S. Self-Defense Exercise, DEP'T ST. BULL., June 1986, at 19.

72. Furthermore, Libya's use of unpublicized but predetermined security lines, *see supra* note 63 and accompanying text, proved inconsistent with the general norm governing the use of peacetime ROE. The latter emphasizes certainty and reserves the use of force as a last resort of immediate defensive necessity. Libya's actions in the incident over the Gulf of Sidra demonstrated a readiness to use force at an earlier point than either the United States or the Soviet Union, and may be viewed as asserting a broader conception of the right to the defensive use of force.

73. "All Members shall refrain in their international relations from the threat or use of force against the territorial integrity or political independence of any state, or in any other manner inconsistent with the Purposes of the United Nations." U.N. CHARTER art. 2, para. 4.

74. "Nothing in the present Charter shall impair the inherent right of individual or

by reinforcing expectations that military aircraft may initiate a limited defensive use of force, but only when confronted with a bona fide danger either to themselves or to their national territory.

Yet the reinforcement of this general norm governing aerial engagement may also have negative consequences for public order. The Gulf of Sidra incident shows that, although certain states with well-established air forces have formulated sophisticated ROE that they are able to apply in a manner consistent with international norms, other states may not fully understand the norms or be capable of assuring their consistent application. The change in Libya's account of the incident, for example, may have indicated its uncertainly about the appropriate norms to invoke concerning aerial rules of engagement. The enforcement of a norm that not all states easily grasp may prove counterproductive to world order if it fails to secure shared expectations regarding appropriate actions and responses.

It is to be hoped, instead, that such reinforcement will function as a catalyst to encourage all parties to accept further pertinent international norms and to formulate ROE consistent with them. Although the norms that govern prescription, application, and appraisal of ROE may appear unnecessarily arcane to certain actors, they clearly offer greater stability than such alternatives as allowing states to fire at will on nearby foreign aircraft or disallowing the use of self-defense in hostile encounters. Although the incident that occurred in the Gulf of Sidra may have caused increased tension between the United States and Libya, the reinforcement of the norms governing rules of engagement should contribute to an atmosphere of greater stability for future military exercises.

---

collective self-defense if an armed attack occurs against a Member of the United Nations, until the Security Council has taken the measures necessary to maintain international peace and security. . . ." U.N. CHARTER art. 51.

THE SHOOTING OF KOREAN AIR LINES FLIGHT 007:
Responses to Unauthorized Aerial Incursions

9

CRAIG A. MORGAN

PROBLEM

In the early morning of September 1, 1983, a Korean Air Lines (KAL) Boeing 747 was shot down by a Soviet fighter while on a regularly scheduled flight from Anchorage, Alaska, to Seoul, South Korea. The Korean airliner had penetrated restricted airspace over a sensitive military base located on Sakhalin Island, on the northern Pacific coast of the Soviet Union. All 269 people aboard were killed. The downing resulted in the greatest loss of life and produced the strongest international reaction of any use of military force against civilian aircraft to date.

The response of effective elites to this incident demonstrates the development and clarification of normative expectations toward the use of force against civil aircraft intruding into territorial airspace. The incident is instructive for three reasons. First, the issues raised by the use of such force have never been formally adjudicated. Second, the only relevant international agreement in effect at the time of the incident did not settle the issue. Third, the most recent preceding incident had resulted in international behavior seemingly inconsistent with that of the four prior incidents.[1]

The KAL 007 incident seems to indicate that the use of lethal force against intruding aircraft is subject to a set of widely shared normative

1. For other discussion of the international legal implications of this shooting, *see,* Kennelly, *Korean Air Lines Flight 007–269 Dead: What Are The Rights of the Passengers? Against Whom?*, 1 AIR AND SPACE LAW. 1 (1983) (evaluating the bases of possible recovery by families of the victims from the Soviet Union, the United States, the airline, the manufacturer of the navigation equipment, and others); Note, *Legal Argumentation in International Crises: The Downing of Korean Air Lines Flight 007*, 97 HARV. L. REV. 1198 (1984) (describing argument in international community based on treaty, custom, and principle); Fox, *International Law and the Interception of Civil Aircraft: Flight 007*, 88 DICK. L. REV. 237 (1984) (discussing four previous incidents involving civil aircraft and concluding that appropriate international action should be taken formally to prohibit the use of deadly force against civil aircraft regardless of their reconnaissance potential); Hassan, *A Legal Analysis of the Shooting of Korean Airlines Flight 007 by the Soviet Union*, 49 J. AIR I. & COM. 555 (1984) (discussing previous incidents involving military or civil aircraft and role of Chicago Convention of 1944, and suggesting that shooting was arguably permissible if clear warning was given and ignored and if there were grounds for reasonable belief that serious threat to national security existed); Note, *Kal 007: A Definitive Denouement*, 8 SUFFOLK TRANS. L.J. 301 (1984) (discussing prior incidents and the Chicago Convention of 1944 and concluding that an amendment of the Convention is the best and only means to prevent a recurrence); Phelps, *Aerial Intrusions by Civil and Military Aircraft in Time of Peace*, 107 MIL. I. REV. 255 (1985) (tracing historical development of sovereignty over airspace through practice and treaty, including post–World War II incidents involving military or civil aircraft, and suggesting that "national security exception" for shooting civil aircraft has not been accepted by the international community in any of the earlier incidents and concluding that it should not apply in this one).Note, *Limitations on the Right to Use Force Against Civil Aerial Intruders: The Destruction of KAL Flight 007 in Community Perspective*, 6 N.Y.L. SCH. J. INT'L & COMP. L. 177 (1984) (discussing the shooting in light of the right to self-defense under Article 51 of the UN Charter and in light of prior incidents, and concluding that the shooting violated international law); FitzGerald, *The Use of Force Against Civil Aircraft: The Aftermath of the KAL Flight 007 Incident*, 22 CAN. Y.B. INT'L L. 291 (1984) (describing the internal process by which ICAO arrived at the proposed amendment to Article 3bis of the Chicago Convention during the spring of 1984); Comment, *Korean Airline Flight 007: Stalemate in International Law—A Proposal for Enforcement*, 22 SAN DIEGO L. REV. 859 (1985) (discussing ineffectiveness of present enforcement mechanisms to prevent such incidents and suggesting amendments to Chicago Convention to authorize establishment of system of fines, security deposits, and boycotts imposed against offending states and airlines). This study attempts a somewhat different approach. Rather than evaluating the legality of this incident in light of existing treaties, *opinio*

expectations among participants in the international community. These expectations require that, at least in peacetime, lethal force not be used against civilian aircraft intruding into territorial airspace unless such aircraft display hostile intent. Civil aircraft are to be presumed nonhostile even when flying at night through restricted airspace over sensitive military installations. The subjacent state has an affirmative duty to identify properly such an aircraft as civilian. Whether an intruder's failure to respond to obvious warnings would constitute sufficient hostile intent to warrant the use of lethal force is still unclear. A number of states, however, apparently subscribe to what could be the emerging norm: the only appropriate response in such a situation is diplomatic, at least when the intruding aircraft does not appear to be armed.

The Previous Incidents

Prior to the downing of KAL Flight 007, there had been five peacetime incidents in which civilian airliners were fired on by the military forces of a subjacent state and casualties resulted.[2] The international community, however, reacted to these incidents inconsistently, indicating no clearly shared normative expectation. Furthermore, there were factual considerations in the KAL downing that were not present in the earlier incidents. As a result, any community judgment of those earlier

---

juris, and prior practice, the focus is upon an assessment of this incident as itself a source of the normative expectations of effective elites in the international community.

2. *See generally* Hughes, *Aerial Intrusions by Civil Airlines and the Use of Force*, 45 J. Air L. & Com. 595 (1980). For an analysis of state practice and response to both military and civil aerial intrusion prior to 1953, *see*, Lissitzyn, *The Treatment of Aerial Intruders in Recent Practice and International Law*, 47 Am. J. Int'l L. 559 (1953). In addition to these five incidents involving airliners, there has been at least one involving a civil air transport plane. On June 3, 1954, a Soviet interceptor fired on a Sabena Airlines transport, en route from London to Belgrade near the Yugoslavian-Hungarian-Austrian border. N.Y. Times, June 4, 1954, at A1, col. 3. The radio officer was killed, the pilot and mechanic were wounded. *Id.* All were Belgians. *Id.* Belgium protested to the Soviet Union, demanding compensation and punishment of the fighter pilot. N.Y. Times, June 10, 1954, at A3, col. 4. Soviet officials claimed that the aircraft had intruded over the Soviet zone of Austria and had ignored orders to land. N.Y. Times, July 10, 1954, at A4, col. 3. Belgian, British, and Yugoslavian officials, as well as the crew, insisted that the transport had been in Yugoslavian airspace when attacked. N.Y. Times, June 5, 1954, at A3, col. 2.

incidents may not provide a complete basis for assessing the expectations of participants in the KAL 007 incident.

The first of these prior incidents occurred on April 29, 1952, when an Air France plane en route from Frankfurt to Berlin was attacked by Soviet fighters over the Soviet-occupied zone of Germany.[3] Three people aboard were injured,[4] but the plane, although badly damaged, was able to land safely in Berlin.[5] The Soviet Union claimed that its fighter had fired warning shots because the plane was not flying in the approved corridor and had thus violated Soviet airspace.[6] The British, French, and American Allied High Commissioners issued a joint statement vehemently protesting the shooting, denying that the airliner was outside the corridor, and arguing that it should not matter if it were: "Quite apart from these questions of fact, to fire in any circumstances, even by way of warning, on an unarmed aircraft in time of peace, wherever that aircraft may be, is entirely inadmissible and contrary to all standards of civilized behavior."[7] They requested that the Soviets conduct an investigation, punish those responsible, and pay compensation for the injuries and property damage.[8] It seems that these requests were never officially answered.[9]

A second incident occurred on July 23, 1954, when a Cathay Pacific airliner flying from Singapore to Hong Kong was shot down by fighters from the People's Republic of China, killing ten of the eighteen people on board.[10] Following protests from the British and American governments,[11] the Chinese, in a diplomatic note to the British,[12] took re-

3. N.Y. Times, Apr. 30, 1952, at A1, col. 1.
4. N.Y. Times, May 1, 1952, at A1, col. 4. Two of the passengers were injured, and one of the crew. *Id.* The aircraft was carrying fifteen passengers and five crew. N.Y. Times, Apr. 30, 1952, at A1, col. 1.
5. N.Y. Times, Apr. 30, 1952, at A1, col. 1.
6. *Id.*
7. N.Y. Times, May 1, 1952, at A3, col. 2.
8. N.Y. Times, Apr. 30, 1952, at A3, col. 2.
9. *See*, N.Y. Times, June 27, 1952, at A4, col. 4.
10. N.Y. Times, July 24, 1954, at A1, col. 1. Six of the ten passengers were killed, including three Americans, and four of the eight crew. *Id.* Curiously, the fact that the airliner may have been over international waters at the time of the shooting did not seem to be a factor in the international appraisal of this incident.
11. N.Y. Times, July 25, 1954, at A3, col. 1.
12. The People's Republic of China consistently refused to deal directly with the United States concerning this incident, a fact seen by some as an attempt to separate the

sponsibility for the incident, claiming that they had mistakenly identified the airliner as a Nationalist Chinese military aircraft on a mission of aggression.[13] They expressed their willingness to consider compensation[14] and subsequently paid in full the British demands submitted on behalf of all claimants.[15]

One year later, on July 27, 1955, Bulgarian fighters shot down an El Al Israel plane near the Graeco-Bulgarian border, killing all fifty-eight on board.[16] Protests and demands for compensation were lodged by the Israeli, British, American, French, and Swedish governments on behalf of their nationals killed in the incident.[17] In an official statement, the Bulgarian government claimed that the airliner had violated its airspace and ignored signals to land, but nonetheless admitted that its air defenses had "shown hastiness" by firing on the airliner before exhausting other means of forcing it to land.[18] The Bulgarian government promised to punish those responsible, take measures to prevent a recurrence, and pay compensation to the victims' families.[19] However, it later denied any fault in the incident, insisting that its offer of compensation was strictly *ex gratia*, and suggested an amount that Israel, the United States, and the United Kingdom all rejected as unacceptably small.[20] These three states then brought suit in the International Court

---

Americans and British as allies. N.Y. Times, July 30, 1954, at A1, col. 3; N.Y. Times, Aug. 6, 1954, at A3, col. 2.

13. N.Y. Times, July 26, 1954, at A3, col. 3.

14. *Id.*

15. N.Y. Times, Dec. 5, 1954, at A82, col. 4. The demand was for 367,000 pounds sterling, US$1,027,600 at the time. N.Y. Times, Nov. 4, 1954, at A7, col. 3.

16. N.Y. Times, July 28, 1955, at A1, col. 5; N.Y. Times, July 29, 1955, at A1, col. 1.

17. N.Y. Times, July 31, 1955, at 1, col. 3; N.Y. Times, Aug. 3, 1955, at 2, col. 6. The British protest was made on behalf of the British, Canadian, and South African victims. N.Y. Times, July 31, 1955, at 1, col. 3.

18. N.Y. Times, Aug. 4, 1955, at A1, col. 7.

19. *Id. See also* N.Y. Times, Aug. 12, 1955, at A1, col. 2. In response to a request from Israel, the UN General Assembly on December 14, 1955, adopted a resolution appealing to all governments to take the necessary measures to avoid such incidents, but did not condemn the shooting or identify Bulgaria by name. G.A. Res. 927(X), U.N. Doc. A/Res./362 (1955).

20. N.Y. Times, Aug. 6, 1957, at A5, col. 5. The Bulgarian offer was 56,000 transferable Bulgarian levas per victim killed, approximately US$8,244 at the exchange rate then current. Memorial of Israel (Isr. v. Bulg.; U.S. v. Bulg.; U.K. v. Bulg.; 1955 I.C.J.

of Justice, but Bulgaria refused to submit to the jurisdiction of the court and the case was never decided.[21]

The most serious incident prior to Flight 007 occurred on February 21, 1973, when a Libyan Airlines plane, en route from Benghazi, Libya, apparently overshot its destination, Cairo, and intruded over the Israeli-occupied Sinai. It was shot down by Israeli fighters and 106 of the 118 people on board were killed instantly or died shortly thereafter.[22] Israel maintained that the aircraft had penetrated airspace "over a most highly sensitive Israeli-controlled military area,"[23] had behaved in a suspicious manner,[24] and had acknowledged but ignored signals to land from the intercepting fighters.[25] Israeli officials claimed that the fighters had shot at the wings of the plane to force it to land, not to

---

Pleadings (Aerial Incident of July, 1955) 45, 79 (Memorial dated June 2, 1958) [hereinafter cited as the Memorial of Israel]. Bulgaria offered no compensation for the loss of the aircraft itself. Its total offer, therefore, was US$461,664 against combined Israeli, American, and British claims of US$2,981,088. See Memorial of Israel at 116, Memorial of the United States (Isr. v. Bulg.; U.S. v. Bulg.; U.K. v. Bulg.), 1955, I.C.J. Pleadings (Aerial Incident of July, 1955) 167, 248 (Memorial dated December 2, 1958) [hereinafter cited as the Memorial of the United States]; Memorial of the United Kingdom (Isr. v. Bulg.; U.S. v. Bulg.; U.K. v. Bulg.), 1955 I.C.J. Pleadings (Aerial Incident of July, 1955) 331, 366 (Memorial dated August 28, 1958) [hereinafter cited as the Memorial of the United Kingdom] See Application of the United Kingdom, Id. at 34, Annex 3, for the exchange rate then current. There was speculation that this shift in the Bulgarian position coincided with its admission to the United Nations in December 1955. The initial apology was made while its application was still pending. See N.Y. Times, Oct. 30, 1957, at 12, col. 3. This shift was repeatedly mentioned in all three Memorials cited above.

21. Gross, *Bulgaria Invokes the Connally Amendment,* 56 AM. J. INT'L L. 357 (1962). There have been reports, however, suggesting that the Bulgarians did eventually pay $200,000 in compensation to the Israelis. N.Y. Times, Feb. 22, 1973, at A11 col. 1; Margolich, *Legal Issues Hinge on Whether Airliner Was Warned,* N.Y. Times, Sept. 2, 1983, at A4, col. 1.

22. N.Y. Times, Feb. 23, 1973, at A1, col. 5. This included 99 of the 104 passengers and 7 of the 9 crew. N.Y. Times, Feb. 22, 1973, at A1, col. 8; N.Y. Times, Mar. 7, 1973, at A8, col. 1. Apparently, either two or four more died by early June. See ICAO Council Res. of June 4, 1973, ICAO Bulletin, July, 1973, at 13 (108 dead); N.Y. Times, June 7, 1973, at A15, col. 1 (110 dead).

23. N.Y. Times, Feb. 22, 1973, at A12, col. 7.

24. *Id.* This included lowering its landing gear as if to descend and then retracting it when the Israeli fighters withdrew. N.Y. Times, Feb. 23, 1973, at A1, col. 5.

25. N.Y. Times, Feb. 23, 1973, at A1, col. 5. Reportedly, the co-pilot, who survived, admitted that the crew had understood these signals but ignored them. *Id.* at A8, col. 1.

destroy it,[26] and had done so only as a last resort.[27] As further justification, they cited intelligence reports, received a month before, warning that Arab terrorists were planning to crash an aircraft loaded with explosives, or a hijacked airliner, into an Israeli city.[28] Nonetheless, Israel admitted that the shooting had been a mistake, although one that could only be known after the fact,[29] and offered to pay compensation on an *ex gratia* basis.[30] The international community condemned Israel for this incident. The Libyan foreign minister declared the shooting a "criminal act,"[31] and Syria, Lebanon, Algeria, and Egypt joined in denouncing Israel.[32] The United Nations Commission on Human Rights called the shooting "cruel and unjustified."[33] The International Federation of Airline Pilots' Associations concluded that it could find "no justification for the excessive use of force,"[34] but decided against calling for sanctions.[35] The International Civil Aviation Organization (ICAO) Secretariat conducted an investigation of the incident. The ICAO Council, after examining the Secretariat's report, adopted a resolution on June 4, 1973, strongly condemning Israel.[36]

The fifth incident occurred on the night of April 20–21, 1978, and involved a Korean Air Lines flight from Paris to Seoul, South Korea, that flew into Soviet airspace over a restricted military area south of

26. *Id.* In fact, it appears that the aircraft was destroyed while attempting to crash-land in the desert rather than in the air. N.Y. Times, Feb. 22, 1973, at A1, col. 8.

27. N.Y. Times, Feb. 22, 1973, at A1, col. 8.

28. N.Y. Times, Mar. 2, 1973, at A4, col. 1; N.Y. Times, Feb. 22, 1973, at A12, col. 7. *See also* Lew, *Shot Down Airliners—Legal Implications*, 123 New L.J. 408, 409 (1973). Although this scenario might have appeared plausible at the time, its use as a justification for the shooting is seriously weakened by the fact that the airliner apparently was on its way out of Israeli airspace when it was shot. N.Y. Times, Feb. 23, 1973, at A1, col. 5.

29. N.Y. Times, Feb. 25, 1973, at A1, col. 1; N.Y. Times, Mar. 2, 1973, at A4, col. 1.

30. N.Y. Times, Mar. 7, 1973, at 8, col. 1. The family of each victim killed was offered US$30,000 and each of the survivors was offered between US$10,000 and US$30,000 depending on injuries sustained—a total in excess of US$3,000,000. *Id.*

31. N.Y. Times, Feb. 22, 1973, at A1, col. 8.

32. N.Y. Times, Feb. 23, 1973, at A9, col. 1.

33. N.Y. Times, Feb. 28, 1973, at A7, col. 1. This was not adopted by a formal vote. *Id.*

34. *Id.*

35. N.Y. Times, Feb. 27, 1973, at A3, col. 2.

36. ICAO Council Res. of June 4, 1973, ICAO Bull., July, 1973, at 13. The vote was secret. N.Y. Times, June 6, 1973, at A4, col. 4.

Murmansk.[37] A Soviet fighter shot the airliner, killing two passengers and injuring sixteen others.[38] The airliner was able to crash-land on a frozen lake[39] with no additional injuries.[40] The Soviet Union released all of the passengers and most of the crew two days later,[41] but detained the pilot and navigator for a week of questioning.[42] This incident is noteworthy for its lack of strong adverse international reaction.[43] The Soviet Union did not publicly charge that the airliner was spying, and South Korea did not condemn the shooting as unjustified.[44] The president of South Korea, in fact, thanked the Soviet Union for the speedy return of the airliner's passengers and crew.[45] Neither South Korea nor the Soviet Union offered a public explanation of why the airliner was several hundred miles off course.[46]

37. This area includes the headquarters of the Soviet Northern Fleet at Severomorsk, eight airbases for nuclear bombers, nuclear missile installations, and several divisions of ground forces. N.Y. Times, Apr. 23, 1978, A1, col. 3.
38. N.Y. Times, Apr. 23, 1978, at A1, col. 3. There were ninety-seven passengers on board and thirteen crew. Id. None of the crew was harmed. Id.
39. N.Y. Times, Apr. 22, 1978, at A1, col. 1.
40. N.Y. Times, Apr. 23, 1978, at A1, col. 3.
41. Id.
42. N.Y. Times, Apr. 30, 1978, at A1, col. 5. The Soviet Union refused to release the aircraft or its flight recorder. N.Y. Times, Apr. 5, 1981, at A41, col. 2. Lloyds of London paid Korean Air Lines US $7,000,000 to reimburse the loss. Id.
43. See Hughes, supra note 2, at 613.
44. As in the other incidents, there was disagreement over the existence and adequacy of warnings. Soviet officials claimed that the fighters had attempted to signal the airliner for over two hours. N.Y. Times, Apr. 23, 1978, at A1, col. 3; N.Y. Times, Apr. 26, 1978, at A3, col. 4. This was contradicted by the reports from the passengers and crew. N.Y. Times, Apr. 24, 1978, at A1, col. 6; N.Y. Times, Apr. 30, 1978, at A15, col. 1. The Soviet Union reported that the pilot and navigator of the airliner had confessed to knowingly disobeying orders to land, a report upon which neither the pilot nor navigator would comment when they were released. N.Y. Times, Apr. 30, 1978, at A1, col. 5. The government of South Korea took no official position on whether the warnings had been given or ignored.
45. On April 24, 1978, Park Chung Hee expressed appreciation for the prompt return of the passengers and most of the crew while appealing for the quick release of the pilot and the navigator still in custody. N.Y. Times, Apr. 25, 1978, at A11 col. 1. This moderate position might have resulted from concern for the safety of the pilot and navigator or, as some speculated, from a desire to normalize relations with the Soviet Union. Id.
46. N.Y. Times, Sept. 1, 1983, at D19, col. 3. Some Soviet officials reportedly told journalists in private that the airliner had been shot because it was thought to have been spying and did not respond to visual commands to land. N.Y. Times, Apr. 27, 1978, at A15, col. 15. This was never substantiated with any physical evidence, however, despite

Prior to this fifth incident, a norm seemed to be emerging that clearly condemned the use of force against civilian aircraft under any but the most extreme circumstances. The muted reaction to the 1978 incident, however, appears difficult to reconcile with any widespread acceptance of such a norm. The lack of condemnation, in fact, could have been construed as vindication of the right to presume hostile intent of an aircraft from its prolonged presence in restricted airspace over sensitive security installations within a nation's borders. The 1973 Israeli incident is the only other incident in which the overflight of sensitive areas was claimed to justify a shooting. The area the Israelis claimed as sensitive, however, was in occupied territory, not in Israel proper, and the occupation of the Sinai was itself an issue of bitter international controversy. Israel's authority to designate the area as critical to its security interests was therefore debatable.[47]

These five incidents suggest that, prior to 1983, international normative expectations prohibited shooting an intruding aircraft simply because it was in one's airspace. "Exclusive sovereignty" over airspace above a state was not enough to justify employing force. In each of these incidents the territorial state felt it had to allege aggravating circumstances—such as failure to heed warnings or presence over sensitive areas—to justify using such force. Beyond this rejection of a rather absolute position, the governing norms were unclear.

In analyzing the prevailing norm prior to the KAL 007 incident, the role of international expectations regarding Soviet behavior may be significant. In two of the five incidents discussed above, the Soviet Union shot down intruding planes. In neither incident did it acknowledge wrongdoing, apologize, or offer any compensation, even on an *ex gratia* basis. This is in contrast to the reaction of the subjacent state in each of the other three incidents. Consistent with this behavior, the Soviet Union could be expected to have acquired a reputation for being peculiarly sensitive to aerial intrusion.[48]

---

the fact that the Soviets retained the aircraft. Officials from Korean Air Lines and the crew of the airliner steadfastly maintained that the course deviation resulted from the malfunction of navigation equipment. N.Y. Times, Apr. 23, 1978, at A1, col. 3; N.Y. Times, Apr. 25, 1978, at A11, col. 1; N.Y. Times, Apr. 30, 1978, at A1, col. 5.

47. Egyptian officials emphasized this as a relevant factor. *See* N.Y. Times, Feb. 23, 1973, at A8, col. 8; N.Y. Times, Feb. 26, 1973, at A9, col. 1.

48. Telephone interview with John Louis Magdelenat, assistant director of the Insti-

Formal Appraisals of the Norm

There have been few formalized international appraisals of the legality of the use of force against civilian aircraft. No international tribunal has ruled on any of the above incidents. Only the 1973 Libyan airliner incident was examined by a international organization. In that case, ICAO issued a resolution condemning the subjacent state, Israel, without elaborating on the standard it had applied.

Moreover, disagreement persists about whether lethal force can ever be used against civilian airlines and, if so, under what circumstances. Particularly demonstrative of this lack of consensus are the memorials submitted to the International Court of Justice by the governments of Israel, the United States, and the United Kingdom in their action against Bulgaria for the 1955 incident. Although all three states protested the shooting of the El Al airliner, they had different views of the norm to be applied. The United Kingdom firmly took the position that the only appropriate response to an intruding civilian aircraft could be diplomatic: "There can be no justification in international law for the destruction, by a State using armed force, of a foreign civil aircraft, clearly identifiable as such, which is on a scheduled passenger flight, even if that aircraft enters without previous authorization the airspace of the territory of that State."[49] Instead, the state whose airspace has been violated should first seek satisfaction from the owner of the aircraft and, failing that, should then protest to the state whose flag the aircraft bears.[50] Yet the British position may not be quite as absolute as it first appears. The British memorial did concede the right of a state to use force against an intruding aircraft "in the legitimate exercise of the right of self-defense."[51] Unfortunately, this cryptic qualification was not further explained.

---

tute of Air and Space Law, McGill University (May 10, 1984) (notes on file with the *Yale Journal of International Law*).

49. Memorial of the United Kingdom, *supra* note 20, at 358. In its diplomatic protest delivered to the Bulgarian Minister of Foreign Affairs on July 30, 1955, the United Kingdom had stated that it "cannot accept that any Government is within its rights in shooting down a civil aircraft in time of peace." *Id.* at 38. On March 15, 1957, the United Kingdom again informed Bulgarian officials that "nothing could possibly justify the shooting down of a civil airliner in peacetime." *Id.* at 356.

50. *Id.* at 363.

51. *Id.* at 358. This is, of course, consistent with Article 51 of the Charter of the United Nations, which states: "Nothing in the present Charter shall impair the inherent

The United States and Israel took more qualified positions than did the United Kingdom. The United States argued that international law permitted only three options in responding to an intruding aircraft: (1) identifying the aircraft and its nationality and thereafter lodging a diplomatic protest; (2) directing the aircraft to land through clearly understandable signals (if it is felt that the security of the subjacent state had already been violated); or (3) escorting the aircraft out of the unauthorized airspace (if it is feared that the aircraft might violate security while still there).[52] The United States stressed the importance of clearly adequate warning.[53] It repeatedly emphasized that only highly unusual circumstances threatening the security of the subjacent state could justify forcing an aircraft to land, and that, even in such a case, care must be taken to safeguard the lives of innocent passengers.[54] Nonetheless, it conceded that there were circumstances in which an intruding aircraft could pose a sufficiently grave threat to justify destroying it,[55] and implied that this might arguably be the case where the aircraft was "flying evasively or erratically over a known prohibited security area."[56]

Israel emphasized the need to exhaust less drastic measures, stating that "the question of warning is irrelevant to the main issue of Bulgarian responsibility."[57] To Israel, this "main issue" was that of proportionality:

> The degree of violence used was quite out of proportion to any possible threat to Bulgaria which [the aircraft] may have presented. . . . [W]hen measures of force are employed to protect territorial sovereignty, whether on land, on sea or in the air, their employ-

---

right of individual or collective self-defense if an armed attack occurs against a member of the United Nations, until the Security Council has taken the measures necessary to maintain international peace and security."

52. Memorial of the United States, *supra* note 20, at 235–36.

53. *Id.* at 210 & 243.

54. *Id.* at 210–11, 241, 243, & 244.

55. *Id.* at 239–40. The United States gave the example of an unauthorized, unidentified, military aircraft, bearing no clear exterior markings, traveling at great speed directly toward a high security area while refusing to comply with reasonable orders to identify itself. *Id.* This is, of course, a rather extreme example. Indeed, in such a situation it is difficult to imagine why it should matter whether the aircraft was identified.

56. *Id.* at 234.

57. Memorial of Israel, *supra* note 20, at 95. *See also Id.* at 87, where Israel states that "the opening of fire on an unarmed civil aircraft in the circumstances of this case, whether or not the aircraft was warned . . . calls for the most energetic protest."

ment is subject to the duty to take into consideration the elementary obligations of humanity, and not to use a degree of force in excess of what is commensurate with the reality and gravity of the threat (if any).[58]

Each of these three positions implies that under at least some circumstances shooting intruding civil aircraft could be justified. Those circumstances, however, are not helpfully discussed and there is no clear agreement on how they would be determined.

The 1944 Chicago Convention

The most important convention governing the use of airspace by civilian aircraft is the 1944 (Chicago) Convention on International Civil Aviation.[59] Article I of the Chicago Convention provides that "[t]he contracting States recognize that every State has complete and exclusive sovereignty over the airspace above its territory."[60] In addition, the

58. *Id.* at 84.

59. The Convention on International Civil Aviation, opened for signature December 7, 1944, 59 Stat. 1693, T.I.A.S. No. 1591, 15 U.N.T.S. 295 [hereinafter cited as Chicago Convention]. Article 80 binds contracting states to denounce adherence to the 1919 Paris and 1928 Havana Conventions. The United States, the Soviet Union, South Korea, and Japan—the principal participants in the KAL 007 incident—are all parties to the Chicago Convention. *See* E.A.S. No. 487 (list of states ratifying Chicago Convention). The Soviet Union submitted a "limited adherence" to the Convention, but the qualifications of its adherence are not relevant to the KAL Flight 007 incident. (They dealt with objections to Article 2, which the Soviet Union took to imply a continued recognition of the legality of colonialization and to Articles 92(a) an 93, which place restrictions on membership in terms of participation in World War II, which the Soviet Union characterized as outdated and discriminatory.)

60. Chicago Convention, *supra* note 59, art. 1. This principal has long been recognized. *See* 21 ANNUAIRE DE L'INSTITUT DE DROIT INT'L 293, 295–302 (1906) (recognizing as customary international law state sovereignty over its airspace comparable to sovereignty over territorial waters). *See generally* Denaro, *States' Jurisdiction in Aerospace under International Law,* 36 J. AIR L. & COM. 688 (1970) (discussing the historical development of the doctrine of "aer clausum"). Three major multilateral conventions since World War I have expressly rejected the airspace–international waters analogy and instead recognized the sovereignty of the subjacent state as a customary rule of international law. The Paris Conference of 1919 produced the International Convention for Air Navigation, U.S. Dep't St. Pub. 2143 (1944), which states in Article I that "[t]he High Contracting Parties recognise that every Power has complete and exclusive sovereignty over the airspace above its territory. . . ." The Commercial Aviation (Inter-American) Convention, Feb. 20, 1928, 47 Stat. 1902, T.S. No. 840, 132 L.N.T.S. 303, states in Article

Chicago Convention expressly authorizes contracting states to establish restricted areas for military purposes and to prohibit all flights above such areas.[61] The contracting states can formulate binding rules of air navigation for entering and leaving their airspace and for conduct while there.[62] They can also prohibit the transport of "munitions of war or implements of war"[63] or the use of photographic equipment.[64] Moreover, contracting states agree to ensure that aircraft registered under their flag will observe the rules of subjacent states.[65] In addition, they will not use civil aviation for "any purpose inconsistent with the aims of the Convention,"[66] which is the development of international civil aviation in a safe and orderly manner.[67]

The recognized right of airspace sovereignty does not, however, grant the subjacent state an unqualified authority to use force against any aircraft within its airspace. All signatories to the Chicago Convention agreed to "have due regard for the safety of navigation of civil aircraft" when issuing instructions to military aircraft to protect their respective airspace,[68] and to aid aircraft in distress.[69] The only expressly authorized response by the subjacent state to violations of its airspace is to force the intruding aircraft in the restricted airspace to land.[70] The text of the Convention nowhere addresses the use of force in intercepting civil aircraft. However, pursuant to the authority granted the International Civil Aviation Organization by Article 37 of the Convention, the ICAO has adopted recommended practices for the interception of civil aircraft by a subjacent state.[71] These guidelines specify identification,

---

I that "[t]he high contracting parties recognize that every state has complete sovereignty over the air space above its territory and territorial waters." As Denaro points out, *supra*, at 692–96, all of these conventions are cast in terms by which the contracting party recognizes the exclusive airspace sovereignty of all states, not just those parties to the convention, while limitations on that sovereignty and exemptions made to it apply only to contracting parties.

61. Chicago Convention, *supra* note 59, art. 9(a).
62. Id. art. 11.
63. Id. art. 35.
64. Id. art. 36.
65. Id. art. 12.
66. Id. art. 4.
67. *Id.* preamble.
68. Id. art. 3(d).
69. Id. art. 25.
70. Id. art. 9(c).
71. Id. art. 37(c). This provision grants ICAO the authority to adopt "international

KAL 007

warning, and signaling procedures, provide that interception of civil aircraft should be "undertaken only as a last resort,"[72] and recommend that intercepting aircraft "should refrain" from the use of weapons in all such cases.[73] Neither the recommended practices nor the Convention, however, indicates how the subjacent state may respond to an intruding aircraft that ignores warnings and instructions to land.

The Chicago Convention reflects basic ambiguities concerning the right of a subjacent state to use force against intruding aircraft. There is an unresolved tension between recognizing the exclusive sovereignty of the state and protecting the safety of innocent airline passengers. This tension is underscored by the fact that the Chicago Convention applies only to civilian aircraft. "State aircraft," defined to include those "used in military, customs, and police services,"[74] are expressly excluded.[75] Thus, an apparently civilian aircraft entering restricted airspace could be regarded as a state aircraft and excluded from the protections of the Convention if it were thought to be performing a military function such as reconnaissance.[76] Conversely, if the aircraft were

---

standards and recommend practices and procedures dealing with . . . (c) Rules of the air and air traffic control practices." Article 12 provides that such rules carry binding force over the high seas, but serve merely as recommendations for flights in a contracting state's territorial airspace. However, under Article 12 each contracting state agrees "to the greatest possible extent" to keep its own regulations uniform with those recommended pursuant to the Convention, and Article 38 requires each state to notify ICAO immediately of any differences between its internally adopted national procedures and those recommended by the international body. Under these provisions, ICAO has adopted Rules of the Air, Annex 2 to the Chicago Convention, *reprinted in* 22 I.L.M. 1154 (1983). The Annex includes, as Attachment A, a provision entitled Interception of Civil Aircraft, *reprinted in* 22 I.L.M. 1185 (1983). The Soviet Union has indicated compliance with Annex 2, subject only to a qualification concerning the use of Greenwich Mean Time on local flights. Amend. 1 to Supp. to Annex 2, Part III, Jan. 31, 1980, *reprinted in* 22 I.L.M. 1189 (1983).

72. Rules of the Air, Chicago Convention, Annex 2, *supra* note 71, para. 2.1, *reprinted in* 22 I.L.M. at 1185.

73. Id. para. 7.1 *reprinted in* 22 I.L.M. at 1187.

74. Chicago Convention, *supra* note 59, art. 3(b).

75. Id. art. 3(a).

76. This does not necessarily mean that the aircraft would be fair game for the subjacent state regardless of the magnitude of any threat it might pose. The principle in international law of proportionality between threat and response would apply even if express treaty provisions did not. *See generally* W. REISMAN & M. McDOUGAL, INTERNATIONAL LAW IN CONTEMPORARY PERSPECTIVE: THE PUBLIC ORDER OF THE WORLD COMMUNITY 964–98 (1981). However, international law and practice has developed a basic distinction

215

not believed to be on a military mission, it could be regarded as a civilian aircraft in distress. In that case, the subjacent state not only would be prohibited by the Chicago Convention from using force to divert the aircraft but would also be under an affirmative duty to render assistance.

FACTS

On September 1, 1983, KAL Flight 007 departed Anchorage, Alaska on a continuation of its service from New York City to Seoul, South Korea.[77] The plane was a Boeing 747 aircraft flying at night with 240 passengers and 29 crew aboard.[78] It was assigned route "Red 20," the westernmost of five routes for crossing the north Pacific, which allows aircraft to pass within fifty miles of the Soviet Union.[79] At some point east of Kamchatka, Flight 007 diverged west of its assigned route and entered Soviet airspace.[80] It crossed the southern Kamchatka Peninsula, left Soviet airspace as it flew over the Sea of Okotsk, and reentered

---

between the status of civil and state aircraft, with the latter entitled to a far more weighty presumption of hostile intent. See generally Hughes supra note 2.

77. Flight 007 was one of five regularly scheduled weekly flights from New York to Seoul. N.Y. Times, Sept. 2, 1983, at A4, col. 3. It had made a 70-minute stop in Anchorage to change crew, refuel, and drop off four passengers. Id.; N.Y. Times, Sept. 8, 1983, at A12, col. 1.

78. N.Y. Times, Sept. 2, 1983, at A4, col. 3. The 240 passengers were from 13 different states, with the largest representations (in declining order) from South Korea, the United States, and Japan. N.Y. Times, Sept. 4, 1983, at A17, col. 1. All of the crew were South Korean nationals. N.Y. Times, Sept. 3, 1983, at A6, col. 5.

79. N.Y. Times, Sept. 3, 1983, at A6, col. 5; N.Y. Times, Sept. 28, 1983, at A3, col. 1.

80. Early speculation seemed to center on the belief that Flight 007 veered off course Red 20 in the vicinity of checkpoint NIPPI, southeast of the Kamchatka Peninsula, the fifth of nine way points along the route. N.Y. Times, Sept. 3, 1983, at A6, col. 6. Later suggestions were that the flight was already well off course when it reported its position at NEEVA, the third way point, located approximately 130 miles from the American base at Shemya Island in the Aleutians, more than 1,400 miles from Anchorage. N.Y. Times, Sept. 23, 1983, at A3, col. 1. The investigation of the incident conducted by ICAO concluded that the flight began to deviate from its assigned path shortly after takeoff. DESTRUCTION OF KOREAN AIR LINES BOEING 747 OVER SEA OF JAPAN, 31 AUGUST 1983: REPORT OF ICAO FACT-FINDING INVESTIGATION, Attachment B to State Letter LE 4/19.4-83/130 (1983) [hereinafter cited as ICAO REPORT]. The point of divergence does not seem to have had much significance in the international debate over the incident.

it while approaching Sakhalin Island.[81] It crossed the island and was within several miles of leaving Soviet airspace once again, when it was struck by at least one air-to-air missile from a Soviet fighter.[82] A missile hit the airliner at approximately 3:26 A.M. local time (1826 Greenwich Mean Time), two and one-half hours after it first entered Soviet airspace. The airliner lost altitude and within twelve minutes crashed into the Sea of Japan, leaving no survivors. The aircraft voice and flight recorders were never recovered, nor were any large sections of wreckage.[83] Most of the remaining facts concerning the incident were disputed.[84]

81. N.Y. Times, Sept. 2, 1983, at A4, cols. 4–5. The area around Sakhalin Island is a major Soviet naval concentration of vital strategic importance to its Pacific fleet. Middleton, *Strategic Soviet Region: Area Where Russians Say Plane Intruded Is Critical Part of Their Far East Defenses*, N.Y. Times, Sept. 2, 1983, at A1, col. 7.

82. N.Y. Times, Sept. 2, 1983, at A4, cols. 5–6.

83. N.Y. Times, Sept. 13, 1983, at A10, col. 1; N.Y. Times, Nov. 6, 1983, at A8, col. 1.

84. Many of these factual disputes have continued and have produced a substantial body of literature debating why the airliner flew the route that it did and whether the United States was culpable, either because it planned the intrusion in advance or because it became aware of it in time to give warning but did not. *See e.g.*, Pearson, *K.A.L. 007: What the U.S. Knew and When We Knew It*, THE NATION, Aug. 18–25, 1984, at 105; Pearson, *New Pieces in the Puzzle of Flight 007*, THE NATION, Aug. 17–24, 1985, at 104 (arguing that U.S. collection capabilities in the area mean that it must have known of the airliner's route and concluding that the most persuasive theory is that the airliner made a deliberate intrusion, with the knowledge of the U.S., in order to activate Soviet air defense systems); Golden, *Seeing a Conspiracy in the Sky*, 5 DISCOVERY 8 (1984) (refuting espionage theory on grounds of technical limitations of U.S. radar capabilities); Sayle, *KE007: A Conspiracy of Circumstance*, N.Y. REV. OF BOOKS, Apr. 25, 1985, at 44 (refuting expionage conspiracy theories on technological grounds and arguing that most likely explanation for the airliner's course was an improperly set magnetic heading switch on the navigation computer); A. DALLIN, BLACK BOX: KAL007 AND THE SUPERPOWERS (1985) (evaluating a number of theories for the airliner's route and, although conceding difficulties with all of them, indicating some preference for that of a deliberate intrusion to active Soviet air defense systems); R. ROHMER, MASSACRE 747 (1984) (arguing that the intrusion was deliberately made in order to fly a shorter route and save fuel for a financially troubled airline); J. ST. JOHN, DAY OF THE COBRA (1984) (suggesting that the intrusion was caused by the Soviet Union through electronic means, hijacking, or substitution of route navigation cassettes inserted in the navigation computer, in order to intimidate Western powers by the subsequent shooting) S. HERSH, THE TARGET IS DESTROYED (1986) (suggesting that the course deviation was caused by errors in programming the takeoff point and subsequent route changes into the pilot's flight computer, and concluding that American intelligence services, for technical, operational, and organizational reasons, did not develop a complete picture of what was happening until after

CONFLICTING CLAIMS

Claims Justifying the Shooting

The Soviet Union justified its downing of the airliner on two grounds. First, it claimed that there was ample evidence to support a reasonable belief that the airliner was engaged in reconnaissance over strategically sensitive areas in Soviet territory, and the airliner had failed to respond to warnings or instructions to land. Second, the Soviet interceptors and air defense ground crews thought it was a military reconnaissance plane. The Soviet Union claimed that its action was fully justified and in keeping with international norms. The Soviets therefore concluded that they were under no obligation to apologize, admit liability, or provide compensation.[85]

In order to show that air defense personnel were justified in thinking that the airliner was spying, the Soviets alleged the following: (a) the aircraft approached from an area where an American RC-135 reconnaissance plane was operating;[86] (b) the airliner did not respond to radio signals from Soviet air traffic control services or from the intercepting fighters, including attempts on the international emergency frequency;[87] (c) while over Kamchatka the intruding aircraft emitted "short coded radio signals" such as those used to transmit intelligence;[88] (d) shortly thereafter, it radioed Tokyo flight control center: "We have safely passed over southern Kamchatka. The plane is proceeding normally";[89] (e) the airliner actively sought to maneuver around air defense

---

the fact); R. JOHNSON, SHOOTDOWN: FLIGHT 007 and the AMERICAN CONNECTION (1986) (concluding that the intrusion most likely was deliberately planned at the direction of the United States CIA in order to trigger defensive radars in the Soviet interior, and that American electronic assets were used to confuse Soviet air defense systems during the flight).

85. *Press Conference Moscow*, Pravda, Sept. 10, 1983, at 4, *reprinted in* CURRENT DIG. SOV. PRESS, Oct. 5, 1983, at 5 [subsequent cites refer to CURRENT DIG. SOV. PRESS reprint].

86. N.Y. Times, Sept. 1, 1983, at A4, col. 1

87. TASS statements of Sept. 2 and 3, 1983, *reprinted in* CURRENT Dig. SOV. PRESS, Sept. 28, 1983, at 1.

88. *Press Conference in Moscow*, *supra* note 85, at 2.

89. Zakharov, *What is Behind the "Incident"?*, Pravda, Sept. 6, 1983, at 4 *reprinted in* CURRENT DIG. SOV. PRESS, Sept. 28, 1983, at 7 [subsequent cites refer to CURRENT DIG. SOV. PRESS reprint].

missile batteries and evade intercepting aircraft over Sakhalin Island;[90] (f) KAL 007 flew without air navigation lights; (g) it ignored visual signals from intercepting fighters of flashing lights and rocking wings as well as 120 rounds of tracer fire;[91] and (h) it persisted in flying through highly sensitive airspace plainly marked on all navigation maps as restricted.[92]

The Soviets also argued that an accidental straying of the 747 was extremely unlikely given its sophisticated triple-redundant inertial navigation system and experienced crew.[93] In addition, they claimed that information subsequently revealed supported their earlier conclusion that the deviation in flight path was deliberate and had been performed as part of an intelligence mission. The Soviet Union, for example, argued that the United States and Japan, by disclosing tape recordings of the radio transmissions of the Soviet fighter pilots, had shown their awareness of KAL 007's peril, yet had neither warned the aircraft nor contacted Soviet authorities.[94] Similarly, the Soviet Union pointed out that U.S. air traffic controllers were responsible for the flight until Japanese controllers took over, but neither the Americans nor the Japanese attempted to warn the plane that it was off course.[95] The Soviets also argued that the flight had been delayed forty minutes in Anchorage to synchronize its penetration of Soviet airspace with the passage overhead of an American intelligence satellite; that the flight carried an extra eleven crew members, presumably needed to operate the reconnaissance equipment, and that several American military planes and ships were off the Soviet coast at the time.[96]

90. *Press Conference in Moscow, supra* note 85, at 2.

91. Romanov, A *Political Provocation with a Far-Reaching Aim,* Pravda, Sept. 5, 1983, at 5, *reprinted in* CURRENT DIG. SOV. PRESS, Sept. 28, 1983, at 4 [subsequent cites refer to CURRENT DIG. SOV. PRESS REPRINT]; *Press Conference in Moscow, supra* note 54, at 3.

92. Zakharov, *supra* note 89, at 7. Official navigation maps carry the following warnings for the Kamchatka and Sakhalin areas: "Aircraft infringing upon non-free flying territory may be fired on without warning." N.Y. Times, Sept. 8, 1983, at A12, col. 1.

93. Bovin, *The Tragedy in the Sky and the Crime on the Ground,* Izvestia, Sept. 8, 1983, at 4, *excerpted in* CURRENT DIG. SOV. PRESS, Oct. 5, 1983, at 6 [subsequent cites refer to CURRENT DIG. SOV. PRESS reprint].

94. Bandura, *U.S. Wants "To Kill Soviet Peace Offensive,"* Izvestia, Sept. 10, 1983, at 5, *excerpted in* CURRENT DIG. SOV. PRESS, Oct. 5, 1983, at 7.

95. Romanov, *supra* note 91 at 5.

96. Kirsanov, *The Facts Expose Washington,* Pravda, Sept. 20, 1983, at 4, *reprinted in* CURRENT DIG. SOV. PRESS, Oct. 12, 1983, at 7. The Soviet account also mentioned

Beyond the primary claim that Flight 007 was on a spying mission, the Soviets also implied that the airliner was, in any case, mistaken for an RC-135 American reconnaissance plane. According to the Soviet Union, the Korean airliner and an RC-135 patrolling off the coast of Kamchatka had approached each other at the same altitude and for ten minutes had flown so closely alongside each other that their radar images had merged.[97] The RC-135 then flew north toward the Aleutians, and the airliner headed into Soviet airspace.[98] The Soviets alleged that the radar profile of a 747 is "analagous" to that of an RC-135,[99] and that its contours in the dark "greatly resemble" it.[100] Moreover, the Soviets claimed that the encounter between the intruding aircraft and the interceptors took place under cloudy conditions and at a great distance,[101] producing such bad visibility that the 747, flying without lights and not responding to signals, was easily mistaken for an intruding reconnaissance plane.

Claims Condemning the Shooting

The United States was the primary voice for the proposition that the shooting was unjustified. Several other states, notably South Korea and Japan, joined in this position. The case against the downing was based on two principal claims. First, the airliner was not on a spying mission, did not act as if it were, and had, in fact, been shot down without adequate attempts to warn it. Second, a Boeing 747 is clearly distinguishable from an RC-135 even at night and reasonable attempts to identify the aircraft would have revealed the difference. The United States, Japan, and South Korea claimed that the Soviet Union was therefore fully liable for the wrongful downing of the airliner and owed reparations.[102]

---

that the pilot of the airliner, Chung Byung In, had boasted to friends of his role in performing special tasks for American intelligence and had even shown them some of the equipment on the plane. Borisov, A *Branch of American Intelligence*, Krasnaya Zvezda, Sept. 16, 1983, at 3, *reprinted in* CURRENT DIG. SOV. PRESS, Oct. 12, 1983, at 9.

97. *Press Conference in Moscow, supra* note 85, at 2.

98. Id.

99. Id.

100. *See supra* note 95.

101. *Press Conference in Moscow, supra* note 85, at 3, 5; N.Y. Times, Sept. 7, 1983, at A16, col. 2.

102. Diplomatic Note from the U.S. Department of State, Sept. 16, 1983, *reprinted in* 22 I.L.M. 1196 (1983).

The United States conceded that the Korean airliner had violated Soviet airspace in a strategically sensitive region, and that there was no convincing explanation for the plane's deviation from the assigned route.[103] Nonetheless, the United States denied that the airliner had been performing reconnaissance or that the Soviet Union had reasonable cause to believe that it was on such a mission. Despite the aircraft's sophisticated equipment, the United States argued that a navigation error could not be ruled out as a possible, though unlikely, explanation. Ambassador Jeane Kirkpatrick referred to twenty-one recorded incidents of such errors with similar equipment.[104] As an example, if the pilot had confused the last three digits in latitude for the last three digits in longitude while programming one of his checkpoints into the computers, the plane would have flown over Sakhalin Island instead of along the correct route.[105] Alternatively, the captain could have switched the automatic pilot from "computer mode" to "heading mode" in order to steer around a cloud or storm mass. If he had then forgotten to return the controls to computer mode, the plane would have continued in a straight line in whatever direction it was last pointed.[106]

In disputing the Soviet factual account of the incident, the United States relied heavily on recordings of radio conversations between the four intercepting Soviet fighter pilots and their three ground control stations. These recordings were made available by Japanese intelligence services and allegedly covered the Soviet pursuit of the airliner during the last thirty minutes of its flight.[107] The Soviet Union did not seriously challenge the authenticity of the recordings, despite a few disclaimers by some officials and by the Soviet media. Yuri Kornilov, a Tass commentator, for example, reported that Soviet officials had de-

103. N.Y. Times, Sept. 6, 1983, at A15, col. 2.
104. Statement of Mrs. Kirkpatrick, Sept. 12, 1983, U.N. Doc. S/PV.2476 (1983), at 63–65.
105. N.Y. Times, Sept. 4, 1983, at 18, col. 6. This appears to be the explanation favored by U.S. officials.
106. N.Y. Times, Sept. 11, 1983, at A16, col. 4.
107. N.Y. Times, Sept. 7, 1983, at A14, col. 1. Only the pilots' end of the conversations were made available, the words of the ground controllers did not appear on the tape or on the transcripts. This use of such recordings is not unprecedented. In February 1957, the U.S. State Department released recordings of the conversations of Soviet fighter pilots shooting down a U.S. Air Force C-130 over Armenia, in order to prove that it had not "crashed" as the Soviets had suggested. N.Y. Times, Feb. 6, 1957, at A1, col. 8.

221

clared that "these recordings could not be believed since they have been falsified from beginning to end."[108] Yevgney Pozdnykov, counselor at the Soviet embassy in Ottawa, said they might have been recorded at another time, perhaps even during a drill several years earlier.[109] Despite these disclaimers, however, no senior Soviet official publicly questioned the legitimacy of the tapes, no alternative recordings or transcripts were offered, and no specific portion of them was ever challenged as inaccurate or falsified even though Ambassador Kirkpatrick offered to make copies of the cassettes available to any interested delegation.[110]

The Soviets instead argued that the tapes both demonstrated that Japanese authorities were aware that Flight 007 was in peril[111] and verified the accuracy of the Soviet account on at least two factual matters.[112] Transcripts of the tapes[113] were offered by the United States to show that: (a) the pilot of the intercepting plane, who eventually shot down the airliner, had it in sight for twenty minutes before firing at it;[114] (b) he twice reported that KAL 007's strobe light was working[115] and once that its air navigation lights were on;[116] and (c) none of the Soviet pilots attempted to contact the airliner by using radio, by flashing lights, or by rocking their wings.[117] The pilot of the lead fighter stated in the

108. N.Y. Times, Sept. 13, 1983, at A10, col. 2. Pravda called the recordings a "forgery." Pravda, Sept. 12, 1983, at 5, reprinted in CURRENT DIG. SOV. PRESS, Oct. 12, 1983, at 4.

109. N.Y. Times, Sept. 7, 1983, at A16, col. 7.

110. Statement of Mrs. Kirkpatrick, Sept. 6, 1983, U.N. DOC. S/PV. 2471 (1983), reprinted in 22 I.L.M. 1121 [hereinafter cited as Sept. 6 Kirkpatrick Statement].

111. Bovin, supra note 93, at 6.

112. The tapes were cited to support Soviet claims that Flight 007 suddenly decreased speed, causing a pursuing fighter plane to pass it, and that the interceptor fired cannon bursts as a warning, N.Y. Times, Sept. 14, 1983, at A12, col. 4.

113. See N.Y. Times, Sept. 7, 1983, at A14, col. 1 (transcript as provided to the United Nations Security Council).

114. Id.

115. Id.

116. Id. The Soviet Union responded that this transmission was inaccurately attributed to the lead aircraft, and was actually a report by the pilot of the second fighter that he saw the lights of the first. N.Y. Times, Sept. 10, 1983, at 5, col. 3. The Soviet Union did not offer a response to the U.S. claim that at 1821:35 GMT the pilot of the lead interceptor, allegedly referring to its strobe light, reported that "the target's light is blinking."

117. Sept. 6 Kirkpatrick Statement, supra note 110, reprinted in 22 I.L.M. at 1124.

transcript that he tried to use I.F.F.(Identify, Friend or Foe) signaling.[118] The U.S. countered that civilian airliners are not equipped with this electronic capability so that its use was irrelevant.[119] The transcripts, as later revised by U.S. State Department linguistic experts, did reveal that the lead fighter pilot had fired cannon bursts six minutes before firing the missiles that hit the airliner.[120] The United States responded, however, that the cannon bursts could have been an attempt to down the plane without using missiles.[121] Even if it was intended as a signal, moreover, the lack of response by the airliner should have prompted the use of other means to communicate, none of which was tried.[122]

In addition, the transcript indicated that the airliner did not change course during the last thirty minutes of flight, although at one point it did slow down.[123] This tended to discredit Soviet charges that the airliner radically altered course, altitude, and speed in order to evade pursuers.[124] Moreover, the last transmissions from Flight 007 to the Tokyo air controller, made while it was being pursued by Soviet fighters over Sakhalin Island and after the cannon bursts had been fired, gave no indication that the pilot knew he was off course or in any danger.[125] This was taken to show that attempts to contact him either had never been made or had been unsuccessful.

Taken in sum, these arguments were marshaled by the United States

118. N.Y. Times, Sept. 7, 1983, at 14, col. 2.
119. Sept. 6 Kirkpatrick Statement, *supra* note 110, *reprinted in* 22 I.L.M. at 1124.
120. N.Y. Times, Sept. 12, 1983, at 1, col. 1.
121. *See* Statement of Mrs. Kirkpatrick, Sept. 12, 1983, U.N. Doc. S/PV.2476, *reprinted in* 22 I.L.M. 1145 (1983) [hereinafter cited as Sept. 12 Kirkpatrick Statement].
122. *Id.*
123. N.Y. Times, Sept. 7, 1983, at A14, col. 3. At approximately the same time, the pilot of the airliner said he was ascending from 32,000 feet to 35,000 feet. N.Y. Times, Sept. 2, 1983, at A4, col. 6. It is possible that the decrease in speed reported by the Soviet pilot, and later described by him as an evasive "trick," N.Y. Times, Sept. 14, 1983 at A12, col. 4, simply resulted from this climb to a higher altitude. According to the transcripts, the Soviet pilot did not report any change in the airliner's altitude. N.Y. Times, Sept. 7, 1983, at 14, col. 1. Yet Marshal Ogorkov interpreted the pilot's communications as indicating changes in altitude. N.Y. Times, Sept. 10, 1983, at 4, col. 3.
124. Krasnaya Zvezda, Sept. 13, 1983, at 3, *reprinted in* CURRENT DIG. SOV. PRESS, Sept. 28, 1983, at 4; N.Y. Times, Sept. 10, 1983, at 4, col. 6.
125. N.Y. Times, Sept. 2, 1983, at A4, col. 6; N.Y. Times, Sept. 4, 1983, at 18, col. 2. *See also* U.N. Doc. S/PV.2473 of Sept. 7, 1983, and SPV.2473/Corr.1 of Sept. 9, 1983, *reprinted in* 22 I.L.M. 1135–36 (1983) (statement of the Japanese representative).

to indicate that the Korean airliner had not, in fact, behaved in a suspicious manner beyond the conceded fact that it was flying without authorization over a restricted area in Soviet airspace. Other allegations indicating that Flight 007 was part of an intelligence collection effort were dismissed.[126]

The United States further claimed that the 747 could not possibly

126. Both the United States and Japan argued that their civilian air controllers had no way of knowing that Flight 007 was off course or in any danger until its last transmission, which was made after it had been hit by the missile. Furthermore, they argued that the military radar, even if it had detected the plane's route, could not identify it as a non-Soviet civilian airliner. The U.S. military radar in Alaska, which under special agreement between the Department of Defense and the Federal Aviation Administration monitors airliners departing south over the Pacific, observed that Flight 007 was on course as it left radar range approximately 200 miles from Alaska. N.Y. Times, Sept. 10, 1983, at 1, col. 5; Wash. Post, Sept. 2, 1983, at A9, col. 1. From that point on, air controllers in both the United States and Japan must rely upon position reports radioed from the pilot until he comes within range of Japanese air control radar. Flight 007 never came within range of that radar, and all of the pilot's position reports were normal prior to the time the airliner was shot down. *Id.*; Statement of Mr. Kurodo, Sept. 9, 1983, U.N. Docs. S/PV.2473 & /PV.2473/ Corr.1 (1983), *reprinted in* 22 I.L.M. 1135 (1983). The U.S. Air Force radar on Shemya Island, moreover, is about 550 miles from Kamchatka and does not cover the point where Flight 007 apparently entered Soviet airspace. Witkin, F.A.A. *Chief Says Jet Was Beyond Radar*, N.Y. Times, Sept. 19, 1983, at A7, col. 4. Japanese Air Self-Defense Force radar at Wakkanai, Hokkaido, recorded an aircraft flying southwest over Sakhalin Island. *Id.* Japanese intelligence services recorded communications between the Soviet fighter pilots and their ground controllers. Because these recordings did not alarm anyone at the time, the Japanese did not analyze the communications until after the fact. *Id.* The RC-135 aircraft that was patrolling outside Soviet airspace that night was on a routine reconnaissance patrol known as the Cobra Dane Spacetrack Radar System, which monitors Soviet missile tests in Kamchatka to ensure compliance with SALT agreements. Shribman, U.S. *Experts Say Soviet Didn't See Jet Was Civilian*, N.Y. Times, Oct. 7, 1983, at A10, col. 3. One such test was scheduled for that evening. Taubman, U.S. *Had Noticed Activity by Soviet*, N.Y. Times, Sept. 14, 1983, at A12, col. 6. The presence of the RC-135 was therefore purely coincidental. Moreover, it had no contact with Flight 007 and was never closer than 75 nautical miles to it. Korean authorities indicated that the number of assigned personnel working on Flight 007 was twenty-three, not eighteen as alleged by the Soviet Union, and that the extra six airline employees on the flight were on their way home or to other assignments. N.Y. Times, Sept. 3, 1983, at A6, col. 5. Korean Air Line officials denied that Flight 007 had been delayed in order to coordinate its flight with the passage of a reconnaissance satellite, pointing out that it was standard procedure to calculate the departure time separately for each flight. ICAO REPORT, *supra* note 80, at 36. No direct response was made to Soviet claims that an American reconnaissance satellite passed overhead during Flight 007's penetration of Soviet airspace, or that the pilot, Chung Byun In, had boasted of spying.

have been mistaken for an RC-135 if reasonable care had been taken. According to the United States, the RC-135 patrolling off the coast had neither entered Soviet airspace nor ever been closer than seventy-five nautical miles to Flight 007.[127] The two aircrafts' radar blips thus could not have "merged" on Soviet radar. A 747, moreover, is fifty feet longer than an RC-135, with a thicker fuselage and a distinctive hump on its back.[128] From the cockpit of a nearby intercepting aircraft, this difference would have been visible even at night—particularly since the night in question was clear with a half moon,[129] and the airliner's lights were on. The United States also pointed out that the fighter pilot had observed Flight 007 for twenty minutes before firing and argued that he should have moved closer if he could not positively identify the plane from two kilometers away.[130]

CONFLICTING CONCEPTIONS OF LAWFULNESS

Conceptions Justifying the Shooting

In several statements, the Soviet Union claimed the right to shoot down an intruding aircraft as an inherent "sovereign right of every state"[131] to protect its "sacred" borders,[132] which no one had the right to violate with impunity.[133] In many of these statements, the Soviet Union stressed the consistency of its actions against KAL 007 with the Law on the USSR State Border, adopted in November 1982.[134] This edict authorizes the Soviet air defense forces to use armed force "against violators of the USSR state border," whether they threaten violence or not.[135] The Soviets did not attempt to explain why this do-

127. Weisman, *Jet Spotted By Russians: U.S. Aides Say Soviet Could Have Initially Mistaken It and Commercial Craft*, N.Y. Times, Sept. 5, 1983, at A1, col. 6.
128. *See id.*
129. N.Y. Times, Sept. 10, 1983, at A6, col. 6.
130. N.Y. Times, Sept. 7, 1983, at A15, cols. 2–3.
131. *See, e.g.*, Pravda, Sept. 7, 1983, at 1, *reprinted in* CURRENT DIG. SOV. PRESS, Sept. 28, 1983, at 9.
132. N.Y. Times, Sept. 8, 1983, at A10, col. 4.
133. *Id.*
134. Law of the Union of Soviet Socialist Republics on the USSR State Border, Pravda, Nov. 26, 1982, at 1–3, *reprinted in* CURRENT DIG. SOV. PRESS, Jan. 19, 1983, at 15–20.
135. *Id.* art. 36. Despite the potential of this statute for a "shoot on sight" interpretation, the aircraft interception procedures issued by the Soviet Union to its military forces

mestic statute might be accepted as dispositive of the international legal issues involved in the incident. It is significant, however, that despite such absolutist rhetoric, the Soviet Union nonetheless sought to justify the incident by claiming that the aircraft was performing a military function and had failed to respond to less severe measures. The norm actually asserted by the Soviets, therefore, was not that any intruder could be shot at will. Rather, the Soviets' proposed norm was that airliners on state missions lose their protected status as commercial aircraft and can be destroyed if they violate territorial airspace, at least after warnings are attempted. As noted above, international conventions and practice do support a distinction between intruding military aircraft and intruding civilian aircraft, with the former entitled to less protection.[136]

Underlying the Soviet argument is the premise that an aircraft's status is determined by its *function* and that a civilian airliner performing a reconnaissance mission may be treated as a military intruder.[137] Implicit in this legal conception are two assumptions: (a) aerial reconnaissance in itself constitutes a threat to the subjacent state sufficient to justify the use of violence in a manner endangering civilian lives; and (b) the territorial state has the right to ascribe a reconnaissance purpose to an aircraft found in restricted airspace when that aircraft does not

---

complied with those recommended by ICAO. See Interception Procedures Used by U.S.S.R., ICAO Report, *supra* note 80, Appendix H.

136. The Chicago Convention, in particular, expressly excludes military aircraft from its coverage. *See supra* notes 74–75 and accompanying text. International reaction to previous incidents, moreover, has been more condemnatory where civilian airliners have been shot than where the aircraft were military. *See generally* Lissitzyn, *supra* note 2, and Hughes, *supra* note 2. The Soviet argument that mistaking the 747 for a military RC-135 aircraft would be a mitigating factor implicitly recognized this distinction.

137. *See, e.g.*, Pravda, Sept. 15, 1983, at 5, *reprinted in* Current Dig. Sov. Press, Oct. 12, 1983, at 6 ("guarantees for flights of civilian planes over USSR territory . . . have no relation to the measures that our country takes with respect to spy planes"); Pravda, Sept. 10, 1983, at 4, *reprinted in* Current Dig. Sov. Press, Oct. 5, 1983, at 1 (press conference conducted in Moscow by the Soviet Ministry of Defense and Ministry of Foreign Affairs, at which it was said that a straying civilian airliner is fundamentally different from one sent "with a preplanned mission"). The underlying premise of the Soviet approach had been previously stated as follows: "Whatever category a plane formally belongs to, its character is *determined by the function it performs*, a plane used for military purposes will always be regarded as a reconnaissance plane, just like a transport plane used as a bomber cannot expect to be treated as a commercial aircraft." Korovin, *Aerial Espionage and International Law*, Int'l Aff. (Moscow) 49, 50 (1960) (emphasis added).

respond to reasonable attempts to warn. This position finds some support in the provisions of the Chicago Convention[138] and in the apparent international acquiescence to the downing of the Korean Air Lines flight in 1978.[139]

Conceptions Condemning the Shooting

The United States argued that no state in peacetime has the right to shoot an intruding aircraft, even over restricted territory, as long as it does not threaten violence.[140] The United States emphatically claimed that the 747 was plainly identifiable as a civilian airliner and would have been so identified had appropriate warning procedures been followed. This argument indicates that the United States nonetheless recognized those international norms distinguishing between civilian and military aircraft.[141]

The norm asserted by the United States was that a state in peacetime may not use lethal force against an airliner, even if the airliner seems to be performing a reconnaissance mission in restricted airspace. The burden, furthermore, is on the intercepting state to identify correctly the aircraft as civilian. Mere suspicion about an aircraft's intentions does not justify treating it as military. This conception also finds support in the provisions of the Chicago Convention,[142] which not only disclaims the use of violence against civil airliners,[143] but also provides that the first interception maneuver should be a close visual inspection of the intruding aircraft.[144]

Moreover, even if a state has a recognized right of self-defense that might in some cases justify action against a civilian airliner on a *combat*

138. *See supra* notes 61–66 and accompanying text.

139. *See supra* notes 43–46 and accompanying text.

140. Sept. 12 Kirkpatrick Statement, *supra* note 121, *reprinted in* 22 I.L.M. at 1145. *See also* Shribman, *U.S. Experts Say Soviets Didn't See Jet Was Civilian,* N.Y. Times, Oct. 7, 1983, at A1, col. 1.

141. This implicit distinction is consistent with the response of the United States to the U-2 incident in 1960, during which the United States never protested the fact that an unarmed military reconnaissance plane over Soviet territory was shot down without warning and its pilot imprisoned. Lissitzyn, *Some Legal Implications of the U-2 and RB-47 Incidents,* 56 AM. J. INT'L L. 135, 135–36 (1962).

142. *See supra* notes 68–70.

143. Id.

144. Interception of Civil Aircraft, Chicago Convention, Annex 2, Attachment A, *supra* note § 3, *reprinted in* 22 I.L.M. at 1185–86.

mission, the United States claimed that such justification would not apply to an airliner on a *reconnaissance* mission. In the latter case, it was argued, endangering civilian lives is an evil far disproportionate to the harm prevented and thus violates the international norm of proportionality.[145] Particularly in light of modern intelligence collection methods, the incremental danger to a state's security posed by a civilian airliner on a reconnaissance mission is so slight that it could hardly justify the use of force endangering civilian lives.[146] The appropriate response would be some form of diplomatic action.[147]

OUTCOME

The Soviet Union never apologized for the shooting, admitted any fault, or offered compensation to the families of the victims. However, there have been reports that the Soviets, profoundly embarrassed by the incident, promptly began a sweeping reorganization of their air defense forces in the Far East.[148]

Despite the considerable attention to the subject, no participant or observer has come forth with convincing evidence that the intrusion of the airliner into Soviet air space was deliberate or manifested a threat of violence.[149]

145. Ambassador Kirkpatrick argued that this proportionality principle was particularly relevant to Flight 007, since the plane was allegedly within 60 seconds of leaving Soviet airspace when it was shot down and had already passed over the sensitive areas the Soviet Union wished to protect. Sept. 12 Kirkpatrick Statement, *supra* note 121, *reprinted in* 22 I.L.M. 1145 (1983).

146. *See* N.Y. Times, Sept. 26, 1983, at A6, col. 2.

147. The United States asserted that there had been seventy-five such incidents in which Soviet aircraft had strayed into U.S. airspace, and that none had ever been shot down. Statement of Mr. Lichenstein, Sept. 2, 1983, U.N. Doc. S/PV.2470 (1983), *reprinted in* 22 I.L.M. 1114 (1983). When an Aeroflot plane in 1981 deviated toward Connecticut from its off-coast route, the Untied States responded by suspending its landing privileges for two flights. *Id.*

148. HERSH, *supra* note 84 at 236–37. A similar personnel shakeup reportedly followed the 1978 incident, *id.* at 225, but not, apparently, because the airliner in that case had been shot down—rather because it had been able to penetrate sensitive Soviet airspace so easily. *Id.* In the aftermath of the KAL 007 shooting, however, the only senior Soviet air defense officer involved in the incident to emerge unscathed was reportedly the one who had cautioned against hastiness. *Id.* at 236–37.

149. Of course, the issue should not be whether subsequent investigation revealed that the intrusion was deliberate, but whether the actions of the Soviet Union were appropriate in light of the facts it knew at the time.

In May 1984, the ICAO Assembly voted to propose an amendment to the Chicago Convention and submit it to the member states for ratification.[150] This amendment is intended to address the problem of interception of civilian airliners and, according to at least one author, "clearly settles the issue concerning the use of force."[151] This result is far from clear. If adopted, the proposed amendment would indeed provide that "every state must refrain from resorting to the use of weapons against civil aircraft in flight."[152] However, this provision is quickly fol-

150. Protocol Relating to an Amendment of the Convention on International Civil Aviation, ICAO Doc. 9437, May 10, 1984 (copy on file with *Yale Journal of International Law*) [hereinafter cited as Protocol]. The amendment would add a new Article 3b to the Convention as follows:

(a) The contracting States recognize that every State must refrain from resorting to the use of weapons against civil aircraft in flight and that, in case of interception, the lives of persons on board and the safety of aircraft must not be endangered. This provision should not be interpreted as modifying in any way the rights and obligations of States set forth in the Charter of the United Nations.

(b) The contracting States recognize that every State, in the exercise of its sovereignty, is entitled to require the landing at some designated airport of a civil aircraft flying above its territory without authority or if there are reasonable grounds to conclude that it is being used for any purpose inconsistent with the aims of this Convention; it may also give such aircraft any other instructions to put an end to such violations. For this purpose, the contracting States may resort to any appropriate means consistent with relevant rules of international law, including the relevant provisions of this Convention, specifically paragraph (a) of this Article. Each contracting State agrees to publish its regulations in force regarding interception of civil aircraft.

(c) Every civil aircraft shall comply with an order given in conformity with paragraph (b) of this Article. To this end each contracting State shall establish all necessary provisions in its national laws or regulations to make such compliance mandatory for any civil aircraft registered in that State or operated by an operator who has his principal place of business or permanent residence in that State. Each contracting State shall make any violation of such applicable laws or regulations punishable by severe penalties and shall submit the case to its competent authorities in accordance with its laws or regulation.

(d) Each contracting State shall take appropriate measures to prohibit the deliberate use of any civil aircraft registered in that State or operated by an operator who has his principal place of business or permanent residence in that State for any purpose inconsistent with the aims of this Convention. This provision shall not affect paragraph (a) or derogate from paragraph (b) and (c) of this Article.

151. Phelps, *supra* note 1, at 303. Others have described it a "an important step" in recognizing the competing interests of state security and aircraft safety, Comment, *Korean Airline Flight 007: Stalemate In International Law—A Proposal for Enforcement*, *supra* note 1, at 884; and as a "useful deterrent" when it becomes effective. FitzGerald, *supra* note 1, at 306.

152. Protocol, *supra* note 150, para. (a). This amendment may be compared to the

lowed by an escape clause to the effect that the amendment "should not be interpreted as modifying in any way the rights and obligations of States set forth in the Charter of the United Nations."[153] This makes clear reference to the elastic concept of self-defense. The proposed amendment, moreover, does not address the questions of when and on what basis a civilian airliner becomes a "state aircraft" not covered by the Convention, or what constitutes evidence of hostile intent. The remainder of the proposed amendment expands the power of the sub-jacent state to require aircraft to land,[154] requires contracting states to punish pilots flying under their flag who refuse to obey an order to land,[155] and directs contracting states to prohibit the use of civilian air-craft "for any purpose inconsistent with the aims of this Convention"[156] Therefore, even if all relevant national elites ratified the amendment, its terms would not fully resolve the traditional ambiguities in the ap-plicable norm. By late April 1987, only thirty-six states out of the 102 needed to enact the amendment had ratified it.[157] South Korea was among these twenty-two, having ratified the Convention on February 27, 1985, but the United States, Soviet Union, and Japan were not.[158]

INTERNATIONAL APPRAISAL

The shooting of Flight 007 caused a far stronger international response than had any of the earlier five incidents. Most states and international organizations that indicated a position condemned the Soviet action as unjustified. Many of these expressly cited the principle of proportion-ality as the relevant international norm that had been violated. Canada, for example, stated: "The opening of fire on the Korean aircraft was in excess of what is commensurate with the gravity of the threat. . . ."[159]

words "*should* refrain" in the current ICAO recommended procedures. *See supra* note 73. (Emphasis added.)

153. Protocol, *supra* note 150, para. (a).

154. The requirement to land on order would apply anywhere in the airspace of the subjacent state, not just in its designated restricted area. Protocol, *supra* note 150, para. (b).

155. Protocol, *supra* note 150, para. (c).

156. Protocol, *supra* note 150, para. (d).

157. Interview with officials of the Legal Bureau of ICAO, April 24, 1987.

158. Id. Even when fully enacted, the amendment will bind only those states that have ratified it. *Id.*

159. Statement of Mr. Pelletier, Sept. 2, 1983, U.N. Doc. S/PV.2470 (1983), *re-*

This principle seemed to endorse the American position: an unarmed civilian airliner in peacetime could never pose a threat serious enough to justify using force that endangered innocent lives, as long as the airliner was being used for a nonviolent purpose. Remaining states generally condemned the shooting without much elaboration of the legal principles upon which they based their decision.[160]

On September 12, 1983, the UN Security Council voted on a resolution to declare the Soviet use of force "incompatible with the norms governing international behavior and elementary considerations of humanity."[161] Only a veto by the Soviet Union prevented its adoption.[162]

Greek opposition was apparently all that prevented the ten members of the European Economic Community from adopting a unified, strongly worded condemnation of the Soviet Union.[163] NATO Secre-

---

printed in 22 I.L.M. 1114, 1117 (1983). The Canadian view was shared by Italy (*Paper on Andreotti Talks with Shultz, Gromyko*, Foreign Broadcast Information Service [hereinafter cited as FIBS] (W. Eur.), Sept. 13, 1983, at L1); Zaire (Statement of Mr. Mapango ma Kemishanga, Sept. 2, 1983, U.N. Doc. S/PV.2470 (1983), *reprinted in* 22 I.L.M. 1120 (1983); and Columbia (Statement of Mr. Holguin, Sept. 7, 1983, U.N. Docs. S/PV.2473 (1983) & S/PV.2473/Corr. 1 (1983), *reprinted in* 22 I.L.M. 1132 (1983)). *See also* the statements by France (Statement of Prime Minister Pierre Mauroy: *Reaction Continues on RoK Airliner Incident*, FBIS (W. Eur.), Sept. 6, 1983, at K1); West Germany (Statement of Mr. Reichardt: *Spokesman on South Korean Airliner Incident*, FBIS (W. Eur.), Sept. 2, 1983, at J1); and Japan (Statement of Chief Cabinet Spokesman Gotoda: *Gotoda, Nakasone Remarks Cited*, FBIS (Asia & Pac.), Sept. 2, 1983, at C3).

160. Spain, for example, called it a "grave violation of international law." *Government Urges Explanation on Plane Incident*, FBIS (W. Eur.), Sept. 6, 1983, at U2. The United Kingdom characterized it as an "inhuman act" and an "atrocity." *Thatcher on Greek EEC Speaker for UN KAL Debate*, FBIS (W. Eur.), Sept. 20, 1983, at Q3. In the past, however, the United Kingdom has made clear its position that shooting an unidentified civilian airliner in peacetime is unjustified unless necessary for self-defense. *See supra* notes 49–51 and accompanying text. Australia called the downing "appalling and inexcusable." *Haydon Asks U.S.S.R. Explanation*, FBIS (Asia & Pac.), Sept. 2, 1983, at M1. Egypt "deplored" the downing. *Government 'Deplores' South Korean Plane Downing*, FBIS (Mid. East & Africa), Sept. 6, 1983, at D1. Brazil regarded the incident as deserving "rejection and condemnation." FBIS (Lat. Am.), Sept. 2, 1983, at D1.

161. U.N. Doc. S/15966/Rev. 1 (1983), reprinted in 22 I.L.M. 1148 (1983).

162. The vote was nine in favor, two opposed, with four abstentions. The Soviet Union and Poland opposed the resolution. The People's Republic of China, Guyana, Nicaragua, and Zimbabwe abstained. U.N. Doc. S/PV.2476 (1983), *reprinted in* 22 I.L.M. 1144 (1983).

163. *Euro MP's Reject Greek Stance on KAL Jet Downing*, FBIS (W. Eur.), Sept. 14, 1983, at A1.

tary General Joseph Luns said that representatives of the sixteen member countries "unanimously condemned" the shooting but did not feel that NATO was the appropriate organization to call for sanctions.[164]

Voices raised in defense of the Soviet action were relatively few, and came primarily from Soviet-bloc states.[165] Most of these simply repeated the Soviet version of the events as reported by TASS.

Surprisingly neutral were Albania and Romania. Both countries gave domestic press coverage to both sides of the issue without publicly taking a official stance.[166] The People's Republic of China stated that shooting a airliner simply because it had entered Soviet airspace without authorization would be "a serious violation of established norms," yet was careful to acknowledge "serious dispute over certain aspects of the incident."[167] As a result, it would neither condemn nor endorse the Soviet action.[168] A cautious stance was also adopted by India[169] and Mexico,[170] both of which implied that the disputed facts would determine the lawfulness of the shooting.

164. *Meeting on Sanctions, Measures against USSR*, FBIS (W. Eur.), Sept. 12, 1983, at C1.

165. The countries supporting the Soviet poition were Afghanistan, *Front Statement on Korean Airline Incident*, FBIS (S. Asia), Sept. 15, 1983, at C2; Angola, *Debates over Downing of ROK Airliner Reported*, FBIS (Mid. East & Africa), Sept. 16, 1983, at U2; Burgaria, *Report on UN Envoy's Speech*, FBIS (E. Eur.), Sept. 13, 1983, at C2; Czechoslovakia, *Daily on Questions Regarding KAL Incident*, FBIS (E. Eur.), Sept. 19, 1983, at D1; Cuba, *Commentary Blames U.S.*, FBIS (Lat. Amer.), Sept. 6, 1983, at Q1; East Germany, *Continuing Commentary on Airliner Incident*, FBIS (E. Eur.), Sept. 12, 1983, at E1; Hungary, *U.S. Version of Air Disaster Losing Popularity*, FBIS (E. Eur.), Sept. 12, 1983, at F1; Laos, *TASS Statement Quoted on KAL Jet Incident*, FBIS (Asia & Pac.), Sept. 6, 1983, at I3; Mongolia, *Reaction to Soviet Downing of Korean Airline*, FBIS (Asia & Pac.), Sept. 12, 1983, at F1; Mozambique, *TASS Report, Pravda on Airline Tapes Cited*, FBIS (Mid. East & Africa), Sept. 15, 1983, at U4; Poland, Reportage on Charge USSR Downed Airliner, FBIS (E. Eur.), Sept. 16, 1983, at G1; and Vietnam, *Nhan Dan Carries TASS Statement on KAL Incident*, FBIS (Asia & Pac.), Sept. 6, 1983, at K2.

166. *See e.g.*, Albania, *Press Cites TASS, Others on Korean Plane Incident*, FBIS (E. Eur.), Sept. 9, 1983, at B1; Romania, *Scinteia Comments on South Korea Plane Incident*, FBIS (E. Eur.), Sept. 12, 1983, at H1.

167. *PRC Abstains on UN Vote*, FBIS (China), Sept. 13, 1983, at A1.

168. *Id.*

169. *Government Urges Investigation into KAL Incident*, FBIS (S. Asia), Sept. 16, 1983, at E1.

170. *Government Urges Investigation on KAL Incident*, FBIS (Lat. Amer.), Sept. 6, 1983, at M1.

The International Federation of Airline Pilots' Associations voted on September 6, 1983, to declare the Soviet Union an "offending state" and to call a sixty-day ban on all flights to Moscow.[171] Fourteen or more states participated to some degree in this boycott from September 12 until October 3, when it was called off because of the anticipated ICAO investigation and a Soviet promise of cooperation.[172]

The ICAO Council adopted a resolution on September 16, 1983, deploring the airliner's destruction, reaffirming that states should not use weapons when intercepting civil aircraft, and expressing concern that the Soviet Union had not yet acknowledged the "paramount importance" of the civilian lives lost. The resolution further recognized "that such use of armed force against international civil aviation is incompatible with the norms governing international behavior and elementary considerations of humanity and with the rules, standards, and recommended practices enshrined in the Chicago Convention and its Annexes and invokes generally recognized legal consequences."[173] The Council adopted this resolution by a vote of 26 to 2 with 3 abstentions and 2 absences.[174] Only Czechoslovakia and the Soviet Union voted against it.[175] The ICAO Assembly endorsed the resolution on October 1, 1983, by a vote of 65 to 10 with 26 abstentions.[176]

A subsequent investigation of the incident conducted by ICAO technical experts produced a report made public on December 30, 1983.[177] It concluded that KAL 007 began to deviate from its planned route soon after departure from Anchorage,[178] probably as the result of the insertion of an erroneous ramp position into one of the inertial navigation units before takeoff.[179] The report also concluded that the air-

171. Press Statement, *reprinted in* 22 I.L.M. at 1218 (1983).

172. N.Y. Times, Oct. 1, 1983, at A1, col. 6. *See also 11 Nations Halt Moscow Air Service to Protest Downing*, AVIATION WK. AND SPACE TECH., Sept. 19, 1983, at 26. The promised Soviet cooperation did not materialize. *See* Resolution of the Council of ICAO of March 6, 1984 (copy on file with the *Yale Journal of International Law*).

173. Resolution adopted by the Extraordinary Session of the Council of the ICAO on September 16, 1983, *reprinted in* 22 I.L.M. 1150 (1983). The "generally recognized legal consequences" to which the resolution refers were not made clear.

174. *Id.*

175. *Id.*

176. *See* 22 I.L.M. at 1149 (1983).

177. ICAO REPORT, *supra* note 80.

178. *Id.* at 55.

179. *Id.* at 51–54. The report concludes that the combination of errors and oversights

liner was not on a reconnaissance mission and did not deliberately deviate from its assigned track for any other reason.[180] The investigating committee determined that the civilian air traffic controllers who were responsible for the aircraft could not have known of its significant deviation, and that military authorities who might have been able to detect the deviation were neither responsible for the airliner's course nor likely to be aware of it.[181] Finally, the report concluded that the Soviets simply had assumed that KAL 007 was an intelligence aircraft and accordingly, "did not make exhaustive efforts to identify the aircraft through in-flight visual observations"[182]

After consideration of this report, the ICAO Council adopted a resolution on March 6, 1984, again condemning the downing of KAL 007 and "reaffirming" that "whatever the circumstances which, according to the Secretary General's report, may have caused the aircraft to stray off its flight plan route, such use of armed force constitutes a violation of international law, and invokes generally recognized legal consequences. . . ."[183]

The international consensus seems to have been that the Soviet Union's actions violated international norms. This consensus rejected the claim that an unauthorized presence in territorial airspace alone raises a presumption of hostile intent sufficient to warrant using violence against an intruding aircraft. The norm was recognized that a subjacent state bears an affirmative duty to identify correctly the status of a civilian airliner, and can shoot down such aircraft only under aggravating circumstances not present in the KAL 007 incident. Most notably, flying over sensitive military installations does not qualify as sufficiently aggravating, even where international navigation maps clearly warn of these installations and although the subjacent state has an express right under the Chicago Convention to prohibit aerial intrusion. Any contrary inferences drawn from the 1978 incident thus seem discredited when compared to this evolving pattern. In addition, na-

---

necessary to cause Flight 007 to deviate so far from its course assumed a "considerable degree of lack of alertness and attentiveness on the part of the entire flight crew but not to a degree that was unknown in international civil aviation." *Id.* at 56.

180. *Id.* at 35–36.

181. *Id.* at 38–40.

182. *Id.* at 56.

183. Resolution adopted by the Council of ICAO on Mar. 6, 1984 (copy on file with the *Yale Journal of International Law*). Again, these legal consequences were left unclear.

tional elites seemed unwilling to recognize as normative any expectations of heightened Soviet sensitivity to aerial intrusion, even though previous incidents might have suggested such expectations. Beyond this consensus, international opinion begins to diverge. According to the U.S. view, only the threat of violence justifies using violence. The possibility that an intruding civilian aircraft may be spying poses an insufficient threat. The only appropriate response in such a case is diplomatic. Many, perhaps most, states currently seem unwilling to recognize so categorical a norm. They take more qualified positions, implying that sometimes lethal force may be employed lawfully against an aircraft identified as civilian even if it does not present a direct threat of violence. This normative conception underlies, for example, the Mexican, Indian, and Chinese statements that unresolved factual disputes prevented their taking sides.[184]

AUTHOR'S APPRAISAL

The KAL 007 shooting may be interpreted in two ways. Focusing on the outcome, some may conclude that the incident has not at all changed norms regarding the use of force against intruding civil aircraft. The Soviet Union, they may point out, never apologized for the shooting, admitted any fault, or offered compensation. Moreover, only thirty-six of the 102 states needed to adopt the ICAO amendment to the Chicago Convention have ratified what is an already timid and inconclusive measure.

This interpretation, however, fails to see the incident in its proper historical perspective. Unlike the 1983 downing, the 1978 KAL incident (which also involved the Soviet Union) did not prompt a strong international reaction. In addition, no amendment to the Chicago Convention was even proposed after any of the previous incidents. Finally, and most important, in 1978 the Soviets did not feel compelled to offer a detailed public justification for the shooting.

If the international appraisal of the lawfulness of the downing of KAL 007 is an accurate indication of international expectations, despite some qualified positions such as those of Mexico, India, and China, one can conclude that this incident has clarified relevant norms. Rati-

184. This more qualified norm may also be inferred from the ICAO Council resolution of March 6, 1984, which condemned the shooting with the observation that it was irrelevant to analyze what had caused the airliner to "stray" from its route. This leaves room for argument that a deliberate intrusion could be treated differently.

fication of the proposed amendment to the Chicago Convention might help to give a formalistic textual base for these norms, but it is not necessary to create them. The principle of proportionality, as a limit upon a state's lawful use of sovereign force, has emerged as an appropriate standard for judging the lawfulness of response to aerial intrusions. Proportionality was affirmed in a way that both has reduced the importance of a nation's security interest in preventing aerial peacetime reconnaissance and has strengthened the value of protecting the lives of international travelers. Furthermore, in implicitly evaluating the issue of hostile intent, the international appraisal reinforced the distinction between acceptable treatment of intruding military and civilian aircraft. Finally, this incident may have strengthened the distinction between civilian aircraft performing reconnaissance functions and those presenting a threat of armed violence.

The subjacent state must justify shooting an intruding aircraft and cannot rely on a presumption that the action is lawful merely because the aircraft violated territorial airspace. Such a shooting must be justified even when the foreign aircraft has penetrated a sensitive and clearly restricted area at night. Some overt demonstration of hostile intent is required to support the use of violence, and the burden rests upon the intercepting state to take reasonable measures to determine that intent and to take measures short of lethal force to divert the plane. Specifically, the ICAO requirement to warn an intruding civilian aircraft has become a widely accepted norm, even though the relevant procedures are technically mere recommendations and despite the fact that warnings may not be needed for military aircraft not obviously in distress.

Moreover, a minority of states feel that during peacetime the threat of an intruding airliner's potential for reconnaissance can never be sufficiently hostile to justify endangering innocent lives. This view may represent the emerging norm. Its rationale stems from two parallel trends in recent history. The first of these is the increasingly important role of civilian air traffic as a conduit of international commercial exchange. Since World War II, the volume of international air travel and transport has vastly increased, and has contributed significantly to worldwide economic growth. Commercial airliners have become instruments of international stability, world public order, and interdependence.[185] A second concurrent trend has been the greatly increasing

---

185. *See* MATTE, TREATISE ON AIR-AERONAUTICAL LAW, at 32–35 (1981).

sophistication of major powers in intelligence collection capabilities, especially with satellites and electronic surveillance,[186] and in swiftly and accurately delivering explosives by missile. In short, as civilian air traffic has become more important as an instrument of international stability, it has become less important as a potential means of aerial reconnaissance and weapons delivery.

Because of these two trends, the use of force against civilian aircraft is becoming more difficult to justify. The presumption in favor of non-hostile intent becomes more stringent as the perceived threats of intruding civilian aircraft become less persuasive and the costs of chilling international aerial commerce increase. The KAL 007 incident has clarified and consolidated norms that reflect these trends.

186. *See generally,* J. BAMFORD, THE PUZZLE PALACE: A REPORT ON AMERICA'S MOST SECRET AGENCY (1982) (analysis of the history and operations of the National Security Agency).

THE BOMBING OF HARRODS:

10 Norms against Civilian Targeting

RONALD J. KUERBITZ

PROBLEM

Military legal theory has long asserted reasoned limitations over military conduct. Current military theory derives prescriptive limitations on military activity from two fundamental principles: military necessity and humanitarianism.[1] These principles find application through the standards of proportionality and discrimination. Proportionality prohibits the excessive use of force to attain a military objective,[2] a standard intended to balance military and humanitarian requirements. Its complementary standard, discrimination, requires military forces to discern between military and civilian personnel and to target only combatants.[3] These traditional rules of warfare, developed out of practical exigencies of war, are, in part, statements of the pragmatic realization that the excessive or misdirected use of force squanders valuable mili-

1. R. Gehring, *Loss of Civilian Protections under the Fourth Geneva Convention and Protocol I*, 90 Mil. L. Rev. 49 (1980).
2. W. Fenrick, *The Rule of Proportionality and Protocol in Conventional Warfare*, 98 Mil. L. Rev. 91, 94 (1980).
3. Gehring, *supra* note 1, at 58.

tary resources.[4] In addition to reflecting military necessity, however, these standards also represent concern for the value of human life. In this sense they reflect the principle of humanitarianism.[5]

Among the proscriptive norms that follow from these reasoned limitations is the norm against targeting civilians, which has generally applied as a standard for conventional warfare. Recent trends in warfare, including the increased use of terror, however, have curtailed the effectiveness of these traditional limitations on the conduct of war, and have raised concerns, at least in the context of unconventional warfare, that the norm against civilian targeting no longer exists. Within this context a Provisional Irish Republican Army (IRA) statement issued December 18, 1983, claiming responsibility for a bomb attack on Harrods department store in London on the previous day, but offering assurances that such an attack would not recur, presents an unusual incident. The Harrods bombing incident indicates that the norm may be extended to unconventional wars such as the conflict in Northern Ireland, despite strong counterpressures.

FACTS

This study reviews the events of approximately one month, beginning with the attack at Harrods and concluding with the responses of the relevant participants. This period, however, must be viewed in the context of a political environment that began to take shape in the early 1980s, when the political wing of the IRA, Provisional Sinn Fein, was becoming increasingly involved in constituency politics.

Background

The major participants can be divided into two groups: the governmental claimants, primarily the government of the United Kingdom; and the nationalist claimants, primarily composed of the IRA and Sinn Fein. Though their voices are many and often disparate, each group's claims tended to be sufficiently homogeneous to characterize them as single "parties."[6]

4. R. Baxter, *Modernizing the Law of War*, 78 MIL. L. REV 165, 166 (1977).
5. Gehing, *supra* note 1, at 56.
6. Assessment of the nationalist group's reactions posed particular difficulties because of the relative dearth of authoritative information about and commentary by the leader-

The IRA is a dominant military organization in the Irish nationalist movement. Its goals include the removal of the British presence from Ireland and the unification of a socialist Ireland. The IRA claims to maintain a centralized command structure directed by the Army Council, a body that formulates and administers IRA policies. The IRA acts through its "active service units" (ASU), groups directed to carry out military operations.

The party Sinn Fein serves as the political wing of the IRA. Sinn Fein has received the electoral support of, and claims to be the authoritative representative of, a substantial portion of the nationalist population (figures range from 30 to 42 percent).[7] Prior to the Harrods bombing the United Kingdom allowed lower level ministerial contacts with Sinn Fein. Gerry Adams, a member of Parliament for West Belfast, was its president when the incident occurred.

During the 1970s, Sinn Fein did not participate in elected institutions. Around 1980, Sinn Fein and the IRA moved away from their abstentionist political stance and began to develop a policy of constituency politics that they continued through the period of the incident. Concurrent with that change, several political parties in the Republic of Ireland and the United Kingdom presented the potential for a working relationship with Sinn Fein.

The IRA's military campaign in Britain began in 1972, when seven people were killed in the bombing of a military installation. The basis for the British campaign lay in the belief that violence in Northern Ireland would not result in a fundamental change in British policy. In a secret meeting with IRA leaders in 1972, William Whitelaw, then secretary of state for Northern Ireland, allegedly informed them that violence against British troops in Northern Ireland would not change British policy, because authorities were prepared to accept the level of military casualties suffered there.[8] This idea remained a motivation for the campaign in Britain. The IRA firmly believed that one bomb in Britain was worth fifty in Northern Ireland, but at the same time they assumed that civilians were not acceptable targets.[9]

---

ship of the IRA. The Army Council of the IRA and people privy to their designs and expectations are, in general, not available for comment. In spite of their general disinclination toward individual commentary, though, this particular incident evoked a relatively large amount of public commentary by IRA officials.

7. *Fortnight*, May 1983, at 4.
8. T. COOGAN, THE IRA (1980), at 491–92.
9. *The Times*, Dec. 20, 1983, at 10.

In their initial attacks the IRA generally selected primarily military or commercial targets, although in 1974 they killed twenty-one people in two attacks on pubs in Birmingham.[10] On December 10, in their most recent attack prior to the Harrods incident, the IRA bombed the Woolwich barracks with a bomb roughly equal in size to the one used in the Harrods attack.[11] The bombing of Harrods, then, was unusual for its civilian targets, not for its violence.

The IRA had not indicated, however, that it would never target civilians in Britain. Its spokesman said that indiscriminate bombings in Britain would be justifiable in the face of British indifference to the violent situation in Northern Ireland. Even the British had recognized that although bombings were facts of life in Northern Ireland, such incidents were largely ignored elsewhere.[12] In reaction to this indifference, the IRA claimed after the Harrods incident, it was under grassroots pressure to initiate a campaign of indiscriminate bombings in Britain.[13]

In addition, improvements in British Army tactics and equipment made military targets increasingly inaccessible.[14] This is evident in the IRA's claim that it had kidnapped a retailing company executive, Don Tidey, in order to gain funds for, among other things, more sophisticated weaponry.[15]

The Tidey kidnapping[16] and the search it engendered for his IRA captors were part of a general increase in military activity just before the Harrods bombing.[17] British security forces were put on a status of maximum alert from the beginning of December. The British claimed to have been aware of IRA plans to step up their activity in Britain around Christmas.[18] They recognized the third weekend of December as one of the last opportunities for the IRA to make good on an earlier threat to bring the war back to Great Britain in 1983, and having discovered caches of explosives earlier in the year,[19] the police knew that

10. *The Times*, Dec. 19, 1983, at 2; *The Guardian*, Dec. 18, 1983, at 2. All references to *The Times* in this Chapter are to *The Times* (London).
11. *The Guardian*, Dec. 20, 1983, at 11.
12. *The Times*, Dec. 20, 1983, at 2; *The Irish Times*, Dec. 19, 1983, at 6.
13. *The Guardian*, Jan. 7, 1984, at 2; *The Irish Times*, Dec. 19, 1983, at 6.
14. *The Guardian*, Jan. 7, 1984, at 2.
15. *Id.*, at 2.
16. *The Guardian*, Dec. 20, 1983, at 11.
17. *The Guardian*, Dec. 19, 1983, at 2.
18. *Id.*
19. *Id.*

the IRA was capable of bombing operations in London. Moreover, Harrods was recognized as a prime target, especially during the pre-holiday shopping rush. It had been bombed almost exactly nine years earlier (on December 21, 1974), was viewed by the IRA as catering to the rich and influential, and, as a London institution, offered certain media coverage. Authorities were also aware of the method of car bombing and its dual attributes for unconventional warfare: the practical value of allowing easy transportation of large amounts of explosives and the terror value of turning an everyday necessity into a weapon.

The Incident

At 1:21 P.M. on Saturday, December 17, 1983, a bomb exploded on a side street across from Harrods department store. The bomb, weighing an estimated thirty pounds, had been detonated by use of a timing mechanism and was contained in a car that had been parked facing the wrong direction on a one-way street.[20] Thirty-seven minutes before the explosion, a warning telephoned to a branch of the Samaritans in London gave a previously unrecognized code word[21] and stated that there was an IRA car bomb outside Harrods as well as two bombs within the store, another bomb on Oxford Street, and a fifth bomb in a shop on Oxford Street.[22] The warning of additional bombs in the store and at the Oxford Street locations were false, as were a reported twenty-two other bomb warnings relayed to the police that day.[23]

The Provisional Irish Republican Army issued a statement the following day, claiming the operation, though carried out by its personnel, was not authorized and would not be repeated. The statement said:

> The Provisional Irish Republican Army have been operational in Britain throughout last week. Our volunteers planted the bomb outside Woolwich barracks and in the car outside Harrods store. The Harrods operation was not authorized by the Irish Republican

20. *Id.*

21. *The Times* reported that the caller told the Samaritans that the code being given would be used in the future as an indication of genuine warnings. *The Times*, Dec. 19, 1983, at 2.

22. The caller is reported to have stated. "This is the IRA. Car bomb outside Harrods. Two bombs inside Harrods. One in Oxford Street. One in Littlewoods, Oxford Street." *The Times*, Dec. 19, 1983, at 2.

23. *The Times*, Dec. 19, 1983, at 2.

Army. We have taken immediate steps to ensure that there will be no repetition of this type of operation again. The volunteers involved gave a 40-minute specific warning which should have been adequate. But due to the inefficiency or failure by the Metropolitan Police, who boasted of foreknowledge of IRA activity, this warning did not result in an evacuation.

We regret the civilian casualties, even though our expression of sympathy will be dismissed. Finally, we remind the British Government that as long as they maintain control of any part of Ireland then the Irish Republican Army will continue to operate in Britain until the Irish people are left in peace to decide their own future.[24]

CONFLICTING CLAIMS

Although it expressed regret for the civilian casualties, the IRA rejected any claims that it was responsible for them. It characterized the bombing as unauthorized and the casualties as avoidable, and said that these facts excused it from responsibility.

The primary IRA claim, as made in its public statement, was that the bombing was undertaken in a manner contrary to the organization's accepted procedures and its policy of appropriate tactics. Initially the IRA stressed that the attack was not authorized by the central command structure, but they also denied there was any factional division in the organization or any other loss of control that would signal an inability to provide assurances of no further civilian targets.[25]

The active service unit responsible for the attack purportedly was forced to act without orders under the difficult conditions imposed by the increased activity of British and Irish security forces. The ASU was under a specific brief from the IRA Army Council authorizing attacks on military targets, such as Woolwich barracks. Because of tight surveillance, greater military security, the maximum alert status in effect, increased public security measures, and the mobilization of military forces in the Irish Republic's search for Tidey, however, the ASU was unable to carry out its authorized strikes.[26] It had also been unable to contact the Army Council for authorization of new targets. A meeting

24. *The Guardian*, Dec. 19, 1983, at 1.
25. *The Irish Times*, Dec. 19, 1983, at 1; Dec. 24, 1983, at 2.
26. *Id.*, at 11.

at which such a request could have been considered was reportedly cancelled because of pressure from the Tidey manhunt.[27] Consequently, the IRA claimed, the ASU acted on its own initiative.[28]

Despite assurances of cohesiveness within the IRA, varying comments issued from its leadership. Gerry Adams refused to condemn the unit. Philip Flynn, a vice-president of Sinn Fein, however, condemned the operation unreservedly as "an incomprehensible offense against innocent people."[29] In addition there were public calls from within the IRA command for punishment of the unit or its leader.[30]

In its statement the IRA placed responsibility for the casualties on the police. The bomb was intended to go off, the IRA implied, only after a complete evacuation. They argued that they had provided a thirty-seven minute advance warning which should have been sufficient to clear the area, and charged the police with incompetence, especially in view of the force's reported awareness of plans for increased IRA activity during that time.[31] Commentators have noted that thirty-seven minutes probably would have been sufficient for evacuation by a highly experienced security force such as the Royal Ulster Constabulary, under the circumstances.[32] The IRA argued that the car had been illegally parked, facing the wrong direction on a one-way street, so that it would immediately attract attention. A competent police force, they said, would have noticed the car and acted in time to avoid casualties. Additionally, the IRA claimed that there would have been no warning preceding any attack signaling a change in the policy of not targeting civlians.[33] The IRA assured the public that it regretted civilian casualties when they occurred and had not changed its standing policy against such attacks in Great Britain,[34] and further assured that there would be no repeat of such an attack.

The public characterization of the incident by British authorities de-

27. *Id.*

28. *The Guardian*, Dec. 19, 1983, at 1; Dec. 20, 1983, at 11.

29. *The Guardian*, Jan. 7, 1984, at 2; *The Irish Times*, Dec. 19, 1983, at 1.

30. *The Guardian*, Dec. 29, 1983, at 22; *The Irish Times*, Dec. 19, 1983, at 1; Dec. 20, 1983, at 1.

31. *The Guardian*, Dec. 20, 1983, at 11.

32. *Id.*

33. *Id.*

34. An unidentified IRA leader, in an interview with the French newspaper *Liberation*, stated, "From now on, IRA targets in Britain would be military. Woolwich will occur again, not Harrods." *The Guardian*, Dec. 29, 1983, at 1.

nied any legitimacy to the IRA as a nationalist organization or to its use of force. Thus, the British claimed to disregard any proffered distinctions between military and civilian targets and stated they would not base any expectations on such declarations.[35] The British also saw the Harrods attack as evidence of a schism in republican ranks, at least between militarists and politicos if not also among the militarists.[36] It was felt that the attack heralded the demise of the new IRA political strategy and a resurgence of a purely military strategy. The British claimed that under either characterization, the bombing demonstrated the valuelessness of the IRA's declaration that its policy permitted economic targets only when civilians would not be injured.

In response to the IRA claim that civilian casualties could have been prevented, the British conceded that they did have some notice but argued that it was insufficient under the circumstances. They claimed that the warning, beginning with an unrecognized code word and coming amid twenty-two additional warnings that involved false reports of bombs, was deliberately vague and confusing. The British did not accept any responsibility for the injuries. Some government personnel said that the IRA caller, by warning of bombs inside Harrods, attempted to induce the police to evacuate the store and thereby move even more people within range of the explosion.[37] It was also alleged that the bomb and warning call were timed to maximize police casualties—that the bomb was set to explode just as police would approach the car. The improbability of this assertion, however, was recognized by government acknowledgment that the bomb was detonated by a timing mechanism rather than by remote control and was therefore subject to limited control by the bombers. Authorities did claim, though, that such a choice showed a clear acceptance of the risk of casualties.

CONFLICTING CONCEPTIONS OF LAWFULNESS

The British government's verbal response both to the bombing and to the IRA's ensuing statement was one of nearly complete contempt, showing a conception of Sinn Fein and the IRA as illegal organizations dedicated to violent change and lacking any legitimacy or authority.

35. *The Irish Times*, Dec. 20, 1983, at 1, 6; *The Times*, Dec. 20, 1983, at 4.
36. *Fortnight*, Oct. 1983, at 15; *The Times*, Dec. 19, 1983, at 1; *The Irish Times*, Dec. 19, 1983, at 1.
37. *The Irish Times*, Dec. 24, 1983, at 6.

Leon Brittan, the Home Secretary, stated in Commons on December 19 that he rejected the IRA's disclaimer of responsibility and viewed it merely as a publicity statement engineered to extricate the IRA from the overwhelmingly negative public reaction to the bombing.[38] He further rejected the statement's implicit distinction between civilian and police casualties, commenting that the bomb was intended to maximize police casualties and denying that there could be any difference in the legitimacy of the killing depending on the status of the victim. In its public comments the government thus seemed to reject any notion of normative limitations on the tactics of unconventional warfare and instead viewed all nonstate violence as criminal.

This response resulted in calls for the banning of Sinn Fein in the United Kingdom. James Molyneaux in Commons asked the government to "remember that political parties in the Irish Republic and elsewhere share the objectives of the IRA and hope for the attainment of those objectives provides the incentive for continuing terrorism."[39] Such sentiments were repeated in the House of Lords, where the legitimacy of Sinn Fein as a political organization was also challenged.[40] Those who believed all violent tactics to be criminal considered Sinn Fein, as the political supporter of the IRA, to be equally criminal.[41]

Opposing voices in the British government, however, argued against a ban on Sinn Fein, warning that the option of political action must be left open to those with grievances or they would never reject military tactics.[42] They argued, moreover, that banning Sinn Fein would criminalize large numbers of people who continued to support it and would likely lead to an increase of violent activity as had been the case with the earlier policy of internment without trial.[43] Those who took this position saw Sinn Fein as a legitimate and authoritative representative of nationalist constituents who legally could not be disenfranchised and, in any case, would not reduce their support for Sinn Fein. Advocates of this view, although opposed to violence, distinguished between the legitimate organization and its illegitimate tactics. They

38. *The Times*, Dec. 20, 1983, at 4.
39. *Id.*
40. *Id.*
41. *Fortnight*, Feb. 1984, at 7.
42. *The Times*, Dec. 22, 1983, at 1; *The Irish Times*, Dec. 21, 1983, at 7.
43. *The Times*, Dec. 20, 1983, at 4.

sought room for an understanding between the parties that could lead to limitations on tactical options.

Contrary to their public statements, however, the actions of both proponents and opponents of the ban on Sinn Fein distinguished between civilian and military targets. The fact that a political ban was discussed at all indicates the seriousness with which the attack was viewed. Such a ban had last been considered in 1981 after the IRA's assassination of the Official Unionist party member of Parliament, Robert Bradford.[44] That attack, like the Harrods bombing, was against a civilian. The intervening attacks on military targets, including the July 1982 bombings of the Household Cavalry and the Royal Green Jackets band, which elicited great public outrage, and the bombing of Woolwich barracks, prompted no such consideration.[45] The ban on the IRA itself did not come until the 1974 Birmingham pub bombings.[46] A ban, apparently, is a serious reaction to a particularly odious attack. Thus, the seriousness of this reaction to the Harrods bombing alone indicates a perceived difference between targets. In addition, the British government had earlier made it clear to the IRA that, at least in Northern Ireland, they were willing to accept the current level of military casualties.[47] In sum, a distinction clearly does exist between the violent tactics available to the IRA. To the British, security forces are significantly more acceptable as targets than are civilians.

The reaction to the bombing in republican circles ranged from Sinn Fein president Gerry Adams's refusal to condemn the ASU involved, to vice-president Philip Flynn's unreserved condemnation, to a call for punishment of the ASU or its leader by the head of the IRA's general headquarters, who said, "Every unit knows it has automatic authority to attack British soldiers and men of the UDR (Ulster Defense Regiment) and the RUC (Royal Ulster Constabulary). But in Britain, targets are carefully selected and it had been decided, before Harrods, not to attack economic targets where civilians would be at risk."[48] The fact that these comments were made public at all is unusual and indicates the seriousness with which IRA viewed the incident.

Additional evidence indicates that the IRA maintained a policy of

44. *The Irish Times*, Dec. 21, 1983, at 7.
45. *The Times*, Dec. 19, 1983, at 2.
46. *The Guardian*, Dec. 19, 1983, at 2.
47. COOGAN, *supra* note 9, at 491–92.
48. *The Guardian*, Dec. 29, 1983, at 1.

military targeting and economic targeting subject to the avoidance of civilian casualties. This claim is given credence by the IRA's attempts to improve its military targeting capability through the acquisition of more sophisticated weaponry. The IRA appeared to reinforce its assurances that civilians were not acceptable targets with a bomb on Christmas Day just off Oxford Street, a major shopping district.[49] The commander of the police antiterrorist unit remarked that the blast could have had much more serious consequences had it not been detonated at a time when the area was relatively deserted. He interpreted the event as a warning that the ASU was still operating in the area but also as an obvious indication that the no-civilians policy was still being followed. The aim of the bomb, like the one at Harrods, was to draw attention during the holidays to the situation in Northern Ireland and to disrupt the normal activity of the Christmas shopping period. Unlike Harrods, however, the bomb was both constructed and timed to minimize civilian casualties. As one policeman said, "If they were planning to kill people they could have chosen a better time and place."[50]

IRA responses to the threats to ban Sinn Fein indicated that such a course would be entirely unacceptable. They condemned such a ban as discriminatory against the nationalist community supporting Sinn Fein and compared it to the disenfranchisement of nationalist politicians in the 1920s.[51] They also threatened an extreme escalation of violence in the event of such a move, saying that it would result in uncontrollable conflict that could expand to include even Republic of Ireland forces if the Republic instituted such a ban. Such escalation, they claimed, would lead to full-scale civil war.[52] Whether or not the IRA was prepared or able to fulfill such threats, they clearly would not have accepted a ban and considered it manifestly unlawful.

The Irish Republic, like the United Kingdom, considered a ban on Sinn Fein, although its response was more to the killing of two security force members by the IRA in connection with the Tidey kidnapping than to the Harrods bombing. Dr. Fitzgerald, President of the Republic, criticized Britain for its policy of allowing ministerial contacts with Sinn Fein and argued that such contacts encouraged Sinn Fein and

49. *The Times*, Dec. 27, 1983, at 1.
50. *Id.*
51. *The Guardian*, Dec. 23, 1983, at 22.
52. *The Irish Times*, Dec. 24, 1983, at 2.

IRA activity.[53] He also called for joint British-Irish action against terrorists and promised no refuge for violent criminals in the Republic.[54] Organized labor in the Republic joined in the condemnation of violence. The Local Government and Public Service Union pressured its acting general secretary, Philip Flynn, to resign as a Sinn Fein vice-president.[55] The Irish Council for Civil Liberties, however, argued against the Sinn Fein ban. The council said such action would increase violence and interfere with a recent move in the IRA toward accepting political methods.[56] The Republic thus expressed disapproval of both the organization Sinn Fein/IRA and the violent tactics it employed.

In summary, the factual claims focused on responsibility for the incident, both sides apparently accepting the unlawfulness of civilian targeting. The conflicting legal conceptions, especially as indicated by the reaction to proposals to ban Sinn Fein, focused on the overall legitimacy of the IRA. All parties, though, drew some connection between the IRA's overall legitimacy and its responsibility for the attack and general willingness to engage in civilian targeting.

OUTCOME

The British government considered many measures to take in response to the incident, including a ban on Sinn Fein, the institution of identity cards, capital punishment, detention without trial, and strengthening the law of incitement.[57] Ultimately it rejected these options, and attempted instead to reach the command structure behind the bombers by applying the existing law of incitement.[58] This minimal reaction is especially significant given government claims of public pressure for action.[59]

The government's reaction was directed at violent tactics alone, especially violence against civilians, rather than the political structure of the IRA. Authorities strengthened security measures.[60] sought to in-

53. *The Guardian*, Dec. 19, 1983, at 2.
54. *The Times*, Dec. 24, 1983, at 2, 10.
55. *The Times*, Dec. 22, 1983, at 1.
56. *The Irish Times*, Dec. 20, 1983, at 7.
57. *The Guardian*, Dec. 23, 1983, at 1; *The Irish Times*, Dec. 21, 1983, at 7.
58. *The Guardian*, Dec. 23, 1983, at 1, 22; *The Times*, Dec. 19, 1983, at 4; Dec. 22, 1983, at 1; Dec. 23, 1983, at 1.
59. *The Irish Times*, Dec. 21, 1983, at 7.
60. *The Irish Times*, Dec. 21, 1983, at 7; *The Times*, Dec. 20, 1983, at 4.

crease joint security with the Republic[61] requested measures in the United States to inhibit the flow of arms and funds,[62] and turned to the law of incitement to reach the planners of violence.[63] The government's restraint is evident when contrasted with the 1974 ban on the IRA, also a decision generated by public pressure.[64]

In rejecting the calls for a ban on Sinn Fein, the British government drew a distinction between the military and political structures of the IRA, noting that the military was responsible for the attack and that the political arm could not consequently be punished by the disenfranchisement of its constituents. They separated the tactics of violence and politics in the nationalist campaign and chose a reaction that discouraged violent tactics while encouraging political action. The only political sanction imposed by the British involved a change of policy by the secretary of state for Northern Ireland that resulted in the cessation of administrative contacts between his office and Sinn Fien.[65] Prior to this action, junior ministers in the Northern Ireland office were able to meet with Sinn Fein representatives, provided they were part of a delegation including representatives of other political parties and the discussions concerned purely constituency matters rather than constitutional issues. Even this reaction, however, was conditional on Sinn Fein's continued support for IRA military operations. Thus the British reaction, though rejecting violent tactics, did not reject outright IRA goals.

Despite the fact that the sanctions were primarily imposed against military activity, Sinn Fein also felt repercussions from the Harrods incident. Sinn Fein had made advances toward its goal of ties with the Labour party before the Harrods attack. In 1983 Gerry Adams had made two trips to London as MP for West Belfast and two Labourites, Ken Livingstone and Steve Bundred, made a trip to Belfast, resulting in a softening of the British image of Sinn Fein as a criminal organization. The Labour Committee on Ireland, a faction within the Labour party, had invited Adams to the Party Conference in Brighton in Sep-

61. *The Guardian,* Dec. 24, 1983, at 1; Jan. 20, 1984, at 2; *The Times,* Dec. 24, 1983, at 4.
62. *The Guardian,* Dec. 23, 1983, at 1; *The Irish Times,* Dec. 20, 1983, at 1; Dec. 21, 1983, at 7; *The Times,* Dec. 21, 1983, at 4.
63. *The Times,* Dec. 23, 1983, at 1.
64. *The Times,* Dec. 20, 1983, at 10.
65. *The Guardian,* Dec. 23, 1983, at 22.

tember, although against the wishes of the dominant party powers. Much of this headway was reportedly lost as a result of the Harrods attack.[66] Thus, Labour too imposed a sanction on Sinn Fein for its breach of the norm against civilian targeting. As long as Sinn Fein sought a place at the negotiating table, Labour or some other British authority would be in a position to ensure the maintenance of at least minimal limits on IRA military tactics.

The Republic of Ireland also rejected the idea of banning Sinn Fein, noting that such action would increase the "romantic appeal" of the IRA and close its available channels for peaceful activity.[67] The Irish also rejected the possibility of internment of IRA members without trial in favor of the use of incitement laws to deal with supporters of military tactics.[68] In addition, they called on the British to end their official contacts with the IRA at all levels.[69] The Irish response, like the British, chose a middle ground for reaction. It provided sanctions for a more broadly defined category of military activities, while attempting to preserve a viable realm of political action for IRA supporters. This reaction implicitly conveyed the view that civilian targeting was unlawful and left the IRA with an opportunity and incentives to concur.

The IRA response, as well, indicated that the attack's potential for civilian casualties was a focal point for deliberations over sanctions. The IRA promised an investigation into the Harrods attack, although they expressed the belief that the ASU did not intend to kill civilians deliberately.[70] The IRA pointed out that their initial statement of responsibility contained an implicit message to the ASU to refrain from any further such attacks.[71] This message may have been, in part, responsible for the character of the Oxford Street bombing on Christmas Day.

The British, Irish, and IRA appeared to agree in rejecting civilian targeting. The British and Irish rejected all violent measures, although apparently not equally; the IRA agreed only to the rejection of civilian targeting in Great Britain.

66. *Fortnight*, Feb. 1984, at 9, 10.
67. *The Guardian*, Jan. 5, 1984, at 2.
68. *The Guardian*, Dec. 24, 1983, at 26.
69. *The Guardian*, Dec. 19, 1983, at 2; *The Times*, Dec. 23, 1983, at 10.
70. *The Guardian*, Jan. 7, 1984, at 2.
71. *Id.*

INTERNATIONAL APPRAISAL

The reaction of the international community is difficult to judge. There was little public commentary and even less press coverage; nevertheless, among the limited international responses was the United States' condemnation of the attack and of all violent tactics. Mario Biaggi, chairman of the Ad Hoc Congressional Committee on Irish Affairs, called for punishment of the bombers, saying that the exchange of political ideas on Northern Ireland should not be suppressed by violence.[72] Shortly after the incident, Charles Price, the U.S. ambassador to the United Kingdom, responded to British requests that American aid to the IRA be stopped by noting that the United States had recently begun to apply the Currency Regulation Act—which requires anyone entering or leaving the United States with more than $5,000 to report it—against known and suspected supporters of violence in Nothern Ireland.[73] Biaggi reacted to this, however, with a statement of concern for the selective enforcement of the law and the consequent possibility for harassment.[74] The American response thus entailed both condemnation of and sanctions against military tactics, but was tempered by elements of support for the republican cause. The only other explicit public reaction to the bombing came from the Nationalistes d'Equerra, a Catalan political organization.[75] They sent notes to Prime Minister Thatcher and Sinn Fein, protesting the suggested ban on Sinn Fein as a repressive attack on the national freedoms of the Irish people and expressing support for Sinn Fein's continued struggle for social, political, and nationalist liberties.

Neither the U.S. nor the Catalan reaction expressed manifest support for the civilian attack or for violent tactics in general, but rather reiterated a belief in the legitimacy of the Irish nationalist cause and its representation through Sinn Fein. The common international appraisal seems to be recognition of the legitimacy of the nationalist struggle coupled with rejection of civilian targeting as a means of attaining goals.

72. *The Irish Times*, Dec. 20, 1983, at 6.
73. *The Guardian*, Feb. 25, 1984, at 4; *The Irish Times*, Dec. 20, 1983, at 1; Dec. 21, 1983, at 7; *The Times*, Dec. 20, 1983, at 4.
74. *The Congressional Record*, Feb. 29, 1984, at H967.
75. *The Times*, Dec. 12, 1983, at 6.

AUTHOR'S APPRAISAL

Development of the Norm against Civilian Targeting in Britain

Assuming the continuation of certain conditions, all parties to the Harrods incident and to the Northern Ireland dispute, as waged in Great Britain, can expect a continued acceptance of the norm against civilian targeting. More generally, the IRA statement, coupled with the British and Irish responses, may constitute a step toward normative limitation of military tactical options in unconventional wars. This limitation can and will continue where the political arena offers a viable forum for reconciliation of disputes.

The basis for this expectation lies in Sinn Fein's desire to be included in any serious negotiation. The IRA has in the past exercised a negative power, the ability to prevent a settlement, in such affairs. What it sought to cultivate in its response to the Harrod's bombing was constructive authority as well. IRA threats to increase the level of violence dramatically and to foment civil war in the Republic in the event of a ban on Sinn Fein indicated the depth of the IRA's desire for legitimate power i n the decision making structure.

There are two related sources of authority and legitimacy available to the IRA. First, the IRA can derive such power and legitimacy and an accompanying position in any decision on Northern Ireland's fate from strong support by the nationalist/republican community in Northern Ireland. Second, such a position could be bestowed by the other powers involved, who would also be the other participants in any negotiations. The most successful strategy would include appeals to both sources. In order to achieve this political authority Sinn Fein had to not only maximize its support at home but also seek British and Irish political ties, thus gaining legitimacy, support, and initiation into the existing authority structure. It was in pursuit of this goal that the IRA recognized its interest in limiting its military tactics, through the prohibition against civilian targeting in Britain.

A key to the expectation that the IRA would accept the unlawfulness of civilian targeting in Great Britain, therefore, lay in the policy change through which Sinn Fein no longer eschewed electoral politics. During the 1970s the IRA generally withheld itself from participation in the electoral process and representative politics. As noted above, however, that began to change in the early 1980s. Danny Morrison, publicity

INTERNATIONAL INCIDENTS

officer for Sinn Fein, expressed this change in November 1981 in language that became a slogan for the new IRA/Sinn Fein direction: "Will anyone here object if, with a ballot-paper in this hand and an armalite in this hand, we take power in Ireland?"[76] The new policy gained impetus from the 1981 hunger strike at the H block of Maze Prison, during which the IRA hunger striker, Bobby Sands, received unprecedented support in an electoral campaign. The IRA capitalized subsequently on this support and in elections Sinn Fein won 35 percent of the nationalist vote, roughly equaling its rival, the Social Democratic and Labour Party (SDLP).

The percentage of the nationalist vote the Sinn Fein had captured largely consisted of a new segment of the nationalist vote, those who had previously boycotted elections. The next step in a drive for political power that could win them a seat at any future negotiations required Sinn Fein to maximize its vote at the expense of its rival, the SDLP, by winning over SDLP supporters.[77] Such a drive, however, would have required a dramatic reduction in military operations, since SDLP supporters were presumed to oppose the IRA's violent tactics and to support the SDLP's nonviolent endeavors. The necessity for a sharp drop in military activity rendered this an uncertain scenario, given the presence and power of old-style militarists within the IRA.

The second basis for normative limitations on military tactics lay in Sinn Fein's cultivation of ties with other political powers. The links Sinn Fein was looking for were with Fianna Fail in the Republic and the left-wing faction of the Labour party in Britain.[78] In order to achieve these ties, Sinn Fein had to limit military operations to the extent that they could present themselves not just as a subordinate support and cover group for the IRA. They had to avoid operations such as the Birmingham bombings or the Harrods attack, which were ultimately counterproductive, and instead wage a relatively low-level, but visible and continuous, British campaign.

The British hope, evident in the decision not to ban Sinn Fein, was that this trend toward politicization and Sinn Fein's desire to forge ties with Labour would continue and that the viability of military options would simultaneously decrease, until the IRA could be drawn within

76. *Fortnight*, Feb. 1983, at 9.
77. *Fortnight*, June 1983, at 4.
78. *Fortnight*, May 1983, at 4.

range of an acceptable compromise achieved through the political process. There was certainly some substance to such a hope; however, it was highly unlikely that the IRA would forsake military activity entirely before a settlement was reached. The IRA, rather, intended to use violence and negotiations in a coordinated strategy, partly by maintaining a level of instability in Northern Ireland affairs until groups were in power that were willing to deal with them. The IRA said that they would continue to fight "until the ink on the treaty document is dry."[79] Instead of dismantling the military aparatus, the IRA planned to update it in order to maintain pressure on security forces and to maintain what they saw as a major basis for their political power. The strategy of the ballot box and the armalite was not merely a slogan.

Although tensions between the militarists and the politicos in the IRA existed because of this strategy, there did not appear to be any sign of a serious organizational split that could end centralized control of military policy and with it British expectations and IRA assurances of limitations. In Craigavon, for example, some prominent Sinn Fein members were expelled allegedly for the disappearance of money from a fund for IRA prisoners and their families. Those expelled, however, were reportedly from the movement's old-style militarist faction, opposed to engaging in electoral politics. Some commentators pointed to this episode as a harbinger of many future disagreements over the new policy. Sinn Fein denied that the expulsions were motivated by factional divisions and that they presaged future divisions, noting that the senior Sinn Fein member in that area supported the new strategy.[80]

Sinn Fein and its opponents recognized its tradition of physical-force republicanism and acknowledged that the ballot box was a new departure, one that was unlikely to usurp its energies entirely. Gerry Adams summed up the IRA's new strategy: "There have always been three tendencies [in republican strategy]: a militaristic and fairly apolitical tendency, a revolutionary tendency, and a constitutional tendency. . . . Since the growth of the two partitionist states there has not been a dominant tendency capable of giving proper leadership to the Irish people on all the issues facing them. Only today, with the protrated [sic] politicization of Sinn Fein and the Republican/Nationalist people, are

79. *The Times*, Dec. 20, 1983, at 10.
80. *Fortnight*, Oct. 1983, at 15.

conditions emerging which if properly developed could lead to success."[81]

The IRA, then, did not give up its traditional military policy. But because of the IRA's desire to pursue a dual tactical strategy that embraced political as well as military action, the IRA had to accept and acknowledge limits on its military tactical options or face the failure of its political initiatives. If Sinn Fein had repudiated its political aspirations there would have been little to ensure the continuation of such a limitation. There would have been no effective sanction against civilian targeting. Nevertheless, as long as Sinn Fein continued to espouse political ambitions, they had to conform to a law of unconventional warfare that prohibited attacks on civilian targets in Great Britain.

The British were willing to accept any limitation on military activity by the IRA. Although they claimed that all violent activity by an unauthorized force was illegal, whether directed against civilians or military targets, they could not reasonably expect a cessation of IRA attacks on military targets or economic targets where civilian life was not jeopardized. They may have claimed disbelief of IRA assurances and have argued the indistinguishable character of military and civilian targets, yet their interests and the interests of the IRA led to mutual agreement on limitations of military activity, at least so far as to exclude civilian targets. British acceptance of the legitimacy of Sinn Fein and encouragement of political activity toward the realization of Sinn Fein's goals indicated their acknowledgement that the disputes in Nothern Ireland were essentially political and required political solutions. Increased security measures were intended to be, then, merely temporary measures to minimize the effects of military activity and did not form the basis for any hope of resolution. The British were eager to limit military activity by encouraging the pursuit of change through political channels.

International Impact of the Incident

The absence of an explicit world response to the Harrods incident makes it more difficult to discern the impact of the incident on the international community. This is not to say, however, that the incident has no application to international normative development. In many instances a single incident may definitely identify a norm. This is es-

81. *Fortnight*, Sept. 1983, at 8.

pecially true when relatively few parties are governed by the norm and the resolution of the incident is agreed upon by all parties. In other instances, however, a single incident may only raise the potential for normative development or initiate a normative trend that may be consumated by later incidents. The bombing of Harrods is such an incident. It indicates an extension of the norm against civilian targeting to the arena of unconventional warfare. However, resolution of the incident is not uniformly agreed upon and no undeniable impact can be identified in the resolution. The incident touches on patterns of conduct that are in flux; an analysis of the incident can yield knowledge regarding the reaction of elites to those changing patterns and may illuminate trends in the normative control of those patterns of conduct.

At the very least, the bombing is an example of one resolution of a typical event, indicative of the concerns and policies of reasonably typical participants in an unconventional war. It provides insights into the dynamics of unconventional war and may signify a development that, in time, will overcome previous impediments to the development of a norm against civilian targeting. As such it has some predictive value with respect to similar incidents globally. In the absence of express world reaction it is this similarity of motive, strategy, tactics, and limitations among unconventional armies and the elites they threaten that gives rise to the generalizability of this regional and situational norm.

The international community has largely been unsuccessful in reaching any formalized consensus on the appropriate limits of unconventional warfare or even the legitimacy of such disputes. The major impediments have been concern for the continued viability of the doctrines of decolonization and self-determination, the inability to devise politically neutral language, and the inability to agree on conditions that legitimize unconventional warfare. One elite's terrorist is another's freedom fighter, and what one elite considers outlaw subversion of a lawfully constituted government another will call an anticolonial struggle for self-determination. Regional agreements condemning particular tactics such as airplane hijackings, letter bombings, or attacks on diplomatic personnel have been reached; the absence of an authoritative and controlling consensus, however, increases the normative significance of a regional incident.

Because of common circumstances many unconventional armies share common characteristics, as do the elites who are threatened by them. These characteristics include individual and group goal-determined constraints, which serve to limit tactical and strategic options and, when one option is exercised, serve to limit further the next range of opportunities.

Unconventional armies must initially determine their individual psychological and physical capacity for violence, but beyond that they are constrained by the need to maintain legitimacy in their opponents' eyes to avoid an overwhelming response that threatens their very existence. Although such a level of violence may be difficult for the IRA to reach, they did feel the effects of this constraint after the Birmingham bombings.

Unconventional armies must also operate in such a manner that maintains support from some constituency, the size and influence of which will in turn partially determine their capabilities. Included in this need for support is the constraint of maintaining their identity as historic victims. Thus, the IRA maintains an image as fighters against colonial oppression to their American sympathizers, while characterizing their conflict as a class struggle to British and Irish constituents. As noted, the ability to maintain some significant constituency in turn largely determines the legitimacy of their power. IRA dependence upon support from the nationalist Catholic community of Northern Ireland and upon sympathetic Irish-Americans, then, dictates limitations on military and political tactics that prevent complete repudiation by the Church hierarchy or by their predominantly capitalist American supporters.

The ideology and self-image of an unconventional army also limits its tactical options. A self-image as a legitimate protogovernment limits the IRA and the PLO in similar ways, just as anarchist motives would impose different limitations. This may be a partial explanation for the fact that although certain unconventional armies could conceivably attain small-scale nuclear weaponry, none has done so to date. The argument that terrorists (as one type of unconventional army) know no limits to the use of violence but engage in random acts of destruction in the pursuit of their goals is certainly incorrect. Although unconventional armies generally reject conventional notions of legal behavior, their need to avoid provoking overwhelming opposition and to maintain some constituency as well as their ideological motivations imposes limitations.

It is acknowledged that the IRA is a unique unconventional army in its long and insular tradition of physical force, anti-intellectualism, and nationalism. As a result, it is distinct in many ways from such groups as the Baader-Meinhof Group or the Red Brigades. This tradition affects its choice of strategy; however, it does not prevent generalization from its experience to other unconventional wars where similar circumstances impose similar limitations on tactics.

Development of the Norm in General

The Harrods bombing incident's potential to reinforce the norm against civilian targeting and extend it to unconventional wars is tempered, however, by pressures on the norm as it applies to conventional wars. The viability of a general norm against civilian targeting has been significantly retarded to the extent that the characteristics of modern warfare have led to the breakdown of traditional restraints.

Several particular and related characteristics of recent wars pose threats to the norm against civilian targeting. The first is the difficulty of distinguishing military personnel from civilians. The growth of guerrilla movements in occupied territories or where battle areas are not defined by "lines," as well as the increasing significance of technical and industrial support staffs, the "civilian infrastructure" of a militarized society, have increased the difficulty of discrimination and enhanced the military value of civilian targeting.[82]

The norm against civilian targeting is also challenged by the general acceptance of strategies of demoralization. In theory, because modern industrial war efforts depend on the high productivity and willing sacrifices of a supportive civilian population, a strategy designed to destroy this support is highly effective. Demoralization of a civilian population through either indiscriminate or selective direct attacks is one such strategy that is employed in both conventional and unconventional war. It is a strategy that generally involves civilian targeting.

Civilian targeting for the purposes of demoralization and terrorization was practiced as early as the American Civil War and has continued through every major war since. It reached a climax of scale in the conventional aerial bombardments of Berlin, Dresden, London, Tokyo, and other cities and the atomic attacks on Hiroshima and Naga-

---

82. R. Gehring, *The Protection of Civilian Infrastructures*, 42 LAW AND CONTEMPORARY PROBLEMS 86 (1978).

saki.[83] The Allied command clearly accepted civilian targeting as a legitimate and militarily efficient tactic.

But the rationale for civilian targeting extends beyond a simple belief in the values of demoralization. Elements of this belief are combined with elements of the problem of discrimination in the rationalization that any member of the opposing system is a justifiable target, simply because of membership in that system. Civilians may be attacked, not just because to do so will weaken their compatriot's resolve and not just because they perform services or produce commodities in support of the military. Rather, civilians are alleged to be viable targets because every element of an opposing system shares the guilt of that system. This characterization, above all, seems to justify and demand total warfare in ideological conflicts and has had advocates in both conventional and unconventional wars. General Sherman remarked that he fought not just a hostile army, but a hostile people.[84] The nineteenth-century anarchist, Emil Henry, argued that there are no innocent bourgeois,[85] and Sartre used this rationale against French citizens subject to Algerian targeting, arguing, "your passivity only serves to place you in the ranks of the oppressors."[86] Such a structure of analysis, dependent upon concepts of generalizable guilt and innocence, is likely to lead to a decrease of humanitarian protections as these concepts become refracted through the lens of the analyzer's values.[87]

A third feature of politics and warfare that challenges the customary prohibition against civilian targeting relates in general to the contemporary character of world politics and war. A basis of law in war, aside from military necessity, is the perceived common interests of all parties to the conflict to maintain a level of humanitarian restraint that sustains their legitimacy as authoritative actors and thus provides some common ground upon which to build a resolution of the dispute.[88] Total war, and certain limited wars such as wars of decolonization,

83. In Hiroshima and Nagasaki the civilian losses were supposedly justified in relation to estimated losses both sides would have suffered had an invasion been necessary.

84. Gehring, *supra* note 1, at 58.

85. N. LIVINGSTONE, THE WAR AGAINST TERRORISM (1982), at 131.

86. LIVINGSTONE, *supra* note 84, at 136.

87. J. Paust, *Terrorism and the International Law of War*, 64 MILITARY LAW REVIEW 1, 34 (1974).

88. P. WILKINSON, THE LAW OF WAR AND TERRORISM: THE MORALITY OF TERRORISM (1982).

however, allow little room for such common understanding. They are the conflict of incompatible systems vying for hegemony. The competing ideologies may claim to allow no accommodation and the resulting highly doctrinaire conflict may contain little from which to build political solutions and common interests.

The tension has intensified between the humanitarian ideals of military law and the reality of modern warfare and politics. The characteristics of total warfare as well as technological developments in weaponry and communication have reduced the validity of prohibitions on civilian targeting based on military necessity. The mobilization of noncombatants for the war effort and the proliferation of indiscriminate weaponry tend to justify efficiency-based claims for the targeting of civilians. Concurrent changes in modes of armed conflict have blurred the combatant/noncombatant distinction and further reduced the viability of the norm against civilian targeting.[89]

To the degree that the Harrods bombing incident reinforces and extends the norm against civilian targeting, it does so in a context of strong counterpressures.

POSTSCRIPT

IRA military activities in Great Britain immediately following the Harrods incident continued generally to follow the norm against civilian targeting. The first major IRA bombing after Harrods occurred in October 1984, when the IRA bombed the Grand Hotel in Brighton. The call claiming responsibility for that bombing stated that the target was the British Cabinet and suggested that future targets would be political or military but not commercial. A policy of attacking political targets added a new dimension to the limitation of tactics that was developing in the wake of the Harrods incident, but an IRA guarantee against com-

89. The Protocols Additional to the Geneva Convention of 12 August 1949, and Relating to the Protection of Victims of International Armed Conflicts and other codifications of proscriptions against civilian targeting attempt to resolve this tension while reinforcing humanitarian principles. Their success remains questionable. Some commentators argue that the most that can be expected from the Additional Protocols is that professional soldiers under organized discipline will observe the customs of war as long as the fighting remains in desolate regions. See M. GLOVER, THE VELVET GLOVE: THE DECLINE OF MODERATION IN WAR (1982).

mercial targeting indicated a continuation of some normative limitations.

An analysis of the continued development of the norm against civilian targeting would require a detailed study of the Brighton incident. A general review of the facts surrounding that incident and of the stable political climate at that time may indicate that, at least to some degree, the normative limitation on military tactics reinforced in the Harrods incident had been maintained. Nevertheless the Brighton bombing, like similar incidents around the globe, appeared to place pressure on the norm against civilian targeting. The attack on the Cabinet may have indicated that the IRA does not acknowledge politicians as civilian targets and may therefore have signaled a diminution of the scope of the norm. Moreover, the IRA displayed a willingness to risk civilian casualties in the attack even when civilians were not the principal targets. To this extent, the Brighton bombing may demonstrate a continued weakening of the norm.

The future of the norm against civilian targeting remains uncertain. The norm may be gaining new strength, as it appeared to in the Harrods bombing. However, twentieth-century pressures on the norm threaten both the strength and the scope of the norms' protections. In the face of these pressures, incidents like the Harrods bombing may represent no more than a temporary aberration in the otherwise slow erosion of a norm.

THE STUDY OF INCIDENTS:
Epilogue and Prologue

11

W. MICHAEL REISMAN AND ANDREW R. WILLARD

It has to be living, to learn the speech of the place
It has to face the men of the time and to meet
The women of the time. It has to think about war
And it has to find what will suffice. It has
to construct a new stage. *Wallace Stevens, "Of Modern Poetry"*

The preceding chapters are a collective effort to develop a systematic method for the study of events in international politics, not for their own sake and not as morality tales, but as prisms for identifying and enlarging the actual expectations of authority entertained by those who are politically relevant in international politics. The incident method does not reject traditional sources of law in toto but starts from the generally acknowledged fact that the effectiveness of law-producing entities in international politics and the correspondence of their pronouncements with elite expectations is lower and more difficult to discern than in advanced national political systems. This is hardly a novel insight, but its implications are honestly faced. The automatic assumption that lawyers in countries such as the United States routinely make, that what is presented as law is law, is not warranted internationally. The point is not that words emanating from formal institutions are always ineffective, but simply that, in international politics, their effectiveness must be routinely tested by examining the expectations regarding them held by politically relevant actors. This can be accomplished economically and systematically by looking to particular incidents and developing a method for studying them for the light they throw on elite expectations of authority and control.

Scholars, like cabinetmakers, sometimes develop curious loyalties to old tools. One of the difficulties in establishing a new focus that does not fit neatly into existing disciplines and then fashioning special intellectual tools for dealing with the problems the focus casts in a new light is that even those who understand and appreciate the purpose of the exercise continue to feel that some of the traditional practices should still be incorporated. What is resented is less the novel idea and more the fact that it makes obsolescent beloved old ways of doing things.

New methods are perforce critical of older methods, but not necessarily of the subject matter to which method is applied. Some may contend that the incidents approach is essentially destructive of international law. That criticism is unfounded. The incident method is based on the realization, shared by many participants and observers of contemporary international politics and law, that the formal international institutional structure established after World War II has decayed; though some of its component parts frequently go through the motions, they do not in fact adequately perform many of the indispensable functions originally assigned to them.

It is equally clear to observers who have reluctantly recorded the deterioration of the formal institutional structure that a great deal of international law is routinely prescribed and applied in many settings and that, at the elite level, there is substantial evidence of both belief in and reliance on expectations of authority and control. The point is not that international law is dead; rather that methods for understanding and manipulating international law that rely solely on formalistic analyses of text are not particularly useful for scholarly, pedagogical, or practical purposes. The incident approach is critical of such formalistic methods, but it is not iconoclastic. The approach was devised as an affirmation of the possibility and reality of international law, through the development of a method for finding and tracking it.

The interest in incidents is hardly novel. Nor is it surprising that scholars have tended to turn to them more in periods of low institutionalization. Prior to the burst of institution building in this century, which began with the formation of the Permanent Court of Arbitration in 1899, international legal scholars who did not believe in natural law perforce collected and published incidents as the raw material of international law.[1] No systematic method for doing this was developed, however, and this scholarly practice receded increasingly through the twentieth century as the institutional superstructure of the international political system became more formally articulated.

Nevertheless, a number of scholars have continued to be concerned with incidents; some, particularly Charles Rousseau and Michel Virally, have maintained a *chronique des faits internationaux*, with valuable raw material for incident studies.[2] Other scholars, such as the late Lassa Oppenheim, in more idiosyncratic fashion, used fact-complexes that were hypothesized but that manifested the same conflict dimension as does our contemporary notion of incidents, for teaching and examination purposes.[3] Others have suggested in more general terms that incidents be studied as a part of custom.[4]

None of these precursors or parallel efforts has a systematic method. Nor does any of them articulate a basic political and legal theory. Without method and theory, the danger that studies of incidents may be unreliable social research hardly needs illumination.[5]

1. *See, in particular,* JOHN BASSETT MOORE, A DIGEST OF INTERNATIONAL LAW AS EMBODIED IN DIPLOMATIC DISCUSSIONS, TREATIES AND OTHER INTERNATIONAL AGREEMENTS, INTERNATIONAL AWARDS, THE DECISIONS OF MUNICIPAL COURTS, AND THE WRITINGS OF JURISTS, AND ESPECIALLY IN DOCUMENTS, PUBLISHED AND UNPUBLISHED, ISSUED BY PRESIDENTS AND SECRETARIES OF STATE OF THE UNITED STATES, THE OPINIONS OF THE ATTORNEYS-GENERAL, AND THE DECISIONS OF COURTS, FEDERAL AND STATE 8 volumes (1906).

2. *See generally,* REVUE GÉNÉRALE DE DROIT INTERNATIONAL PUBLIC (C. Rousseau & M. Virally eds. Quarterly).

3. L. OPPENHEIM, INTERNATIONAL INCIDENTS FOR DISCUSSION IN CONVERSATION CLASSES (1909).

4. *See* A. D'AMATO, THE CONCEPT OF CUSTOM IN INTERNATIONAL LAW (1971).

5. For conceptual and theoretical orientation, *see* M. McDougal, H. Lasswell, & M. Reisman, *Theories about International Law: Prologue to a Configurative Jurisprudence,* 8:2 VA. J. INT'L L. 189 (1968), reprinted in M. McDOUGAL & M. REISMAN, INTERNATIONAL LAW ESSAYS (1981) and *The World Constitutive Process of Authoritative Decision,* 19 J. LEGAL EDUC. 253, 403 (1967), reprinted in 1 THE FUTURE OF THE INTERNATIONAL LEGAL ORDER (C. Black & R. Falk eds. 1969) and M. McDOUGAL & M. REISMAN, *supra.* See generally H. Lasswell & M. McDougal, *Criteria for a Theory about Law,* 44:2 S. CAL. L. REV. 362 (1971); *Trends in Theories about Law: Comprehensiveness in Conceptions of Constitutive Process,* 41:1 GEO. WASH. L. REV. 1 (1972); *Trends in Theories about Law: Maintaining Observational Standpoint and Delimiting the Focus of Inquiry,* 8:1 U. TOLEDO L. REV. 1 (1976); and *The Relation of Law to Social Process: Trends in Theories about Law,* 37:3 U. PITT. L. REV. 465 (1976). *See also* M. Reisman,

The incident studies that were carried through to completion in our seminar did bring to the surface a number of methodological problems that had been unanticipated or underestimated. One of the first seen was that certain types of events are better suited to this format than others. Events that engage normative expectations pertaining to the shaping of values other than power—for example, well-being, affection or skill—may have significant impact on world public order, but lack of coverage may make the events unsuitable for study in terms of an incident. Apparently, it is easier to carve incidents from headline stories than from material buried on page nine. Dramatic character, perceived importance, and, perhaps in causal relation, media attention create a popular perception of a matrix or boundary to a set of events that simplifies its subsequent treatment as an incident by an international legal scholar. On the other hand, the very diffuse but often far more important processes by which new demands are raised to an increasingly overt level of consciousness and are refined as claims for law and, in some cases, ultimately become installed as norms in the international system may be too unorganized and complex to lend themselves to study as incidents.

The incident method depends on some baseline of expectations from which the scholar charts normative developments—reinforcement, change, or termination. The practical problems of establishing baseline expectations proved to be greater than anticipated. It is no secret that the incident method is animated by a certain skepticism about the continuing empirical correspondence and reliability of much international doctrine and formula. Yet normative baselines must be drawn from some sources. In certain instances, the process of research itself revealed, in empirically verifiable fashion, the relevant expectations. In other studies, our collaborators found themselves using as evidence of provisional baselines many of the same conventional sources about which they entertained doubts. In reviewing the production of the seminar, we were surprised at the extent of reliance on or at least reference to more traditional indicators of international law. As the number of incident studies grows, this practical difficulty may be mitigated some-

A *Theory about Law from the Policy Perspective*, in LAW AND POLICY (D. Weisstub ed. 1976), reprinted in M. McDOUGAL & M. REISMAN *supra*, and *International Lawmaking: A Process of Communication*, Lasswell Memorial Lecture of the World Academy of Art and Science, American Society of International Law, April 24, 1981. PROC. AM. SOC. INT'L L. 101 (1981).

what, but it is now clear that it will continue. We hasten to add that this is not intrinsically or inevitably a problem. The genre of incidents is only one of a number of methods for identifying a much larger body of international law. Other methods with suitable procedures should be maintained alongside it.

A potentially rewarding avenue of study involves the examination of what might be termed "the averted or aborted incident," that is, those events that seem to be leading up to an incident-type conflict but in which a resolution or settlement is reached prior to the culminating events that would have generated the accessible international reactions characteristic of full-blown incidents. Normative expectations about international matters may be important factors in such instances and they may reveal baseline expectations; the matter remains to be researched.

Oppenheim used hypothetical incidents for teaching purposes. We, too, have used them for purposes of explaining, in an abbreviated fashion, what we mean by an incident. But we have been reluctant to push further, lest we find ourselves simplifying complex situations and excluding the richness of factors that make international decision making difficult and the study of international incidents exigent. However, there may be additional uses for hypothetical or adapted incidents in gaming and simulation exercises.

Because incidents are selected with primary reference to elite expectations and without regard to many of the boundary assumptions of traditional international legal studies, it is not surprising that many will challenge the classic conception of what international law is. Dividends of realism and relevance must be set against political costs. To study, for example, terrorist activity *within* a state in terms of the international norms regulating the use of force touches on one of the major controversies in this area of contemporary international law. Merely choosing the subject for study has disturbing political implications.

We understand and share the revulsion over the indiscriminate targeting and killing of civilians and certainly do not want to endorse it or in any way to legitimize it. Yet, international lawyers must begin to find out what norms, if any, have come to operate in those transnational processes in which resources are mobilized for the prosecution of unconventional warfare, for it is likely to be the most common form of large-scale violence of international concern in the foreseeable future. In the light of events of the last few years, it is difficult to see how anyone can seriously contend that this is not an "international" prob-

INTERNATIONAL INCIDENTS

lem whose appraisal ineluctably uses the most familiar and conventional international legal norms.

For the incident method to make a continuing and effective contribution to the study of contemporary international law, it will be necessary to establish an incident data bank into which regularly updated "deposits" can be made. That sort of activity will necessarily involve many scholars in many different universities and institutions. The endeavor will lose the structural concentration achievable in a single seminar in a single school that tends toward a certain uniformity of method and result. Whether the divergence will introduce dialects and creoles of incident studies, rendering them so different that they can no longer be considered part of a single method, is a question one cannot answer. This problem may be anticipated and mitigated somewhat by creating a coordinate system of organization and diffusion. A number of scholars have indicated interest in establishing such a system. It is hoped that it will be one of the results of the studies collected here.

There are many factors that operate in favor of the adoption and diffusion of the incident method. The more pragmatic international lawyers are eager for a valid method that encourages realistic orientation and provides conceptual tools whose use yields both insight and practical results, because the traditional methods' lack of utility has become increasingly evident. At the same time, the decay of international institutions and the incredible discrepancies between statements of doctrine and formula and actual expectations of authority and control have become more and more apparent. Finally, even among political scientists, there is an increasing sense of the relevance of authority in political behavior and of the need for a legitimate place in contemporary political science for the central function of law: understanding and clarifying common interest.[6]

6. *See generally* the discussion of "Authority" in 1 INTERNATIONAL ENCYCLOPEDIA OF THE SOCIAL SCIENCES (D. Sills ed. 1968), which includes a brief but useful bibliography, and the HANDBOOK OF POLITICAL SCIENCE (F. Greenstein & N. Polsby eds. 1975). Among many pertinent studies, *see* C. MERRIAM, POLITICAL POWER: ITS COMPOSITION AND INCIDENCE (1934); C. BARNARD, THE FUNCTIONS OF THE EXECUTIVE (1946); AUTHORITY (C. Friedrich ed. 1958); A. BRECHT, POLITICAL THEORY: THE FOUNDATIONS OF TWENTIETH CENTURY POLITICAL THOUGHT (1959); THE PUBLIC INTEREST (C. Friedrich ed. 1962); H. ECKSTEIN & T. GURR, PATTERNS OF AUTHORITY: A STRUCTURAL BASIS FOR POLITICAL INQUIRY (1975); R. BENDIX, KINGS OR PEOPLE: POWER AND THE MANDATE TO RULE (1978); AUTHORITY AND POWER: STUDIES ON MEDIEVAL LAW AND GOVERNMENT PRESENTED TO WALTER ULLMANN (B. Tierney & P. Linehan eds. 1980); J. SCHAAR, LEGITI-

EPILOGUE AND PROLOGUE

<small>MACY IN THE MODERN STATE (1981); L. DOOB, PERSONALITY, POWER, AND AUTHORITY: A VIEW FROM THE BEHAVIORAL SCIENCES (1983); COMPLIANT BEHAVIOR: BEYOND OBEDIENCE TO AUTHORITY (M. Rosenbaum ed. 1983); W. BLUHM, FORCE OR FREEDOM? THE PARADOX IN MODERN POLITICAL THOUGHT (1984); E. PAGE, POLITICAL AUTHORITY AND BUREAUCRATIC POWER: A COMPARATIVE ANALYSIS (1985); and A. Wildavsky, *The Once and Future School of Public Policy*, 79 PUB. Interest 25 (Spring 1985). Studies with a focus on world community and international politics include E. CARR, THE TWENTY YEARS' CRISIS, 1919-1939: AN INTRODUCTION TO THE STUDY OF INTERNATIONAL RELATIONS (1940); THE WORLD COMMUNITY (Q. Wright ed. 1948); M. KAPLAN & N. KATZENBACH, THE POLITICAL FOUNDATIONS OF INTERNATIONAL LAW (1961); S. BROWN, NEW FORCES IN WORLD POLITICS (1974); ON THE CREATION OF A JUST WORLD ORDER: PREFERRED WORLDS FOR THE 1990's (S. Mendlovitz ed. 1975); E. MORSE, MODERNIZATION AND THE TRANSFORMATION OF INTERNATIONAL RELATIONS (1976); H. BLANEY III, GLOBAL CHALLENGES: A WORLD AT RISK (1979); C. BEITZ, POLITICAL THEORY AND INTERNATIONAL RELATIONS (1979); and S. KIM, THE QUEST FOR A JUST WORLD ORDER (1984).</small>

Index

INDEX

Brezhnev, Leonid, 167
Brezhnev Doctrine, 88
Brittan, Leon, 246
Brzezinski, Zbigniew, 79
Bulgaria, 129, 206–207, 211–13, 232

Callaghan, James, 125–27, 130
Camp David accords, 154, 158
Campbell, Donald, 99
Canada, 35, 230. *See also* Cosmos 954
    incident
Carrington, Lord, 118, 131, 133–34,
    140–42
Carter, Jimmy, 70, 93, 189
Carter Doctrine, 88
Casebooks, 10
Caudillo system, 9
Cheysson, Claude, 171
Chicago Convention on International
    Civil Aviation (1944), 203, 213–14,
    233, 235–36; state aircraft and, 215–
    16, 226–30
China, People's Republic of, 3, 205–206,
    231, 232, 235; Soviet Union and, 59,
    98; Taiwan and, 4
Civilian aircraft incidents: Air France
    (1952), 205; Cathay Pacific (1954),
    205–206; El Al (1955), 206–207, 211–
    13; Korean Airlines (1978), 208–210;
    Libyan Airlines (1973), 207–208. *See
    also* Korean Airlines Flight 007 inci-
    dent
CoCom (Coordinating Committee for
    Multilateral Security Export Controls),
    91–92, 103
Collective security, 55, 87–88, 102–106,
    111–12, 114
Commercial goods, 86, 91, 109–114
Confidentiality, 75–76
Constitutional law, 11, 18
Corfu Channel Case (1949), 19, 64
Corfu Channel incident (1946), 62, 64
Cosmos 954 incident: appraisal of, 78–84;
    conflicting claims in, 71–72; facts of,
    68–71; lawfulness of, 72–78; outcome
    of, 80–81; radioactivity from, 69–70,

72, 78, 81, 82; settlement, 71, 77, 79,
    81
Costa Méndez, Nicanor, 118–19, 126,
    133, 138–39
Council on Mutual Economic Assistance
    (CMEA), 74, 80
Critical defense zones, 88
Currency Regulation Act (U.S.), 252

Decolonization, 116, 121, 127, 136,
    138–39, 257
Denmark, 58, 60
Détente, 92–93, 110
Dobrynin, Anatoly F., 79
Domestic law: behavior and, 11–13; court
    decisions and, 7–11, 15–17, 22; factual
    information and, 20; statutes and, 7
Druse Moslems, 163
Druzhba oil pipeline, 92, 100

Egypt, 208, 231; Lebanon and, 169, 179;
    Libya and, 189, 190, 198; PLO and,
    161, 179
Endurance, HMS, 126, 131–35, 139,
    142
European Economic Community (EEC),
    97, 106; Argentina and, 137; KAL 007
    and, 231; Lebanon and, 171, 177,
    178–79
Export Administration Act (U.S.): 1969,
    92; 1979, 92, 105–107, 110
Export Control Act (1949)(U.S.), 90–91
Export-Import Bank Act (Dec., 1974)
    (U.S.): Stevenson amendment, 93

Falk, Richard, 148, 149
Falkland Islands: condominium over,
    124–25; Council, 122, 124, 134, 141;
    described, 116–17; Franks Report on,
    120–30, 134, 140; Memorandum of
    Understanding and, 122–24, 141; Na-
    tionality Act (1981) and, 139; Opera-
    tion Condor and, 121–23; population,
    117, 123; self-determination and, 122–
    25, 138, 141; territorial boundaries,
    130–31; vulnerability of, 121, 122, 141
Falkland Islands War, 3–5, 15, 32; ap-

INDEX

International law: conception of, 267–68;
court decisions and, vii, 13–17, 19, 64;
effectiveness of, 6–7, 67, 264; formal
sources of, 5–6, 13, 68, 263–64, 266;
incidents and, vi–viii, 4–6, 15–24, 34–
39, 263–68; jurisdiction and, 106–108;
political factors in, 4–5, 14, 263–64;
practice in, 16; signals and, 115–16,
135–38, 143
International legal science: development
of, 16–18, 23–24, 263–65; methodology, 25–27, 38–39, 263–68
International norms: attenuation of, 37;
codification of, 30; consensus and, 36;
development of, 4–6, 15–16, 18, 22–
25, 29–37, 263–68; extension of, 37;
identification of, 30–31
International political economy, 85–90
Iran, 20, 29, 83, 154
Iran hostage crisis, 83, 189
Iraq, 29, 154, 161
Ireland, Republic of, 240, 243, 248–49,
251, 254
Irish Council for Civil Liberties, 249
Irish Republican Army: active service
units (ASU) of, 240, 243–44, 247–48,
251; aid to, 250, 252; Army Council
of, 240, 243–44; banning of, 247, 250;
Birmingham bombing and, 241, 247;
Brighton bombing and, 261–62; Catholic Church and, 258; disunity in, 245,
254–55; hunger strikes and, 254; as nationalist organization, 240, 245–46,
250–54, 258–59; law of incitement
and, 249–51; politics and, 253–56; support for, 253–54, 258; Ulster Defense
Regiment (UDR) and, 247; Woolwich
bombing and, 243, 247
Islamic Conference, 196
Israel, 64, 98; arms sales and, 178, 179;
Bulgaria and, 212; ceasefire and, 145–
46, 151–54, 160, 170, 175; disunity in,
147, 179–80; Egypt and, 169, 208;
Libya and, 207–208; occupied territories and, 154, 157, 210; Phalangists
and, 147, 174; right to exist, 148; Syria
and, 146, 147, 156, 158–64, 166–69,

172–73, 180, 208; United Nations and,
161, 170–71, 175–77, 179–80; West
Bank and, 157. *See also* Lebanon, war
in; Palestine Liberation Organization
Israeli Defense Forces (IDF), 144, 146–
47, 151, 153, 168, 174; West Beirut
and, 162, 177, 179
Italy, 231; energy dependence and, 101,
108; Israel and, 178; Lebanon and,
179; territorial waters and, 60; trade
sanctions and, 92, 94, 96–97, 112
Iyad, Aby, 167

Jackson, Henry, 93
Japan, 220, 221–22, 224, 230, 231; energy dependence and, 100; territorial
waters and, 60; trade sanctions and, 35,
91, 92, 94, 96, 112
Jellinek, G., 6
Jobert, Michel, 111
Jordan, 154, 161
Judicial systems: history and, 18–20; importance of, 7–11, 13–14, 17; neutrality and, 21; power of, 9, 11, 22; precedent and, 22
Jurisdiction: extensions of, 102–108; principles of, 106–107
Jurisdictional immunity, 40–41, 52–53,
57–67, 186–89, 194, 196–97

Kirkpatrick, Jeane, 175, 221, 222, 228
Kissinger, Henry, 175
Korean Airlines Flight 007 incident: appraisal of, 230–37; conflicting claims
in, 218–25; espionage and, 217–21,
224, 228, 234; facts of, 202–217;
ICAO report on, 233–34; lawfulness
of, 225–28; navigation error and, 216–
17, 219, 221; outcome of, 228–30
Kornilov, Yuri, 221
Kreisky, Bruno, 178

Lambsdorff, Otto von, 95–96
Langdell, Christopher Columbus, 9–10,
14
Law; academic, 11–13, 15; context and,
11–13; constitutive process in, 86; de-

Library of Congress Cataloging-in-Publication Data

International incidents: the law that counts in world politics / edited by W. Michael
Reisman and Andrew R. Willard.
    p.   cm.
    Papers originally presented at the Yale Law School Spring 1984 seminar on The
incident as a decision unit in international law.
    Includes index.
    ISBN 0–691–07772–X (alk. paper)   ISBN 0–691–02280–1 (pbk.)
    1. International relations—Congresses. 2. International law—Congresses. 3. World
politics—1945—Congresses.   I. Reisman, W. Michael (William Michael),
1939–   .   II. Willard, Andrew R.   III. Yale Law School.
JX54.Y35I58 1988
341.5—dc19   87–25846 CIP